Starstruck

Starstruck

The Business of Celebrity

Elizabeth Currid-Halkett

Farrar, Straus & Giroux
New York

Farrar, Strauss & Giroux
18 West 18th Street, New York 10011

Printed in the United States of America
First edition, 2010

Library of Congress Cataloging-in-Publication Data
Currid, Elizabeth, 1978–
    Starstruck : the business of celebrity / Elizabeth Currid-Halkett. — 1st ed.
    p.   cm.
    Includes bibliographical references (p.   ) and index.
    ISBN 978-0-86547-860-2
    1. Fame.   I. Title.

BJ1470.5.C87 2010
306.4—dc22

                                                2010014393

Designed by Abby Kagan

www.fsgbooks.com

To my husband, Richard,

the light of my life,

brighter than a million camera flashes

Contents

Starstruck

1

Celebrity Today

M and I met briefly several years ago on a tree-lined street in New York City's West Village. He knew the man I was with, and when M said hello he introduced himself to me as well. We spoke for perhaps ninety seconds. I have not seen him since. He did ask for my e-mail address, and at some point I got an e-mail asking if I would like to be friends with him on Facebook. I accepted in the way that most of us accept Facebook friends, as long as they're not Charles Manson.

In the several years since I first met M, I have learned a lot about his life. He works in media. He seems to fly back and forth between Los Angeles and New York at least once a week. I don't think he has a girlfriend, but from his Facebook photos he seems to spend time with attractive women and semifamous people, and he goes to lots of parties. I pretty much always know when he's watching a movie, getting brunch, listening to new music, unable to sleep, or feeling pensive, gloomy, or euphoric. I know what parties he goes to, what he ate for breakfast, and when he's in Los Angeles or New York, running late for a flight to Los Angeles or New York, or anywhere else.

I am not a stalker. Every time I go on Facebook and see my "News Feed" I am assaulted with information about M. Between my log-ons, M has updated his "Status" multiple times, sometimes several times in an hour. I know about him and really about everything in his daily life with minimal effort. I can also tell that I'm not the only one fascinated with his fascination with himself. Recently, M uploaded a picture of his sofa with a laptop open and the status update, "This is my sofa view when I'm not living the glamorous life," to which a flurry of friends commented: "all too familiar" and "without love it ain't much" (the latter of which made no sense to me), and M was able to respond in kind. For someone who several posts later wrote "M is busy" (which also received several comments by friends), he sure has an amazing amount of time to spend online. Many people (any of his three thousand–plus Facebook friends) are reminded of the intimate details of his existence several times a day. Whether they want to know these things or not, no one ever forgets that M exists. Ironically, I've grown attached to M. The other day there was an entire nine-hour hiatus between status updates. I genuinely wondered what the hell was going on. As much as I'd like to say that people like M are annoying, in truth, I click on their Facebook profiles more than on the people who never update their statuses, and I notice when they have gone silent. I can't help myself.

All of us know characters who seem to have no job, hobby, or chore other than updating their blog or Facebook status. Twitter, the online social-messaging and "microblogging" system accessible by personal digital assistant (PDA) applications, short message service (SMS) text messaging, or computer, tantalizes with the question: "What are you doing?" Users are challenged to answer in 140 characters or fewer, and they do. Dozens and dozens of times per day. We "follow" (in Twitter-speak) people's lives via a click of a button, and people follow ours as well. Britney Spears does it. So does British comedian Stephen Fry and Hollywood heartthrob Ashton Kutcher. So does one of my favorite economists. And my graduate school adviser. And my husband (though, recently, I've put a stop to that). And yet their status updates, or tweets, as it were, would lead us to believe they have extraordinarily exciting lives (which some of them surely do) . . . so extraordinary it's a wonder they have time to do anything other than live it. They are "off to Brazil," "heading to the Super Bowl," "eating brunch with Mickey in Santa Monica," "stayed out waaaayyy too late" "pondering between steak frites and a cheeseburger at Balthazar."

I choose to pay attention to M's news feeds more than those of any of my other friends on Facebook for reasons I can't fully explain. I don't know M personally and I don't think he is particularly remarkable, and yet I find him fascinating. But here's something you might have picked up on already: My seemingly banal, casual interest in M, or any of the Facebook or Twitter characters each of us develops a personal affection for, is no different from our interest in the average celebrity gracing the cover of OK! magazine. The socialite may feed gossip about herself to the tabloids while M employs Twitter and Facebook, but these distinctions are pretty academic: Our interest transcends any talent these individuals may or may not have; they provide us with personal information that we really shouldn't know, and we remain consistently engaged in their lives and want to know more. My "friend" M, the perpetual Facebook updater, is as much a star as the high-profile socialite giving us constant new information about her boyfriends, new shoes, and where she goes clubbing. We can find versions of celebrity—that collective obsession with someone—in all of our lives. And just like with Hollywood fandom, in our desire for information from him, his friends (including me) are the essential participators in cultivating M's celebrity.

I have a particular affection for M's updates in the way that someone else may have an interest in the New York socialite, or perhaps his or her own Facebook celebrity. I'm not entirely sure if M's updates are true, but then again, Hollywood publicists have been spinning stories to the media since the beginning of time. Asking whether his updates are credible is missing the point. M is able to create a fabulous persona that engages a wider public in a way never possible before. M's star power is a function of new forms of social media that allow him to share intimate information about himself and enable his "fans" to attain his personal details with very little effort.

The phenomenon of celebrity—that collective fascination with some people over others—is everywhere. The way we use Facebook and Twitter demonstrates that star power is not just about "special people in special places." This disproportionate interest exists in the most prosaic and ordinary places and is directed at people who are not conventional stars. In fact, we confuse celebrity and its accoutrements of tabloids, TV programs, and flashbulb lights with a basic maxim: We just care about some people more than others. Celebrity on the big screen and plastered across glossy magazines is just a magnified version of a phenomenon present in our own lives.[1] M is a celebrity in his Facebook world, in the way Paris Hilton is in the world at large. The high school quarterback is as much a celebrity in his small town as Joe Montana of the San Francisco 49ers was to America at large. And in this respect, celebrity has a significant importance in illustrating some of the fundamental principles of human and social dynamics. This process of selecting some people over others happens everywhere and almost always requires the same elements: a collective public, some type of mechanism for distributing information (whether *People* magazine, Facebook, or the small-town local newspaper), and interest in these people for reasons other than any contribution they make to society.

Celebrity is the special quality that some individuals possess that propels society to care more about them than about other people. This quality, most visible on the big screen, is present in every layer of society, in every pocket of the world, and in all types of social circles from Hollywood to the family reunion. Some celebrity can be chalked up to charisma, the magical trait that catalyzed the public frenzy surrounding Barack Obama and John F. Kennedy, for example. Some celebrity is sheer determination to be noticed: M spends way more time updating his Facebook page than most other members, and as a result, I'm more aware of his existence. Some celebrity is the luck of being born beautiful or being in the right place at the right time. Undoubtedly, the attainment of celebrity on the big screen or Facebook or in small-town America is not a simple formula. Not all stars achieve their status through the same means or characteristics. Yet these diverse individuals are tied together by the basic fact that we are interested in them.

This book is about celebrity as a social phenomenon that exists everywhere. Far from being frivolous, celebrity permeates our social dialogue and generates millions of dollars in revenue for celebrities themselves and the various people and companies that latch onto these individuals. A person who possesses celebrity may win elections, get the lead role in a movie, or become homecoming queen. Despite the seemingly vast difference between M and Paris Hilton, they are connected by their common attribute of being interesting to their respective collective publics. This assertion leads to many questions. What basic "rules of stardom" do celebrities abide by? Can we predict who will become a celebrity? What makes someone so captivating? What makes us want to know more about someone over another? How does celebrity work?

Before getting into the different aspects of stardom, it's worth taking a moment to look at where we are now, which is in a state of unprecedented oversaturation and decentralization. Yes, undoubtedly, in order to be a film star one must pass through Los Angeles. But the deluge of social media has provided a virtual geography with no barriers to entry, such that people like M can permeate a collective consciousness around the world like any other celebrity. No, he will not grace the cover of *US Weekly*, but his wide and diverse social circle will be aware of all the intimate details of his life and may discuss him just as they would a conventional star. Similarly, Bollywood film stars (and their fans) care not at all about breaking into Western markets, and why would they? Hollywood is not the only pinnacle of celebrity. As such, celebrity is a definitive example of cultural multipolarity. Just as many argue that a central political superpower or financial center no longer exists, the point should be extended to celebrity, which increasingly has no one particular type, market, or fan base.[2] People can become extraordinarily celebrated and reap the financial rewards of their celebrity without ever stepping into a film studio executive's office. The ability to ignore the conventional channels of stardom is due to celebrity's changing definition. Today's celebrity is different from the past in three interweaving ways. First, anyone seems to have the chance of becoming a star. Second, we want more from our celebrities than ever before. And finally, new media and technologies make both of these trends possible.

Let's start with the first defining trait of contemporary celebrity: anyone can be a celebrity. Yes, celebrity has always existed in smaller versions in our own lives, whether the high school quarterback or our favorite aunt. People like M have always existed on a smaller scale, but our awareness of so many people like him is a product of the massive rise of new democratic media forms. YouTube celebrities, the Gosselins, and Tila Tequila are not just celebrities within their own proximate social worlds; they are everybody-knows-your-name stars who are on the tongues of average Americans and yet for reasons we cannot pinpoint. They are not notably talented, beautiful, or starring in blockbuster films. Instead, these individuals emerge, by their own volition, through the various new entry points made available. Otherwise unknown people come out of the woodwork in the form of YouTube videos, reality TV, MySpace profiles, and obscure web-based phenomena like ROFLCon, an organization and annual conference devoted to promoting what we now call "Internet celebrities." Great Britain is abnormally fixated on *Big Brother*, a reality show (with splinter series in multiple countries) that bunks up complete strangers in a confined space and records their every move in creepy, overexposed Orwellian style. Each week, a housemate is "evicted." Meanwhile, the housemates are sequestered from all forms of media, news, or information from the outside world. Needless to say, extraordinary things occur.

Mark Frith, former editor of Britain's celebrity tabloid *heat*, had an epiphany while observing Britain's obsession with the show. He was presciently aware that despite the utter ordinariness of these people, society was fascinated with their inner workings. Voyeuristically, Britains peeked into the housemates' lives and wanted to know everything about them, despite—or almost because of—their banality. Just by putting the characters of this reality TV show on the cover of the magazine, *heat* increased its circulation by 50 percent. "Anyone is now a celebrity," Frith said. "We've [*heat*] been the first to realize this and it's something that is helping us immensely. No one else has picked up on it."[3] Frith was onto something big. These individuals being obsessed about went on to be rewarded with TV contracts, book deals, and so forth.

Big Brother was only the beginning of a worldwide trend of making celebrities out of nobodies. Tila Tequila got a reality TV show because she was the most popular girl on MySpace (based on number of page views), and lonelygirl15 captivated the world just hanging out in her bedroom *doing nothing* (or so it seemed) and recording all of this nothingness on gritty YouTube footage. In Britain, Katie Price, otherwise known as

"Jordan," went from a tabloid pinup girl to reality TV star to equestrian clothing designer, author of children's books, and novelist, earning more than £50 million for just being an ordinary girl from Brighton with a nice smile, giant breasts, and an affection for bad language and hot pink.

As celebrities themselves have changed, so has our relationship to them. Celebrities have existed since the formation of social and economic stratospheres in society. Anyplace where differences exist in social class, there will be an elite group that is revered and focused upon more than the rest.[4] Early cultivation of celebrities had two important qualities. First, the public accessed stars primarily from a distance. Sightings were limited to official events, like the Oscars, which showcased the stars looking glamorous and perfect. Second, stars' public personae were carefully constructed and micromanaged: The public rarely got a taste of them as regular people. Even though Marilyn Monroe's life was filled with sordid and tragic tales, she still maintained an aura of glamour and sexiness. She did not truly unravel or become pathetic in a way that would challenge her stardom.

The other quality of past celebrity is that stars historically attained that position through possessing something special, whether power, talent, social status, wealth, or achievement. Leo Braudy notes in his definitive book on the history of fame, *Frenzy of Renown*, that Alexander the Great attained celebrity through conquering much of the known world. Later, Julius Caesar achieved renown through his creation of the Roman Empire. The French saw their aristocrats as celebrities, and the British still do. Yet possessing something special and extraordinary is not necessary to attaining contemporary celebrity. So what changed?

Madame Tussauds Wax Museum has been the definitive celebrity monument for almost two hundred years. Tussaud's wax representations are a reflection of society's changing relationship to stars throughout history. Born Marie Grosholtz in 1761, Tussaud herself was a young woman from Strasbourg, France. Her mother was housekeeper to Phillipe Curtius, an affluent doctor with a skill in waxworks. After years as his apprentice, Tussaud finally produced her first solo waxwork, a statue of the French Enlightenment writer and philosopher Voltaire. In the following years, Tussaud built an empire of wax museums documenting the celebrities of her day, a blend of notable intellectuals, such as Benjamin Franklin and Jean-Jacques Rousseau, along with French aristocracy and high society. Ahead of her time, Tussaud was a keen appraiser of the public's tastes and an expert on the perpetual "cult of celebrity." As early as 1849, Madame Tussaud's wax museums were viewed as litmus tests of the cultural zeitgeist, with one magazine coining the phrase "the Tussaud Test of Popularity." Or as the magazine put it, "Madame Tussaud's has become in fact the only dispenser of permanent reputation."[5]

Tussaud's original ambition adhered to our modern-day understanding of celebrity: The people she immortalized in wax (even the talented ones) had always been individuals whose stardom rested as much on their personae as their work; they were individuals the public was captivated by. The result of her efforts was to bring, as the historian Kate Berridge put it, "the gods down to earth." But over time, there were changes in how the museum presented its stars. When it first opened in the early 1800s, a rope protected the wax figures and no photographs were allowed.[6] The public could observe these icons only from a distance. But in the last few decades, as a recent visit I made with my father showed, we can now go right up next to them. We can touch them. The museum has not only allowed cameras but actually encourages visitors to be photographed next to the statues. In fact, if you're my father, you can take a tedious tour around the museum and compare your height to all of the U.S. presidents, reporting back with smugness that you inched out Nixon, even if by just a hair.

And thus we are today at a moment in which we strive to be near celebrity by any means possible. Contemporary celebrity is defined by our desire to know everything about stars, not as icons but as people "just like us," to use *US Weekly*'s mantra. An 1850s French aristocrat whose life was followed with great intensity was surely a celebrity, and surely many wished for more information about her daily existence. However, her public did not have access to it. In other words, the modern appetite for celebrity is greater, but perhaps partially because we have been given more material, which in turn created a yearning for more—this need is not so different from an addiction to a substance or activity. Today's reportage of celebrity is different because we have expanded the list of things we want to know about stars. No longer is it enough to see them at the Oscars in Chanel; we want to see them at Starbucks without makeup, getting their nails painted, fighting with their boyfriends, see what they ate for breakfast—we want to know everything about them. Just as in Tussaud's wax museum, we want to remove the protective rope and be as close to them as possible. And we do not care so much about their talent anymore (if they even have any); celebrities, even the talented ones, are focused on for things that have nothing to do with their talent.[7] Stan Rosenfield, one of the most famous and respected publicists in Hollywood, explained the evolution of celebrity to me. "There was a time when most media coverage had to do with their [stars'] ability to perform. Frank Sinatra [was covered by the media] because of the crowd he ran with and the lifestyle he lived, but he was still a [music] star. But these days, he wouldn't need the profession."

With this greater emphasis on personal narrative, the talentless celebrity has become just as legitimate a star as the actors, musicians, writers, and other talented celebrities.[8] And gone are the days of the Hollywood studio system and well-oiled PR departments, where actresses were under strict contract to give interviews only to a very select group of media outlets and those outlets' output was tightly controlled. In the old world of celebrity, stars were rarely reported doing anything second to perfection. In our modern celebrities, we have all the tawdry and dull stuff of human existence. Celebrities and aspiring ones are willing to trade their intimate moments—some seemingly mortifying and embarrassing—for the chance that the world might take notice of them. The collective interest in the everyday or oddly unglamorous, decidedly "un-Hollywood" parts of celebrity life has saturated us.[9] In fact, the banal details of one's personal life are the currency of contemporary celebrity. In the process, we ordinary (even talentless) individuals have ever more potential ways to enter the state of celebrity.

In one of the more grotesque examples of this phenomenon, former U.K. *Big Brother* reality star Jade Goody (a classic example of how anyone can be a celebrity) allowed the *Sun* to document a graphic daily account of her rapidly deteriorating health as she battled the cervical cancer that would ultimately kill her. We watched her quickie marriage, leaving her doctor's office, sucking on a pain medication stick, losing her eyesight, and feebly getting in and out of cars as the paparazzi flashed the camera lights. *We watched her die.* I knew as much about Goody's failing health as I would know of that of a close friend.[10] Initially, it was hard to understand why someone in the throes of cancer thought it would be a good idea to pose on the cover of *OK!* magazine, bald from chemotherapy and needing two naps just to make it through the photo shoot. Goody, it turned out, was actively raising money through these media gigs to provide for her soon-to-be motherless children (she made £700,000, or $1 million, for photos of her wedding). But our rationale for watching Goody's tragedy unfold was more ambiguous. What was wrong with us that we wanted such devastating updates about a woman we didn't even know? According to *OK!* the week Goody's hurried and tragic wedding was on the cover, the magazine sold two million copies, almost four times the average.[11] Even the *New York Times*, the BBC, and the *Financial Times*, which generally deal with world events and "real news," felt compelled to cover the story in feature articles.

Despite M and Goody being such different cases, their celebrity was manufactured in a similar manner. M posts his deluge of status updates on Facebook and his friends read and comment. And we create M's celebrity, much as we create Goody's, through our insatiable interest in his goings-on. Today anyone can be a celebrity: We define a celebrity as someone we want to know everything about, whether she likes it and maximizes the benefits of such exposure (the Jade Goodys of the world) or she crumbles under the pressure and invasiveness (the perpetually derailed Britney Spears, for example, who seems to both abhor and desire her participation in this drama).

This transformation has been made possible through the essential element of contemporary celebrity: the rise of new forms of media and entertainment and the change in what constitutes media. Media has been not only an observer of these processes but also part and parcel of creating this new kind of stardom that enables anyone to place himself or herself front and center of the public's eye, even if just for a minute. The media—from print to television to blogs and online paparazzi sites—gives us up to the minute visuals and news snippets on every star we could ever want to hear about while symbiotically giving those stars a channel to be heard.

The Hollywood studio system no longer can control what is being written about their stars. Nor can they control their stars, who tweet away about their breakups, mishaps, and any other traditionally private information they choose to share. In the last few years, celebrities haven't just dominated the media; they have actually created and fed entirely new forms. Dozens of blogs, magazines, and TV shows devoted to their every move began to appear. In 2000, *US Weekly*, the definitive celebrity glossy, had a circulation of 872,000, and stood at ninety-fourth place in U.S. circulation rankings, just inching out *Arthritis Today* and the *Handyman Club of America*. Today, *US Weekly* boasts a circulation of 1.9 million, making it the fortieth best-selling magazine in the United States. *People*, the classic celebrity middle-brow magazine, had a circulation of 3.6 million in 2009, up from 3.5 million in 2000. Magazines like *OK!* and *In Touch* didn't even exist in 2000 and yet in 2009 each boasted a circulation of almost one million. Since 2000, the presence of celebrity tabloids in the top two hundred best-selling magazines has nearly doubled. This figure doesn't include hybrids like *Rolling Stone*, *Harper's Bazaar*, *W*, or *Vogue* (which are also in the top rankings). Contrast this increase in celebrity media demand to the rest of the publishing world. Since 2000, circulation has declined by almost 11 percent for non-celebrity-focused magazines overall, but celebrity-focused magazines are actually *up* by 10 percent. In other words, in an era when the publishing industry has struggled, and sales for print media have taken a drastic dive, celebrity tabloids are not just defying the trend but also producing substantial growth.[12]

Why Celebrity Matters More Than Ever

What can explain the dominance of celebrity, and this new form of celebrity, in this particular moment in time? Those of us old enough remember where we were when Princess Diana married Prince Charles. We remember John Lennon's murder and Kurt Cobain's suicide. We recall, all too recently, the real-time reportage of Michael Jackson's legal travails and, later, his cardiac arrest, rush to the hospital, and subsequent death. Even the commonplace details of modern celebrity—the love lives or rags-to-riches stories of stars like Elizabeth Taylor, Madonna, Sean Connery, and Jennifer Lopez—are a part of their legendary status as much as their acting or music. Lopez grew up in the Bronx and lived on pizza. Before Madonna became Madonna, she grew up in Detroit, lived in squalor in New York City as a Dunkin' Donuts waitress, dated Basquiat and Warren Beatty, married Sean Penn and later Guy Ritchie, and dated A-Rod, America's most famous baseball player of the twenty-first century. Connery grew up in rural Scotland, one of eight children in a house with no toilet. Taylor grew up in the affluence of London and Los Angeles and was married eight times to seven men (she married Richard Burton twice and, as I write this, is set to wed again). Because celebrity is a magnified version of the human experience, we can't help but watch as all of the things that are important to us in our own lives—love, children, family, divorce, or vacations in exotic locales, as the case may be—play out across the stage of stars' lives.

A crucial part of modern celebrity is our desire to access celebrities through new forms of media and the creation of new types of stars. Society's desire for information about both conventional and democratic stars appears more acute than ever. Perez Hilton, whose salacious gossip blog that documents almost live footage of celebrity antics is one of the most trafficked sites in the world, wouldn't have a job if we didn't troll his website by the millions, giving advertisers a pretty strong signal to keep paying for ads there. Gawker Stalker, the application on Gawker.com that allows readers to post exact celebrity locations in real time, wouldn't exist if readers didn't send tips in. (There's no criticism here: I too am fascinated with stars picking up dry cleaning, reading the newspaper, and leaving the hair salon. And in high school the way the homecoming queen, Mandy Hendershot, was able to get her hair that precise blond with those perfect curls was a mystery I desperately wanted to solve.) The media creates stars and new shows, magazines, and blogs because there is a built-in audience for whom celebrity fulfills a particular acute need.

A fundamental part of celebrity's heightened importance in current society can be explained by the last fifty years' radical changes in how we work, live, form relationships, and interact. In a superglobal world, where many coastal twenty- to thirty-year-old urbanites don't live down the street from our parents, have anything in common with our coworkers, or attend the same events as our neighbors, celebrity offers an adhesive that binds us together.[13] Consider, for example, how much later we marry: In 1970, the median age at first marriage for men was 23.2 and for women 20.8. By 1990, the age for men bumped up to 26.1 and 23.9 for women, a 12 percent and 13 percent increase, respectively. By 2000, the age moved up to 26.8 for men and 25.1 for women, increasing women's average age of first marriage by yet another 5 percent in just ten years.[14]

Many of those who are late to marry live in big cities and spend most of their twenties toiling away at their careers.[15] And these metropolises are nothing like the small towns they might have grown up in. In New York or London it's unlikely that we know the names of more than a few of our neighbors. In fact, because our communities are not as close, the chance we even care what our neighbor is doing and feel the urge to talk about it is pretty minute.[16] While there are exceptions to these generalizations (people in suburban New Jersey or small-town America do tend to be more neighborly), there is a broader, changing definition of community and social structure taking form. Sociologists call this transformation one from gemeinschaft to gesellschaft, going from a community of strong and close ties among neighbors and family to less personal relations among a society of almost strangers. These latter connections are more economic (jobs, networking, picking up groceries, and so forth) than the previous close social ties of smaller communities.[17]

This classic theory on the transformation of society is played out in contemporary society. In *Bowling Alone*, Robert Putnam found that, since the 1960s, Americans have become less and less "civically and socially engaged." People have less face-to-face contact, do not vote as much, and do not participate in civic organizations, whether the bowling league or the PTA. Putnam blames watching television and the rise of the Internet as substitutes for human engagement, and believes these new behaviors cause an overall decline in social capital. Without joining clubs and spending time with one another, we lose collective experiences that allow us to bond and form close relationships. One sociological study corroborating Putnam's thesis concludes that we are lonelier than ever. Comparing U.S. national data from the General Social Survey from 1985 and 2004, the researchers found that the number of people who have no one to talk to about important matters has tripled, and individuals' personal networks have declined by almost a third.[18] The sociologist Dalton Conley calls this new form of community the "Elsewhere Society," whereby our community is increasingly constructed through technology and social media, causing us to be slightly disengaged from any particular physical moment and less likely to form bonds with those immediately around us.[19]

And yet, despite all of these changes, because we're human, our desire for community and social belonging has not left us. Our ability to simply talk to one another about something or someone we all know about—to gossip—is limited in an age when most of us wouldn't know each other's aunts, uncles, or the village idiot. It's not surprising that we live to talk about others and that we seek out those topics of conversation that will socially glue us together and help prevent us from feeling lonely in a society marked by weak personal relations and anonymous communities. A friend of mine recently remarked that the only way she could talk to her coworkers was by reading celebrity tabloids, because then at least she'd have something to chat with them about. Gossip, the media scholar Henry Jenkins points out, is a way for us to create social ties. "It's not who you are talking *about*," Jenkins writes, "but who you are talking *with* that matters."[20] A Social Issues Research Center study found that more than half of both men and women spend most of their "conversation time" talking about other people's lives.[21] Another study found that women who gossip are actually happier than those who do not, because such bonding actually produces feel-good hormones.[22] Historically, people gossiped about what was going on in a particular place; the subject matter was localized. Now that our societies are organized in different ways, gossip has been institutionalized and commercialized and revolves around people we have no direct contact with and thus celebrity is a prime topic of conversation. Celebrities are the global water cooler topic, so to speak.

We can also explain the new role of celebrity through the fact that we simply have a lot more information from a variety of both old and new media, what Jenkins calls "convergence culture." Technology is both inexpensive and efficient in giving us the immediate information that defines current celebrity. As *Wired* editor in chief Chris Anderson points out in *Free*, so much of our access to news and entertainment is at no cost and abundant. If we have any interest in celebrity gossip, and most of us do, why wouldn't we saturate ourselves with updates when they are there for the taking, at the click of a refreshed computer screen? Our relationship with new media is mutually reinforcing. We want abundant and varied information about our celebrities, and social media enables more and different types of people to try to become celebrities. Technology provides us with an easy way to indulge our curiosities and voyeuristic tendencies. But instead of satiating us with its copious news updates and a cult of oversharing, technology has actually whetted our appetites. This process builds upon itself: If just one news source provides instant and free access, then every other website must follow suit or be left behind. Thousands of magazines, millions of blogs, and news from the BBC, *Financial Times, Wall Street Journal*, and every other news media source are updated by the second. That picture of Britney Spears stumbling out of a nightclub can be uploaded in real time to a blog so that millions of viewers can see it less than ten minutes after the photo was taken. We found out about New York governor Eliot Spitzer's call girl, Ashley Dupré, not just through news reports or press conferences but through her MySpace page, where Dupré posted all sorts of juicy things about her life, including a few music singles she was hoping would take off. For the most part, stars are happy to share instant updates through various social media too. (There are hundreds of Coffee Bean & Tea Leaf shops in Los Angeles, but Paris Hilton and the rest of the Hollywood star posse choose to stop by the one Perez Hilton is blogging from.)

Celebrity Today

There was a time when celebrities were a compartment of society like professional athletes, popular TV shows, or *Star Trek*—a part of our lives by choice, not foisted upon us. The fusion of technology, free information, and our need to socially bond has created a perfect storm: the current, frenzied moment of celebrity taking on every shape and form. There's no possibility of standing in line at the grocery store, pumping gas, turning on the radio or TV, or walking through an airport without a constant barrage of celebrity. Even the most respected media outlets have paid homage, such as the *New York Times*'s "serious" profile of Angelina Jolie and *Atlantic Monthly*'s coverage of the paparazzi covering Britney Spears. We can't escape the allure of celebrity, and the presence of celebrity virtually defines contemporary society.

Even if we choose not to engage with it, and whether we like it or not, celebrity has become an intrinsic part of modern society, dominating our newspapers, magazines, and television with a ubiquity unlike ever before. Celebrity news stories crowd out other topics from the issues agenda and distract the public from more serious matters: Tiger Woods's extramarital affairs were covered at the expense of discussing President Obama's health care plan; former presidential candidate John Edwards's love child and separation from his wife dominated news headlines more than the contentious confirmation of the Federal Reserve chairman and America's increasingly tense relations with China.[23]

Economically, the importance of celebrity is clear (people get wealthy from stardom, products are sold through celebrities), but the social impact of celebrity might be the most profound reason why it cannot be ignored. People live vicariously through celebrities, people talk about celebrities, and, truthfully, many people actually want to be celebrities. A 2007 survey by the Pew Research Center revealed that 51 percent of eighteen- to twenty-five-year-olds said that their first or second goal in life was to become famous. "Certainly, the consumption of celebrity has become a part of everyday life in the twenty-first century," writes the media critic Graeme Turner, "and so it is not surprising if it now turns up as a part of young people's life plans."[24] Like it or not, celebrity matters and is more present than ever before.

So how does contemporary celebrity—as people, as an industry, as a social phenomenon—work? Are all celebrities the same? Why do so many individuals want stardom and what does society want from those who attain it? We know that only a very small fraction of people who aspire to celebrity actually become stars (certainly not 51 percent). Even if that select group is expanding, how does that selection process work? Why does society hand-pick some to be celebrated and callously discard others? What makes stardom happen for some and not for others, and why should we care? And for those of us who have no interest in personal stardom, what does it mean for us that our airwaves are dominated by celebrity? How much does it distract us from "the things that matter"—unless celebrity really does matter? Does it? This is what *Starstruck* is all about.

2

The Celebrity Residual: The Inexplicable Brew of Talent, Fame, and Celebrity

That mysterious confluence of presence and reserve on which stardom relies. —**Anthony Lane,** "Carrie," *New Yorker*, June 9, 2008

The difference between being recognized in restaurants and being talked about in restaurants. —**Louis Menand,** "The Iron Law of Stardom," *New Yorker*, March 24, 1997

Consider Paris Hilton and Tara Reid. Two young Hollywood actresses, both attractive, blond, blue-eyed, tanned by the Los Angeles sunshine, strikingly thin, and well proportioned. Both wear stylish, couture clothing, which they occasionally accessorize with some indecent exposure. (Paris was caught on camera without underwear and Tara's dress fell off, exposing a breast). Both are seen about town with various handsome men, in and out of trendy clubs, drunk, dancing on tabletops, getting in fights, falling into limousines, and looking pretty and providing endless content for celebrity blogs and magazines. Both have appeared in fairly camp, unsuccessful films, but both have also been involved in some hits: Paris in a TV series (*The Simple Life*), Tara in the *American Pie* films. On paper, Paris and Tara are almost the same person. Yet their career paths could not be more different.

Paris has built a perfume, clothing, and jewelry empire, and has been paid tens of thousands of dollars to appear at a party for ten minutes. Tara is a joke. Paris is an A-lister while Tara is in the bottom rungs of the C-list. Paris is collectively obsessed about, a cultural zeitgeist, admired and hated. Tara is viewed with indifference or pathos, if thought of at all. Despite her heiress background, Paris could live like a queen for the rest of her days on the money she has made from the Paris brand (not the Hilton chain), which is estimated to be worth between $15.5 and $50 million, depending on where you look.[1] Tara makes the news with reports of liposuction gone awry, alcohol abuse, and an exposed breast at rap mogul P. Diddy's birthday party. She has trouble getting into nightclubs and, as the story goes, got turned down for a slot on the go-to gig for D-listers, the reality TV show *Dancing with the Stars*. Why does Paris get rewarded for being a beautiful but ditzy woman, capable of absolutely idiotic antics (including a sex tape), while Tara is shunned?

The Paris-Tara paradox provides good insight into why celebrity is hard to predict and why it's not always about what's on a résumé. On the one hand, people rarely become celebrities without "handlers"—the agent, the stylist, the publicist, and so forth—yet even the best agent can't guarantee the success of a fledgling potential star. Is there a smoothly running machine of publicists, managers, and media, a masterminded system that spits out Tara Reid and anoints Paris? Or are some handlers working harder for their clients than others? Maybe it's simply that Paris puts in more hours than Tara? Is there something in their brief bios that explains Paris's true talent and Tara's lack thereof?

Both stars applied the formula "noise plus naked equals celebrity,"[2] yet that prescription worked only for Paris. It probably should be acknowledged that Tara is from central Jersey and Paris grew up in the Waldorf-Astoria. Some might argue that Paris already had a leg up because she comes from one of the richest families in America and came of age during a moment when society celebrated the excess of wealth. Paris's wealth and social standing at such a young age certainly gave her special access to the media and events the media cared about. But plenty of rich socialites don't become the legendary celebrities they want to be, and plenty of ordinary girls do. Just look at New York girl-about-town Tinsley Mortimer, who, blond, pretty, and rich, just like Paris, has never made it into the limelight in any meaningful way, despite clear attempts to be noticed. So yes, Paris had an advantage, but that advantage isn't surefire, the same way that being born in Jersey doesn't doom a girl. Consider America's sweetheart, the television personality Kelly Ripa, another pretty blond, from Camden, New Jersey, whose mother was a homemaker and father a labor union president and bus driver. The thing about celebrity that makes it so difficult to attain is that there is no obvious recipe for success. What allows Paris and Jersey girl Kelly Ripa to rise to the ranks but leaves Tara behind? Does it come down to that magic X factor that captivates the public—what Hilton's former publicist, Elliot Mintz, has called "the light"?

If anyone knows the answers to these questions, it is Mintz. He has built his entire career on representing the biggest internationally known celebrities, like John Lennon, Yoko Ono, Bob Dylan, and Christie Brinkley. And Paris Hilton. Mintz's life is devoted to preserving and promoting that special thing, the "light" (as ambiguous as that might be), that stars have and the rest of us do not. Talking to Mintz generates the same relaxing sensation as rubbing suntan oil over one's body. His voice has a trance-inducing quality regardless of what the topic is. He could sell fur coats to the president of PETA. Despite being in his midsixties at the time I interviewed him, Mintz is out into the wee hours at every Hollywood club that matters, emerging from a dark car, tan and trim, dressed impeccably (often in a monotone suit-tie-shirt combo), with immaculate nails and perfectly combed blond hair slicked to one side with an exact part. Mintz exudes an almost kitsch Hollywood glamour, as the *New York Times* put it in a profile of him in 2006.

Representing Paris is hard work. While Mintz's arrival at a club or restaurant can be viewed as a sure bet she'll show up later that night, what she might do at the club is anyone's guess and Mintz's job is to put the multiple fires out. Paris may dance on tables, kiss someone else's boyfriend, get wildly drunk, or urinate in public, or she may just sit there, looking her well-groomed self. Should disaster strike, Mintz has to put down his glass of chardonnay and rise to the occasion. And after all of these years and all of Paris's antics (including her jail time for a DUI), Mintz and his suntan oil voice seem able to maintain Paris's legendary celebrity status—despite the fact that her behavior has been no different from Tara Reid's, our poster child for the cocktail joke. If you ask Mintz what separates the stars from the wannabes, as I did point-blank, he will not comment on Paris (or any of his clients, for that matter, which is the key to being a good publicist). Rather, he will only remark that in the vicious competition for celebrity, stardom comes down to the fact that some people have "the light," and some simply do not.[3]

Richard Johnson, legendary editor of the *New York Post*'s gossip column Page Six,[4] has a somewhat different angle on Paris's celebrity. If Mintz is credited with maintaining Paris's star power, Johnson and Page Six are contenders for starting the Paris Hilton phenomenon in the first place. As Johnson tells it, Paris entered the socialite scene at the age of sixteen, when she was brought around the party circuit by her parents, Rick and Kathy.[5] Their access and high profile were initially a function of being a part of the Hilton hotel fortune, but that all became irrelevant as Paris was being noticed increasingly in

her own right. Unquestionably she was always pretty and pho-
togenic, but it was her tabletop dancing and wild partying that
made Page Six take notice. "Paris may have invented table-
dancing," Johnson remarked, "not what happens in topless
bars, but the technique of climbing atop a table . . . and dancing in nightclubs."

Before Paris, socialites (bar a few exceptions like Edie Sedgwick, Andy Warhol's infamous sidekick who died of a drug
overdose) were well-behaved young ladies. But Paris was the
trailblazer of high society as we know it now. "Paris changed
the rules," Johnson explained. "Socialites were supposed to be
paragons of virtue—at least in public. So Paris is a socialite in
that she has no discernible talent. But she behaves more like a
Hollywood starlet. She combined two archetypes into a mon-
strous new hybrid." Paris was good-looking and stylish in the
way that most socialites are, but she also ignored etiquette,
danced where she pleased, and demonstrated her sense of entitlement in ways from butting in line to taking copious
amounts of "swag" (valuable goodies given to stars). As Johnson himself tells the story, "Paris was caught more than once
urinating on the floor. Once she had her posse form a ring
around her for privacy before she left a puddle. I kid you not."

Then in 2003, a sex tape mysteriously leaked of Paris and
her high-flying financier boyfriend, Rick Salomon. As video-
taped bedroom interludes go, Paris's footage was banal (even
to her, it seems, because she answered her phone midact), but
it did the trick. "[The sex tape] really put her on the map,
timed as it was to the launch of her reality TV show," Johnson
commented. "Paris was well known in New York before the
sex tape, but the sex tape made her famous all across the
world. She's big in Japan you know." In an instant, Paris
Hilton became a star. The celebrity PR guru Matthew Freud
quipped, "The velocity by which Paris became famous [was
impressive] . . . It took Jesus a thousand years [to attain that

fame]." And Mintz spent many years controlling the flames that spread her star power.

These are competing theories on what makes Paris one of the biggest celebrities in the world. Contrast Mintz's glamorous but vague description of celebrity with that of Richard Johnson, who bluntly points out that it was hard not to notice Paris; she was a platinum blond miniskirt-wearing bull in a china shop filled with pearls and cashmere twin-set-clad sheep. She forced the media to remark upon her inappropriate and unseemly behavior.

So what about Tara Reid? She also behaved badly in public, but instead of being fascinated by her, the public dismissed her. Johnson has an explanation: Paris behaved badly, but she looked good while doing it. As he explained to me, "Despite her image as a red-carpet-hogging party monster . . . she is intensely aware in public that she is being watched and photographed, and she rarely takes a bad picture." Tara, on the other hand, didn't strike Paris Hilton's optimal balance of scandal and glamour; she was pitied, not revered. As Johnson summed it up, "Tara Reid seemed to have a problem at parties, and regularly became, as the Brits say, 'tired and emotional.' She also had a weight problem at one point, and then she had the bad plastic surgery. People just lost interest in her as she continued her descent. And her reality show made matters worse."

Depending on whether you believe Mintz or Johnson, Paris is either a born star or an acutely sophisticated manipulation machine while Tara is neither. But the interesting element in both stories is that neither one of them points to a societal contribution Paris makes with some distinguishable talent. They do not speak of her poignant acting skills, her work as a musician, or even her beauty. She wasn't vetted by the big studios, she didn't win an Oscar or a Grammy or a Golden

Globe, yet she appears in all the same media outlets that cover Hollywood's industrious denizens.

Mintz may call it the light and Johnson may describe it as urinating on bathroom floors, but both are getting at something central to celebrity: Celebrity requires a collective obsession regarding things about a person that are unrelated to and unexplained by that individual's talent. The public and the media pay an inordinate amount of attention to the lives and personal trivia of celebrities rather than to what they contribute to their field or to society, and the attention foisted upon them cannot be explained by their talent alone. They *might* be talented, they *might* be beautiful, and they *might* have built an empire. But the public's interest in them centers on their lives, their personaes, and has very little to do with their work or skill. Stars understand that the essence of stardom often lies in making something more than their talents or contributions to the world visible to the public.

There is no question that some celebrities have talent. But let's be clear: The thing we care about and invest in is rarely their obvious skill. Even among similarly talented and well-known people, however, some are simply more "celebrated." What are the differences, then, among talent, fame, and celebrity? How do these different qualities intermingle? Let's start with some rules of the road.

Talent describes a person's inherent extraordinary ability— whether that is running at a faster speed, acting with poignancy, writing with lyricism, or orating with special power.

Fame is pure renown—literally the sum of all the people who have heard a person's name and can connect it meaningfully with something else—a face, a brand, a voice, or an idea.

Celebrity is the phenomenon of society collectively caring about certain people for reasons that far outweigh (or have nothing to do with) their talent or deserved fame. The difference between how much we should care about someone (their measurable talent) and the amount that we actually do (their fame) can be called the "celebrity residual."[6] Our interest in these people transcends their talent in their field of specialty, whether this is scoring touchdowns, winning Oscars, or bi-coastal blogging, like my friend M. The people who possess this residual are celebrities—one could also call them stars and the quality stardom; I used both terms as interchangeable with celebrity throughout this book.

None of these attributes are mutually exclusive, but as this chapter will show, celebrity, fame, and talent are different from one another in important ways.[7] Some people are talented and then become well-known and then become celebrities. Sports stars are a very good example of this path to celebrity. Ac-tresses who lead public lives also may become celebrities in this capacity: Elizabeth Taylor and Angelina Jolie, for example. Paris Hilton, on the other hand, exemplifies a celebrity that is independent (completely devoid, even) of talent. Paris Hilton is almost all celebrity residual—a person with no discernible tal-ent who has nevertheless become one of the most talked about individuals of the first decade of the twenty-first century. Her "extra something" is her only something.

The Difference Among Celebrity, Talent, and Fame

In order to fully appreciate what celebrity is, it's useful to look at what celebrity is not. Consider being famous for one's tal-ent. Contrast Brad Pitt with Bill Gates. People like to think of Gates as a celebrity, but actually he's just famous for being a genius. He built the biggest software company in the world. Microsoft transformed how people work and communicate. He's the second-richest man on earth. *Of course* he's famous. There's no gap between his talent as a technology and business

guru and his world fame—the ratio between these two measures is 1. In other words, Bill Gates deserves every ounce of
his world renown. When people talk about Bill Gates, they
mention his extraordinary intelligence, his business savvy, and
his unparalleled philanthropic contributions to AIDS research
and other humanitarian and health issues. They do not talk
about where he has dinner, where he works out, or what he
and his wife did for Valentine's Day. Bill Gates isn't a celebrity
for two reasons: His fame is proportionately the same as his
talent, and our interest in him can be explained by his talent
and doesn't have anything to do with other elements of his
persona. In other words, Gates has no residual.

These distinctions are not to say that Gates is the only individual in the world who could achieve such success. The
Microsoft story is far more complex than that. There are multiple, unquantifiable factors that help explain Gates's strato-
spheric rise. And given a different context or point in history,
there are likely similarly gifted individuals who, with the right
opportunities, could be as successful as Gates. His is a blend of
genius, ambition, and luck.[8] Despite the circumstances that
might explain his rise, however, it is clear that his renown is
fundamentally different from that of Brad Pitt (and Paris
Hilton, for that matter)—and not simply because they have
different occupations. It's not that Brad Pitt isn't talented. He
is, of course, one of the most highly regarded film stars of his
generation. But we are far less interested in any talent he possesses compared to our obsession with him as a person.

Really talented people do not necessarily become famous.
We all know those people who are talented, who may even
make a living out of their talent, but are virtually unknown to
most of the world: innovative mathematicians, the guy who
created the Linux operating system (Linus Torvalds, known by
computer scientists but not to most of us), great pianists. But
let's take it a step further. Even famous people do not neces-

sarily become celebrities. When you achieve extraordinary recognition for your talent, people will know your name, but that doesn't mean they are interested in you for anything other than your talent. Consider the distinctions like this: Society knows about brilliant scientists but rarely, if ever, cares about their personal lives. On the whole, despite major contributions to economics, we don't project ourselves onto the Nobel Prize winner. Notwithstanding his necessity in keeping our financial system humming along, we don't emotionally invest in the secretary of the Treasury. Unless we are economics whizzes or politics aficionados, we likely do not know what these individuals look like, nor do we follow the quotidian aspects of their lives despite the fact that their talents have more effect on our daily lives than do any stars. You can be very talented but unknown. You can be really famous for being really talented. But neither of these is the same as being a celebrity.

Even with regard to the most talented of individuals, those who become celebrities do so through means unrelated to their skills. Barack Obama, to use an obvious example, may be an extraordinary politician, the first African-American president, a brilliant, Harvard-educated man, but we also care about how many times he goes to the gym, whether he drinks coffee and how he likes it, and where his wife, Michelle, likes to go shopping. We first noticed Obama because of his talent and political charisma, but now we're interested in all aspects of his life. Even the *New York Times* profile of the first lady couldn't resist a blurb about her favorite food being french fries, her affection for pleated skirts, and her secrets to staying thin.[9] While the first lady is often profiled, the media's interest in her extends far beyond her charitable works or the occasional comment on her gowns at state dinners. The public's affection for Bill Clinton, who is also a celebrity, seems subdued compared to Obamamania. The collective interest in the Obamas has transcended the president's talent as a political leader. Despite Obama's seemingly tranquil personal life, his prosaic interest in basketball, the quiet time he spends with his wife, his clean living (he doesn't drink alcohol, is trying to kick his smoking habit, and is a total health nut), we're obsessed. Unquestionably, the media helps create the narrative surrounding President Obama, perhaps even actively portrays his personal life as worthy of our interest, but the public eats it up. Yes, Obama, like all presidents, interacts with celebrities and world leaders, which naturally generates media attention. But his public is also interested in the mundane aspects of his life, despite the fact that nothing exciting or abnormal seems to be going on. Our desire for personal information about Obama is insatiable, as if he lives the never-a-dull-moment life of a rock-and-roll star. Ask yourself if you had the same interest in George Bush Sr. or Jimmy Carter. John F. Kennedy was the last president to captivate the world to the same degree as Obama. Kennedy too was not "just a president" (irony implied), but a celebrity.

How the Residual Emerges; the Visual and the Ambiguous

Hollywood, politics, music, and sports are most likely to produce individuals with high celebrity residual. The preponderance of stars in these industries links to two important traits of celebrity. First, celebrities are more likely to emerge in fields or social realms when we can see them. Unsurprisingly, psychological studies have found people tend to respond to visual stimuli more than anything else.[10] Pictures, videos, and Internet coverage that show us more information about people—what they look like, how they dress, and so forth—enable us to establish a collective interest and investment in particular individuals. Hollywood is a visual industry, and most of the information surrounding the industry comes in the form of photos, specials on TV, and glossy tabloids. We know what every star in Hollywood looks like because the media's reportage is not just text but also pictures; in other words, their work and existence are documented through a visual medium. The same holds true for sports and pop stars and, to a certain extent, high-profile politicians.

Second, celebrities emerge when it's hard to discern who is the most talented. In fields where talent is either ambiguously measured or subjective, there are a greater number of stars.[11] Let's take the case of film and former TV star Jennifer Aniston. It's not entirely clear whether Aniston is a talented actress. She hasn't won any film awards and her movies tend to bomb, but some people genuinely think she's given fabulous performances (I, for one, think her acting in *The Good Girl* and *Friends With Money* deserved awards). She also has a legacy as the character of Rachel from *Friends*, one of the most popular and successful TV sitcoms of the 1990s.

On the one hand, it could be argued easily that the bad reviews mean her film acting isn't good. On the other, she's one of the most successful TV stars in history, and her movies, bad as they seem to the critics, regularly bring in millions of dollars at the box office. Similarly, Megan Fox didn't win an Oscar for her role in *Transformers*, but the movie had one of the biggest opening weeks in Hollywood's history. Does that make her more or less talented than Kate Winslet, who won an Oscar for her role as a Nazi prison guard in *The Reader*? Who is the better film star? The one who brings in the bucks or the one revered by the industry? Further, even though Oscars or Golden Globes are ostensibly awards for exceptional acting, since only one Best Actor and Best Actress award is given out each year, they cannot be the only measure of talent.

Even though sports use quantitative measures of talent, the statistics can be misleading. Sports statistics are both direct (home runs, goals, touchdowns) and indirect (contributions that enable winning or prevent the other team from winning, such as tackles, passes, sacks), and thus measuring talent can be ambiguous.[12] The stats we use to evaluate a player (RBIs, home runs, batting average) are not always the stats that win the game. Baseball and football are such complicated and team-oriented sports that it can be difficult to measure where a player's input is most valuable. In soccer, winning a game involves many different contributions. While goals seem straightforward (they directly increase the score), the percent of passes completed is also a crucial part of the game that ultimately contributes to the final score. Additionally, soccer statistics have a qualitative aspect. For example, not all completed passes are equal. A completed pass that results in a goal two minutes later is better than a pass in midfield that just keeps the ball moving around. Similarly, some goals are simply harder to score than others.

Football, inherently a team sport, is even more difficult to measure. For a running back, his "yards per carry" (the number of yards a football player covers when he has the ball) is a good statistic, but it still depends significantly on other people—the quality of those players on the offensive line. In this respect, football is more of a team game than soccer and thus it's very hard to isolate individual stats that would determine whether a football player was on his own definitively "the best." Even a quarterback depends on his offensive line and his wide receivers to a great extent. Matt Cassel, when he was a quarterback for the New England Patriots, became a star partially because of the Patriots' impressive offensive line. Even truly talented players need an exceptional team in order to win games.

Michael Lewis has studied in depth the ambiguous and misleading nature of sports statistics. In his best-selling book *Moneyball*, Lewis analyzed how the Oakland A's became one of the best baseball teams in the American League, despite lack of money and celebrity players. He found that the team's general manager, Billy Beane, decided to sign the baseball players who actually won games, rather than those with star power. Lewis contends that most of the time, recruitment scouts are looking for the wrong signals in determining whom to recruit. There are two ways scouts make decisions about baseball players. First, they look at conventional stats like RBIs, home runs, and batting average that are supposed to demonstrate talent but are primarily useful for signaling individual performance rather than how a player helps his team overall. Second, scouts recruit players who "look like baseball players." When Beane looked at the baseball players with stats that determine successful game outcomes (on-base percentage, slugging percentage, and high number of walks are crucial), he found that they can be chubby and unfit-looking, and thus unappealing to the average scout. For example, when Beane tried to recruit Jeremy Brown using these unconventional statistics, he was met with dismay from the scouts who deemed the player a "soft body." "We're not selling jeans here," Beane retorted during the standoff over Brown.[13] But actually, at least metaphorically, they were. Attracting ballplayers who look the part is crucial to building stars and drawing in big crowds. Lewis concludes that baseball teams tend to pay a premium for players who look the part and possess stats that are exciting to talk about, and conversely undervalue players who lack such celebrity qualities.

Politicians are learning to promote themselves and increase their celebrity in ways that have little to do with their ability to win elections or talent at passing legislation. The 2008 presidential election campaign was a great celebrity maker. Republican candidate Mike Huckabee had rallies that drew thousands and thousands of people, and yet in the end he was able to pony up only 12.3 percent of the vote in the Republican primaries. Despite the buzz surrounding his candidacy, when it was time to vote, it became clear that Huckabee had no shot at winning. He carried Iowa with great fanfare and then proceeded to become increasingly unlikely. Yet Huckabee was every bit the political celebrity because people were fascinated with his persona rather than his policies: guitar playing, his Chuck Norris endorsement, and his weight-loss story. On sheer celebrity, Huckabee blew McCain out of the water, but, as it turned out, McCain nevertheless got the votes. Post-election, Huckabee became a commentator on Fox News, turning his ephemeral celebrity into a new job.

Sarah Palin, the former Alaska governor and John McCain's 2008 vice presidential candidate, may have seemed like a joke in political circles, but she was nonetheless a bona fide star on the campaign trail. In the aftermath of losing the election, she resigned from the governorship, wrote an autobiography that sold over 2 million copies, hit the talk show circuit, and made over 1.5 million Facebook friends, even if she could barely identify countries on a map. Palin is also set to participate in a TLC reality TV show about Alaska.[14] As the newspaper and blog Politico put it, "D.C. may be facing something now commonplace in Hollywood: a true bifurcated standard of fame, i.e., real movie stars and those who reality producers refer to as 'celebrity adjacent.' The former try their best to stay out of *US Weekly*; the latter crave it. One is defined by a certain suaveness and subtlety; the other, by red carpet revelry."[15] Within political celebrity, we observe the same spectrum of pure celebrity residual and talent-driven stardom. There are those who rise to acclaim through demonstrating a great ability to transform policy and the public dialogue, while there are others who appear to offer no tangible contributions to the political agenda and resonate with voters nonetheless.

The Absence of the Residual

If celebrity plays a role in Hollywood, music, sports, and politics, consider the types of industries where the residual is hard to cultivate. Bill Gates comes from an industry where celebrity rarely exists. When the market is efficient and transparent in determining talent and winners, celebrity is much less likely to emerge. In meritocratic-driven fields where talent is unambiguous, celebrity cannot masquerade or make up for inadequacies in talent or competence. People may be famous for being good at their job; slackers and failed entrepreneurs are unlikely to have a shot at the "all-residual" star power that Paris Hilton's entire public existence rests upon. Either you're making money or drumming up successful inventions, or you're not. In merit-driven industries, the public tends to fixate on the people who have achieved success as defined by the market. In the uncertain, taste-driven worlds of music and film, it's much easier to be a celebrity.[16]

For example, financial fame is not divorced from merit. The public is unlikely to spend hours obsessing over individuals who have been determined to be mediocre. Not only do most successful financiers loathe the media, they also couldn't attain a profile without having the deals, the flair, as well as the salaries that make them mediaworthy, and even then, many top financiers remain out of the public eye.[17] Most investment bankers and hedge fund managers do not seek out media attention, because it is not a requirement to make money, which is the essential goal of their job.[18] In 2008, James Simons, a hedge fund manager at Renaissance Technologies, made $2.5 billion. The next year, after the 2008 tallies of earnings were available and Simons was publicly known to be at the top of the heap, his name made it into only 246 news stories. John Arnold of Centaurus Energy made $1.5 billion and was named in a mere 408 stories; Raymond Dalio of Bridgewater Associates generated $780 million in earnings and yet he was mentioned in just 16 news stories.

Contrast these figures to those of the most powerful and richest celebrities. Between June 2008 and 2009, *Forbes* magazine calculated that Angelina Jolie earned $27 million. She generated some 34,400 media hits during approximately the same period.[19] Oprah Winfrey, earning $275 million from 2008 to 2009, is the richest celebrity almost two times over the second-highest-paid star (Steven Spielberg). Her annual earnings are just on par with the seventh-highest-earning hedge fund manager, David Shaw of D. E. Shaw & Co. But in terms of media, Oprah generated over 21,000 news hits versus Shaw's 700 mentions.[20] Being most successful in finance does not necessarily produce a public profile in the way that being a multimillion-dollar entertainer translates into celebrity.

Additionally, finance and technology do not rely on a visual presence and, by extension, an audience, in the way that sports, politics, and the performing arts do. The "stars" are the quarterly earning reports and the products or the brand. Thus the drumming up of individual celebrity is less likely because a public is not necessary for them to do their job. Financiers do most of their work behind the scenes. In fact, it's imperative that most of their "talent" is under the radar, for fear that a competitor will sniff out a deal or attain market information. They are not photographed with such frequency. The *Wall Street Journal* does not even photograph the financiers and business gurus profiled in the paper. Contrast this with sports, and to a greater extent with Hollywood, where an audience and visual persona is part of a star's dossier of success.[21]

Financial celebrity emerges at times, but it is usually predicated on two conditions: when someone has done something really bad or when someone has actively created a persona that transcends his or her talent. Financial celebrities tend to be cultivated through notoriety. The 1991 Salomon Brothers' outrage when trader Paul Mozer was found to be submitting false bids to buy U.S. Treasury Department bonds or the $50 billion Ponzi scheme that Bernie Madoff was busted for in 2009 were some of the most speculated about and discussed scandals of their time. Madoff's private life was endlessly dissected in *Vanity Fair* and even *Tatler*, including a tell-all by his secretary and an examination of his privileged (and now broke) social circle. But again, the collective public interest was directly linked to extraordinary circumstances.

Consider the other type of famous financier. The world's obsession with Warren Buffett has everything to do with both his savvy as an investor and the way that he portrays himself and his relationship to money. In Alice Schroeder's best-selling biography of Buffett, *Snowball*, we are told of his knack for spotting "the deal" in the most mundane of circumstances. One of the most telling stories is that of him staying at the house of *Washington Post* publisher Katharine Graham, where he was so preoccupied with the free shampoo in the guest bathroom that he did not even notice the original Picasso. We are fascinated with how the third-richest man in the world (after Carlos Slim Helú and Bill Gates) makes his money but also with his complete lack of interest in spending any of it. Despite being so rich and successful, Buffett remains an Omaha denizen who lives in the same house he bought for $31,500 in 1958.[22] One might argue that the public is intrigued by Buffett's folksy, frugal, and unpretentious persona, thus our interest in him is like that in any other star. Not to mention, the media loves Buffett's sound bites. But as with Bill Gates, our curiosity in Buffett revolves around his extraordinary talent as a financier. Our fascination with him as a person is due to his ironic relationship with his wealth. Like Gates, Buffett's star power is a function of his talent and there is no gap between his talent and fame. Buffett has no residual.

Celebrity is rare in fields where determining talent is transparent and the public is less able to obtain personal information about the individual. Sure, some people in finance or technology are famous, but this fame is directly linked to their success in the field (thus not conforming to the definition of "celebrity"). Can you imagine a conversation about an entrepreneur with an obviously failing business where one would say, "I wonder what he's all about. I really want to learn more about his failure as a businessman"? But in film, sports, and politics, we obsess about individuals who aren't the most talented of their peers and those who demonstrate questionable contributions to their field. We may be more interested in Larry Page (founder of Google and the 24th richest individual in the world) than the Swedish businessman Hans Rousing (ranked 64th), but both are clearly extremely good at what they do, and Page has an edge being the founder of one of the most revolutionary companies of the twenty-first century. Google is not only a world-changing innovation; the company itself (and Page as one of its representatives) also has actively sought to cultivate media attention and buzz. When an actress's film bombs or an athlete has a bad season, fans tend to find ways to rationalize the poor performance, or they simply don't care. In finance, business, or technology, if you're not successful you're not worth talking about. So if the Google model fails, Page will no longer be a regular news item (except in the short duration after the fall when people would speculate, analyze, and gossip). And if we are talking about people because they have made smart business decisions or have been innovative, then we're talking about them for their talent, which means these entrepreneurs, as notable and world renowned as they may be, are not celebrities—they're just famous.

There are financiers and businesspeople who are celebrities and who are not total scoundrels nor are they at the top of the pack. But these individuals have created personalities that transcend their talent. Donald Trump gained fame for rising like a phoenix from the ashes of company bankruptcy. Twice. That's pretty impressive, but this renown is linked to his talent as a businessman. Trump's *celebrity*, on the other hand, has much to do with his affection for beautiful women (he owns the Miss Universe pageant), his TV personality and show (he is the star of the extraordinarily popular *The Apprentice*), and being thrice married, each time to a fabulously good-looking model-actress type. Trump's fame rests on his business acumen and his rags-to-riches-to-rags-to-riches story.[23] But his celebrity is due to his glamorous and exciting personal life, which at times is covered with media fervor as intense as that of Paris Hilton. Undoubtedly, our interest in Trump as a person was helpful in his regaining financial success—he wrote best-selling books and his presence on the show is what makes *The Apprentice* such a hit.

Similarly, Richard Branson is a billionaire entrepreneur who gained fame through his transportation and music companies (the Virgin brand includes Virgin Atlantic, Virgin America, Virgin Trains, and Virgin Records). But he also owns a spaceship company, Virgin Galactic, and an island (Necker Island in the Caribbean), which may be related to Branson's entrepreneurial talent but also generate a fair amount of admiration and/or amusement with Branson the person. Not to mention that Branson actively generates a high profile. He writes books (including his autobiography *Losing My Virginity*), appears on TV shows (*Baywatch*, *Friends*), and starred in his own Fox reality TV show (an attempted rival to Trump's show; it failed). Branson attempts to break world records, including traveling around the world in a balloon. Anyone who wants to watch a movie during a Virgin Atlantic flight often must sit through an introduction featuring a golden-locked and grinning Branson chatting away on the miniature screen. There is no question that Trump's and Branson's public personae—their celebrity—are part and parcel of their overall success story.

Who Gets the Celebrity Residual?

By this point, we know what celebrity is, what it is not, and how talent, fame, and celebrity intermingle. But what enables some people to attain celebrity while others do not is still not straightforward. If some people—Hollywood actors, baseball players, Facebook friends, or politicians—have the celebrity residual, the question becomes: Why are some people more interesting to us than other people *seemingly* just like them? What makes Jennifer Aniston talked about, despite the fact that she doesn't appear to demonstrate movie star talent? Why Paris, not Tara? The celebrity residual rests on the public's assessment of these individuals as interesting relative to others like them. We want to know about them in the way we like to know about our best friend or our high school crush. Celebrities attain their status by cultivating their personae as multifaceted individuals. They are not just actors or football players. M is a celebrity not because he's successful in media. M is a celebrity because his Facebook and Twitter profiles are more interesting than everyone else's (at least for me, and apparently most of his friends). Part of this celebrity rests on his constant status updates and sheer determination to be noticed. But within this context of abundance, his updates (where he's traveling, his thoughts on the world, what he ate for lunch) become individually interesting. M spends an awful lot of time making himself seem more exciting and more fabulous than everyone else. M projects his celebrity to the public, which is exactly what any other star who is interested in media profiles and public interest does as well. His celebrity is a result of his active cultivation, and social media provides him this opportunity. Twitter, Facebook, and MySpace demonstrate the purest form of cultivation of celebrity because, for the most part, their entire purpose is to feed us unessential personal information. However, because celebrity is not meritocratic, it is predicated completely on us *remaining* interested in them as people, based on what they tell us about themselves.

Paris Hilton, the ultimate celebrity, embodies this maxim. She is skilled at catching our interest and recognizes that celebrity (not fame, not talent) rests on perpetuating this public interest. Without us remaining interested, she's just famous. And that's exactly what has begun to happen. Over the past few years it's become clear that Paris, the all-residual celebrity, is on the decline. Sure, people know who she is and her name still appears boldfaced here and there, but the peak of her celebrity was in 2006, when she was the most searched person on Google. From the middle of 2007 to the present, however, aggregate Google search hits revealed she was far down the list of searched individuals.[24] There is no doubt that the public has grown bored with her antics. In the spring of 2009, Paris was interviewed on the red carpet and she mentioned that her boyfriend, Doug Reinhardt, would be her future husband. There was a time only a few years back when her remark would have landed her a tabloid cover and speculation about wedding plans.[25] By 2008, Paris's comments—even declarations about marriage—barely made the blogs. Partially, Paris's decline has much to do with the zeitgeist and the winds of change. Paris had become a celebrity during a time of glorious wealth and conspicuous consumption, when wearing flashy clothes and driving a pink Bentley was de rigueur. In 2009, in an economic climate second only to the Great Depression, with unemployment rising every month and the real estate market in disarray, Paris was no longer the sign of the times. The era of flash and the good life was over, and with it Paris

Hilton's celebrity was on the wane. One could argue that Paris was a reminder of all the excess that got us into the financial meltdown to begin with.

Luckily, a perfect storm was brewing. In June 2009, Paris dumped that boyfriend, the would-be husband. And almost simultaneously (as in the very next day), some six thousand miles away, it was announced that Cristiano Ronaldo, a Portuguese footballer, had left Manchester United to sign a $132 million contract with Real Madrid, topping David Beckham's previous record. Ronaldo was now far and away the highest-paid footballer in history. And Ronaldo was also a celebrity by anyone's definition, the papers detailing his Louis Vuitton man bags, famous "wink" (both on and off the field), tiny white bathing suit, and immaculate metrosexual upkeep. Of course, his contract with Real Madrid along with his celebrity profile made him a major headline story. Interestingly, the very day his deal was announced, another major Ronaldo development swept the world. He happened to be feting his deal in the sunshine and nightclubs of Los Angeles, paired up with none other than Paris Hilton, just fresh from her breakup of the day before. The Ronaldo-Paris love affair dominated the tabloids for several days, with rumors swirling about her long-held crush on the Portuguese sports star. Within a month she announced she had dumped Ronaldo because she didn't want to be a footballer's wife. Then she got back together with the potential-husband boyfriend. But all these details are just noise. More to the point, Paris Hilton managed to get the media to write about her and maintained her status as a public obsession. Knowing that her star power rests on the public's constant fascination with her life, Paris has somehow figured out the exact formula for keeping us interested.

3

The Relative Celebrity (or, The Biggest Star
You Never Heard Of)

About an hour and a half out of London on a slow-as-molasses train, one arrives in the gray city of Nottingham, a former center of lace making and bastion of the Industrial Revolution, known for its Sherwood Forest, the legendary home of Robin Hood and his band of thieves. Today, however, while progress has passed this city by, Nottingham has become renowned within some circles as the headquarters for one of the most byzantine and zealous subcultures in the world. Seemingly far removed from anything most of us experience in our daily lives, this subculture tells us something very important about the way celebrity operates.

Within one of the city's dreary industrial estates there is a compound filled with moats, sculpted castle walls, and strange creatures that draws thousands upon thousands of visitors from countries as far away as Japan. Couples plan their honeymoons to include a stop at this compound, still others travel thousands of miles to attend the annual autumn event that brings up to fifteen thousand fans. One man I spoke with packed up all his belongings and moved from Indiana to Nottingham, knowing not a soul there, just for the chance to work at the compound. His story is not unique. In fact, countless people from around the world come to Nottingham for the same reason: to be a part of an exclusive world with its own media, jargon, exciting members-only events, and of course, access to the celebrities who reign supreme within this subculture.

Welcome to Warhammer World, where Tyranids (bioengineered races of evil creatures) relentlessly attempt to control the world and only the Tau (aliens working for the greater good) are able to save you. Aggressive battles take place in space, in the Milky Way Galaxy, for example (controlled by the Imperium of Man), and can play out over the course of one thousand years. Warhammer is one of the oldest and most popular fantasy creations, alongside Dungeons and Dragons and *Lord of the Rings*. Like its counterparts, Warhammer has been the subject of novels and comic books and provides great entertainment for ten- to fourteen-year-old boys around the world. Also similar to Dungeons and Dragons, Warhammer fans have a chance to role-play and act out various battles and scenarios within this fantasy world, which they do with miniatures standing 1.1 inches high. The Warhammer World fantasy games use an intricate collection of props, rule books, miniatures, and paints to enact the battles among the various creatures. Armies are designated by the special colors used to paint them.

Do not let the fantastical nature of this enterprise fool you; Warhammer World is also the name of the Nottingham compound that acts as the headquarters for Games Workshop, the company that produces very profitable war games revolving around science fiction or fantasy themes including Warhammer and Warhammer 40,000 (the latter takes place in the forty-first millennium).[1] The compound also acts as the meeting place for hobbyists from around the world, hosting events and open game nights where enthusiasts can bring their miniatures and stage battles on one of the many Astroturf tabletops. At any given time, half a dozen battles might be going on throughout the compound. Similarly, in all Games Workshop stores, tables covered in fake grass are set up so that hobbyists can come in to play each other. At the same time, battles, dramatic climaxes, and great defeats are going on around the world in workshops from Los Angeles to Jimbocho, Tokyo.

Warhammer World defines the very existence of those who live and breathe the games. Besides younger boys, the active hobbyists are men in their late twenties and early thirties, who picked up the hobby again later in life, and who, with more disposable income, are able to establish the large collection of miniatures necessary to become serious players. Thousands upon thousands of people devote mind-boggling amounts of time and money—some their entire lives—to participating in Games Workshop. Unlike playing with Barbie or miniature cars, participating in Games Workshop requires real skill. One must learn how to paint the miniatures required for playing and acquire extraordinary knowledge of the rules of the game. Even to participate requires a hobbyist to make it a top priority. Specialist games have been created for "veterans" who have been playing for many years and need more challenging scenarios. One Games Workshop manager who gave me the lay of the land was, like most employees, a hobbyist himself, which is why he became manager of a local store. In general, managers are not usually working at Games Workshop to pay the bills. They know the games intimately, who the major players are, and a bit about the groups of kids who come in, day after day, to play. And they too have their own miniatures, read the hobby's glossy events magazine, *White Dwarf*, and participate in battles. Some hobbyists join the Facebook groups that allow them to talk about their favorite battles, the people they respect the most in Games Workshop, and the events they're attending. Games Workshop has become such a distinct subculture that hobbyists would no sooner compare themselves to other war games such as Dungeons and Dragons (despite the obvious similarities) than they would to American Girl doll or Barbie collectors.

To understand the Games Workshop phenomenon, one must go back to when it all began. Originating in a bedroom in London in 1974, the hobby company was initially a small mail-order gig founded by Ian Livingstone, John Peake, and Steve Jackson. In the beginning, they sold wooden board games and distributed Dungeons and Dragons to British consumers. In their effort to expand the company, the trio started creating games of their own. In 1975, to spread the word, they produced a company newsletter called *Owl and Weasel*, superseded shortly thereafter by *White Dwarf* in 1977, which still functions as Games Workshop's key publication and is sold around the world. It contains listings of upcoming events, updates on major battles, and profiles of leading gamers. In 2001, their coup was landing a licensing deal with *Lord of the Rings*, which is now their most popular game next to Warhammer 40,000. There are more than a thousand Games Workshop locations around the world, and the number grows each month. Gauging the number of hobbyists is virtually impossible given that such an estimation would have to include those who use the websites that sell secondhand or painted miniatures, along with people who play the games, people who don't play but paint miniatures, people who simply buy miniatures in the Games Workshop stores (or Hobby Centers, as they are also called), those who buy them from other outlets, and those who do not own their own sets but borrow their friends' miniatures. While Warhammer World was not forthcoming with many exact numbers, the Nottingham compound alone is a destination for more than fifty thousand visitors a year. The business has developed into a multimillion-dollar enterprise, complete with rights to *Lord of the Rings*, *The Hobbit*, Doctor Who, and Judge Dredd.

White Dwarf and the Games Workshop's annual Games Day (the annual conference, established in 1975, that attracts thousands of hobbyists) were game changers, quite literally. By creating a worldwide publication and an annual event, Games Workshop was able to connect localized communities and enthusiasts to other avid hobbyists around the world. While there are Games Days held around the world, the Birmingham Games Day is the biggest event worldwide and has become an important backdrop to put hobbyists and Games Workshop creators into physical contact, while also generating more buzz about the hobby. *White Dwarf* created a platform for gamers to regularly exchange information, showcase upcoming events, and celebrate top gamers. Like in any other industry or hobby, the high-profile gamers are known for a particular talent: whether it's battle strategy, painting miniatures, or winning games. These "experts" are covered in great detail in *White Dwarf*, with photos and profiles, and consequently enthusiasts recognize the top gamers and celebrated designers when they walk into a Games Workshop location. Through the Tournament Circuit, gamers are able to compete with one another, accrue points, and increase their rankings.

Holding court in the Warhammer universe is Jervis Johnson, Games Workshop designer, columnist for *White Dwarf*, revered in the Games Workshop subculture for the past two decades, and by far the most renowned member of the Workshop community. A slight, balding man of about fifty, Jervis is one of the key contributors to the Warhammer 40,000 game (also known as Warhammer 40K). There is one guaranteed time and place where avid fans will get the chance to meet Jervis: Games Day. Even in the pouring rain (which tends to be frequent in England), hobbyists stand in lines round the block from early in the morning, waiting to get in. Some come early to get the limited-edition miniatures, others to heckle the rule book authors about new criteria in a particular game, and still others to talk to the miniature designers, who are revered in the community. Jervis is mostly adored, sometimes criticized, but world renowned within the Games Workshop community.

In the same moment that one gamer is proudly uploading photos of himself and Jervis playing Warhammer at the compound, another will be ranting on the Facebook discussion board about the publication of another Games Workshop rule book. One angry hobbyist ranted, "What a pile of shit the new rules are they need to stop thinking about MONEY all the time and think about the people who have been doing the hobby for years . . . This all happening about 4pm today it's now 1.20am and am still pissed off." No matter their opinion of Jervis, however, it is undisputable that he has achieved legendary, iconic status among Games Workshop players. One enthusiast's photo uploaded on a Facebook discussion board came with the explanation, "That's actually [Jervis's] shoulder next to me in the picture."

Celebrity Everywhere

You might notice something that I discovered myself: Despite the apparent discrepancy between Games Workshop and, say, the Academy Awards ceremony, these events and their attendees are connected by an important concept: *Relative celebrity, whereby small-scale celebrity is a fractal version of mainstream stardom.* Games Workshop is as far removed from Hollywood as possible, but the Nottingham-based subculture creates stars and fans just like its glamorous Los Angeles counterpart. Jervis's celebrity oversteps his talent: He is a brilliant designer, but fans also get excited about photos that capture a few inches of his shoulder. Fan obsession with gaming stars and Jervis mirrors obsession with Jennifer Aniston, Brad Pitt, or any other conventional star. And, just as Jennifer Aniston's fan base ebbs and flows, there are opportunities for the relative celebrity to increase or decrease his star power.

When I asked one Games Workshop store manager about

stars like Jervis, he wasn't sure why this question needed to be asked. As far as he was concerned, there was nothing unique about Games Workshop fandom and the celebrity of particular members of the community. To him, this story could be found in all realms where celebrity and an audience exist. As he put it to me in a rather no-duh fashion, "You always get that, with everything. It's the same as everything else, isn't it?"

Relative celebrities exist in all of our own worlds, in our hobbies, social groups, and families. Jervis is a perfect example of someone removed from traditional versions of celebrity—Hollywood, baseball players, supermodels—and yet just like them. There are five important lessons about relative celebrity that we can learn from Jervis and Warhammer World. First, to be clear, relative celebrities are not necessarily on the road to full-fledged everyone-in-the-world-knows-your-name celebrity.[2] Relative celebrities are not subsets of the "real thing." Relative celebrities exist autonomously within their own professions, on their own scale, and with their own adoring public.[3] Make no mistake: Jervis Johnson is the star of his show. Jervis showing up at Games Day means as much to Workshop hobbyists as Barack Obama's acceptance speech means to America at large and Angelina Jolie's presence at the Academy Awards means to her fans. Hobbyists queue for hours for the chance to meet him. But his celebrity is independent of Hollywood, politics, or other versions of conventional stardom. Jervis is not on a path to being bigger or better known. Jervis has reached his peak in his relative celebrity world.

Second, context is everything. Relative celebrities are distinctly linked to the particular context in which they become stars. Jervis from Games Workshop is a star around the world but only within the Games Workshop community. In the Nottingham compound or at the Birmingham Games Day, fans clamor to speak with him, but the average person on a New

York City street could not pick him out in a lineup. This lopsidedness goes the other way too: Stars like Paris Hilton would not be nearly as interesting to Games Day attendees as is Jervis. Although she may stop traffic in the streets of Los Angeles, most gamers view Paris Hilton as a minor distraction (more likely an annoying interloper) as they make their way into Warhammer World to speak with Jervis.

Let's return to M. M continues to be a Facebook celebrity, but if we removed Facebook he would cease to be a star in my microworld. The same can be said for anyone's high school crush: Did you ever notice that the person who you crushed on in high school often had an extensive trail of admirers, making you feel all the more certain he or she would never give you the time of day? In high school, most crush objects are relative celebrities: Lots of people have crushes on the same few crushees and collectively speculate about all aspects of their life, from where they hang out on a Friday night to whom they're going to the prom with. But the crush's celebrity rests on being in high school. Without high school, there is no context in which to attain information about this individual or for him or her to cultivate a collective group of admirers. Almost all relative celebrity emerges from four different (but not mutually exclusive) channels: career, geographic ties, social network, and subculture.[4] Without the fan base that surfaces from these particular contexts, a relative celebrity ceases to exist.[5]

Third, like major athletes or film actors, relative celebrities rely on certain outlets and events, which are also context specific, to establish and affirm their celebrity status. For Jervis, it is Games Day and the pages of *White Dwarf*. For Hollywood stars, it is the Oscars and the *Vanity Fair* Oscar party and various celebrity magazines from *US Weekly* to *OK!* to *People*. For the local sports star, it is the Friday night football game, the write-up in the local newspaper, and homecoming, where he is not only the star football player but also likely on the homecoming court. M, our definitive example of the relative celebrity, attains his stardom through various social media sites that distribute information about him and his fabulous life.[6]

The fourth lesson is that relative celebrity is fluid. Just like any Hollywood star who moves from B- to A-list, relative celebrities have the chance to move up the food chain, becoming bigger versions of celebrity *within* their relative worlds. A truly talented high school football player who is recruited to play for Notre Dame or Ohio State or the University of Southern California moves up his relative-celebrity hierarchy. In a few years, if he is successful in his collegiate playing, he may be given another chance at moving up if offered a contract with the NFL. If he takes the offer, he becomes that small-town football player who went pro, thus increasing his celebrity locally while moving up a tier within his sport. Not everyone moves up all or even any of these steps. The football player has the option to decline the mountains of scholarships awaiting him and stay in his small town. He will remain a relative celebrity, for sure, as that former high school athletic star, taken from Springsteen's "Glory Days," but his rank in his relative celebrity world remains static and with time his stardom will decrease as new former high school football stars take his place. Jervis, however, has not chosen the static option. He's been moving up the ranks of relative celebrity for decades. As a columnist for *White Dwarf*, the chief designer for Warhammer World, and one of the main attractions of Games Day, there's no higher echelon of stardom for Jervis to achieve in his world.

Finally, relative celebrity relies on an element of exclusivity. Gamers may want stardom in their world, but they're not interested in anyone invading it, just like *Vanity Fair* keeps a strict list of who gets to enter its Oscar party. I've found it harder to gain access to the top members of Warhammer World than to the top Hollywood publicists. Games Workshop has zero interest in being documented or capitalized upon by hungry mainstream media looking for innovative stories and topics to cover. When MTV inquired about doing a documentary on Warhammer World, the network was denied access. (You can bet if MTV wanted to do a documentary on the average indie rock band or Hollywood starlet, doors would open before they finished their request.)

These principles of relative celebrity demonstrate that celebrity exists everywhere, in many forms. Stars as seemingly dissimilar as Jervis Johnson and Jennifer Aniston emerge from the same fundamental conditions: Particular contexts, events, and outlets create and affirm each star's celebrity status and exclusivity; fans are uniquely obsessed with these stars within these contexts; and both Aniston and Johnson are able to become more or less celebrated within their respective worlds. Most people tend to view subcultures like Games Workshop as something akin to a carnival's House of Oddities and Freaks. We judge these worlds differently, as if Hollywood actors and annual Academy Awards and Oscar parties in Los Angeles are fundamentally different from gamer aficionados and their annual Games Day in Birmingham. However, when you get down to it, there is very little distinction between how these two remarkably different worlds create celebrity. While Games Workshop celebrities do not seek representation in the pages of *US Weekly*, they do appear on the game message boards, are written up in *White Dwarf*, and make the rounds at Games Day. Hollywood has a larger market and is followed more in popular culture, but Games Workshops and small-town football players are simply smaller versions of Hollywood's star system.

The Mainstream Celebrity

Scale is an important factor that explains the radical difference between Aniston's and Johnson's position within the larger phenomenon of celebrity. So far, we've seen that celebrities exist in many cultures, industries, and places, and that relative celebrities tend to be created and perpetuated through similar processes. Yet there are celebrities that both Games Workshop hobbyists and my mother are aware of—Aniston is and Jervis is not one of these shared stars. Mainstream celebrities are those everyone knows about, usually emerging from sports, politics, music, or Hollywood. Like other celebrities, mainstream celebrities arise from specific contexts and industries, but because the creation and reportage of their celebrity are cultivated through mainstream, widespread media, lots of people know about them. This amplification and exposure set them apart from the relative celebrity.

Angelina Jolie is revered by Hollywood, but even if her Hollywood public ceased to exist, she would have a collective public stretching from Kansas City to Paris that would buy magazines with her face on the cover. Sure, Jervis has *White Dwarf*, but *US Weekly* and *OK!* are sold at newsstands around the world.[7] Jervis's celebrity has to be actively sought out if one is not a Games Workshop hobbyist. Mainstream celebrities attain such status not because they are fundamentally different from relative celebrities but because there are so many more avenues to learn of their existence.[8]

Yet even mainstream celebrities are relative in certain contexts. Tom Cruise, perhaps the definitive example of a mainstream celebrity in Western culture, is for all intents and purposes a relative celebrity in India. He is known by Indians, but he is not nearly as celebrated as his Bollywood counterparts. Bollywood, the term used to describe India's film industry, centered in Mumbai, produces some eleven hundred films a year (twice the number of films produced in the United States) and sells 3.6 billion movie tickets (compared to America's 2.6 billion).[9]

Shahrukh Khan, arguably the most famous Bollywood actor, reigns front and center. Known as "King Khan," he began as a television actor in the 1980s and then burst onto the film scene in 1992 with *Deewana*. Since then, Khan has appeared in seventy-five films, produced nine films, and appeared on and hosted multiple television programs. His 2007 film *Chak De India* was the third-highest-grossing film that year, generating $20 million.[10] At forty-five, Khan is a handsome man who is every bit the archetypal film star, and one often sees photographs of him splashed across India's celebrity tabloids (which are even more feverish in their documenting of stars' lives than their American and British equivalents).

Many Westerners may not be aware of Shahrukh Khan's existence (despite the installation of a Khan wax figure in the London Madame Tussauds), but calculating the total number of films Khan appears in and the number of tickets that are purchased to see him shows that he is far and away more worshipped than any Hollywood actor.[11] "On a global scale, Khan has twice as many fans as Tom Cruise," explains Mark Lorenzen, a professor at Copenhagen Business School and an expert on Bollywood. "All the Indians, both in India and abroad, all the Pakistanis, all the Bangladeshis, lots of Arabs and lots of Asians are Khan fans." Shahrukh Khan is by all accounts the biggest movie star in the world.[12]

India's population of 1.13 billion versus the U.S. population of 304 million ensures a superior fan base, and the Indian diasporas of the 1990s that spread to the United States, Britain, and the Middle East distributed Bollywood culture and Khan's celebrity worldwide. The United States and Britain alone account for 50–60 percent of Bollywood's export rev-

enue, and Bollywood is the largest foreign contributor to the
U.S. entertainment market.[13] And it is growing larger all the
time: In 2009, Reliance, a Bollywood film company, invested
$325 million in Hollywood's Dreamworks.[14]

Yet the same cannot be said for Hollywood's influence on
India's film market, where Hollywood has just a 4 percent
share.[15] "Hollywood has tried to enter into India unsuccess-
fully," Lorenzen explains. "Fox and Universal Pictures have
tried to lure the big Indian stars over. They were not able to
lure the biggest stars because the biggest stars didn't really care
about Hollywood . . . because their home market is so enormous. Indian stars are very, very wealthy, just as wealthy as
their A-list Hollywood counterparts. If you can compare what
they get for their money, they're actually wealthier. Many of
them have massive personal fortunes." Indeed, Khan turned
down one of the lead roles in Danny Boyle's Academy
Award–winning *Slumdog Millionaire*, a film about a young
boy growing up in the slums of Mumbai who becomes a contestant on *Who Wants to Be a Millionaire?*[16]

For many Westerners, both Bollywood and Khan seem like
far lesser examples of star power than their own A-listers.
However, on a global scale, Indian celebrities have a much
greater fan base than most Western stars (barring perhaps
Michael Jackson). By definition, our Western top-tier celebrities are relative in the sense that their renown is created from
the perspective from which we are viewing them; they are not,
in other words, absolute. "Indians know the Tom Cruises and
Brad Pitts," Lorenzen remarks. "They are impressed with
them, but Cruise's and Pitt's impression upon the Indian public is very weak compared to the Indian stars. Indians are so
unimpressed with Western stars compared to Bollywood and
their cricket stars."

Bollywood celebrity is so tantalizing and so mainstream
that no aspiring star in the industry views going to Hollywood

as an enticing prospect because Hollywood does not offer them a greater form of celebrity. "For those who haven't made it to the highest level," Lorenzen explains, "it would be a real opportunity cost to disappear to Hollywood." Bollywood may seem like a source of relative celebrity to the average American, but the converse is true as well: Hollywood celebrities are smaller stars to a fan in India. Celebrity almost always rests on context, whether geographical, cultural, or through the media channels necessary to create it.

The Currency of Star Power

In 2003, the *Observer*, the Sunday edition of Britain's left-leaning newspaper the *Guardian*, ran a faintly ridiculous article titled, "Why Brits with Brains Are the Big Apple's New Blondes," which was a treatise on the rise of the British academic as American celebrity.[17] The reporter, barely concealing her amusement, observed that British professors were being wined, dined, and handed fabulous apartments in New York City and Cambridge, Massachusetts, fully embraced by American academe. Case in point was Niall Ferguson, the dashing Oxford-educated Scottish historian with a knack for writing best sellers on economic history. At Oxford, Ferguson felt that all professors were treated as, in his words, "equally brilliant," but individual stardom was frowned upon. He greeted American academic celebrity with bemusement. The article went on to comment on rumors that Ferguson, having been lured from Oxford to New York University, was being poached from NYU by Harvard. Sure enough, within a year, Ferguson was a chaired professor at Harvard. On his trajectory from Oxford to Harvard, Ferguson achieved a major multibook contract from Penguin and his own TV series.

After reading the article, one might initially think that the reporter was making much of a random anomaly. How many good-looking, well-dressed professors could the halls of academe really produce? But something in her story rang true. The *New York Observer* picked up the article, and New York's snarky gossip blog, Gawker, reported on the *Observer* story with great fanfare. A few months later, David Kirp, a professor at Berkeley, wrote a *New York Times* op-ed on the "star wars" of academe, devoting much of his argument to Ferguson's case.[18]

I met Ferguson in the summer of 2009 to quiz him about financial celebrities (he believes they don't exist). I met him at the Union Square Cafe, a publishing industry see-and-be-seen hangout, where Ferguson had just finished lunch with a fellow academic superstar. During our meeting, some seemingly Important Person stopped by our table and made plans with Ferguson to meet up in the British Airways lounge at JFK that evening, before they both caught a flight to London. After our meeting, Ferguson had to race to a TV interview. In an immaculate linen suit and with perfectly disheveled hair, Ferguson was the picture of what *Vogue* would mock up should Anna Wintour create a fantasy fashion shoot on academics. He sure didn't look like any of the professors I had at Columbia. A few weeks later, a friend happened to see Niall Ferguson's name in my e-mail in-box. She gasped, "Is that *the* Niall Ferguson? The author? Oh my God, he is so hot." How, I ask you, is this any different from the average reaction to Brad Pitt?

Ferguson is the new face of academic celebrity. He is good-looking, charismatic, articulate, and not painfully esoteric. He does his research, but he knows how to write in plain English. In the last decade, the image of the professor with a corduroy jacket and pocket protector has rapidly given way to a figure more engaging and interesting to the wider public.[19] Websites have sprung up where students can anonymously but publicly evaluate their professors' charisma (or lack thereof); Rate-

MyProfessors.com allows students to vote on whether their professors are "hot" or "not." Professors get mentioned in gossip columns and blogs, write best-selling books, and travel around the world with celebrities. The Columbia economist Jeffrey Sachs promotes poverty awareness with Angelina Jolie and Brad Pitt. U2's Bono wrote the foreword to Sachs's *The End of Poverty*. The former Harvard sociologist Cornel West produces music, appeared in *The Matrix: Reloaded* and *The Matrix: Revolutions*, and made front-page news around the country when Harvard president Laurence Summers told him to put the hip-hop gear away and conduct some more serious research. West left for a more appreciative Princeton. This development was covered by popular media, with every turn detailed on the front page of the *New York Times*. Again, I ask, how is any of this different from the mainstream celebrity coverage we are accustomed to?[20]

Academic celebrity is a perfect example of relative celebrity.[21] It's always existed in the form of the academic star system, which for the most part remained inside the university. In recent years, however, the star professor has attained a public following among people unrelated to his or her field. And thus we get to a final facet of relative celebrity: All relative celebrity has an exchange rate between relative and mainstream. Like any currency, the rate changes continually, and some relative celebrity has a stronger exchange value than others.

Consider it like this: Ferguson was a star within academia for quite a while. His rapid moves from Oxford to NYU to Harvard would have made his star power fodder for gossip in the halls of universities. But when mainstream publications like Gawker started covering Ferguson as they might Angelina Jolie, his star power ceased to be merely relative and constrained within the context of the university. By virtue of being written about by popular media, Ferguson was now known by people who read Gawker, the *New York Times*, the *New York Observer*, and so forth, people not necessarily affiliated with academic politics or gossip. Ferguson's celebrity was becoming less relative and more mainstream. Of course Ferguson had not attained the visibility of Brad Pitt, but he was not relevant only within his immediate academic context. Ferguson's celebrity was transforming, and not simply because his books were being read by a wider audience. By the very definition of celebrity, his stardom was transcending his talent as a historian. Mainstream journalism was speculating about him as a person, and regular folks were gushing about his attractiveness (including my friend and, in full disclosure, my aunt as well). When Ferguson's marriage broke up in February 2010, the *Daily Mail* ran a huge story on its demise, including gossip about his new girlfriend, Ayaan Hirsi Ali, a lawyer and a former member of the Dutch parliament who penned the highly critical and controversial script for the film *Submission* in addition to the widely acclaimed books *Infidel* and *Nomad*. *Submission*'s director, Theo Van Gogh, was murdered in 2004 and Ali, currently under police protection at all times, has a fatwa over her head. The article discussed in detail Ferguson's multiple homes, jet-set lifestyle, and hobnobbing with the British political elite. One source claimed that Ferguson's wife was shocked that he had begun "conducting a private life in a manner more akin to that of a Premiership footballer than a professor."[22] Gawker summed up the Ferguson report simply: "Sex! Scandal! Murderous Muslim Clerics! This Story Has It All."[23]

Ferguson contemporary Nouriel Roubini is another academic transforming from relative to mainstream celebrity. Roubini, a New York University economist, became renowned due to his prescience in predicting the burst of the real estate bubble and the potential collapse of the U.S. economy several years before these events occurred.[24] Roubini, also known as

"Dr. Doom," for his dark economic forecasts, unfortunately turned out to have been remarkably accurate in his predictions.[25] Consequently, Roubini has attained a worldwide following, giving speeches and interviews around the world and penning opinion pieces. Roubini is also a regular subject of Gawker's gossipy posts. Gawker, however, is not interested in Roubini's economic analysis as much as his celebrity lifestyle. The site has devoted several postings to the NYU professor's "very hard partying,"[26] including an uploaded photo album of the economist with young ladies (and fashion designer Marc Jacobs) at Russian oligarch Roman Abramovich's 2010 New Year's bash in St. Barts.[27] Back in March 2009, in a posting titled "Nouriel Roubini Copters His Way Back Home," Gawker dissected both the photos the economist uploaded on his Facebook profile documenting him alongside good-looking women, and his status updates, including one stating "Nouriel is taking a coptor to the airport as São Paulo car traffic is THE worst in the world." The article commented, "Roubini, a doomsaying economist who's as well-known for his Tribeca loft parties as his increasingly grandiose predictions of worldwide economic collapse, took a break from wooing young women on Facebook to post a few photos of a copter ride in Brazil." When asked in a *Financial Times* profile what he thought of his newfound stardom, Roubini merely sighed, "Celebrity has become a burden."[28]

Partially, Ferguson's and Roubini's increasing relevance to a more mainstream fan base can be explained by the media's new interest in academic stars as viable people to report on and speculate about. In another era, Gawker might not have cared about Ferguson's or Roubini's rising star power; and if the media hadn't cared, these academics would have remained relative celebrities, moving up the ranks of academic celebrity but unknown to the mainstream public. Like Jervis, Ferguson and Roubini would have been at the pinnacle of their relative celebrity but nothing more. However, to use the currency metaphor, academics with relative celebrity now have a stronger exchange rate with mainstream celebrity than ever before. Best-selling academic authors like Richard Dawkins, Jeffrey Sachs, and Steve Levitt made the idea-driven book de rigueur reading, catalyzing a deluge of more best-selling books by academics and public intellectuals. Academics no longer shy away from mainstream media, many of them showing up on TV shows, writing opinion pieces, and hiring agents like anyone interested in becoming a celebrity might do.

Two things must happen for a relative celebrity to become mainstream: Mass media needs to report on the individual and the public needs to respond with interest. Exchange rates between relative and mainstream celebrity fluctuate because they reflect changes in consumer tastes and media interest. At the turn of the twenty-first century, the relative celebrities who have become mainstream are Internet stars and reality TV contestants. Conversely, when the public grows bored or moves on to a new fixation, the exchange value of a particular type of star goes down.

Consider the rise and fall of artists as mainstream stars in the United States.[29] At the turn of the twentieth century, most artists were still fairly unknown. They may have painted portraits of famous people, but the mainstream media and public did not celebrate them as stars. In the 1950s, however, the Abstract Expressionists had a general public who recognized and was fascinated by their lives.[30] By the 1980s, Andy Warhol and his crew of pop artists were genuine celebrities, hanging out at Studio 54 with Mick Jagger and David Bowie, and being written up by columnists everywhere.[31] It was Warhol himself who said, "Don't pay any attention to what they write about you, just measure it in inches." Since the late 1980s, however, American visual artists' relative-celebrity currency exchange with mainstream stardom has decreased. In the mid-

2000s, barring a few exceptions like Damien Hirst and Jeff Koons, the general public does not obsess about the art world. Artists are stars of their own (relative) worlds, but society is not collectively interested in them in the way it cares about Hollywood actors or musicians or reality TV stars.

The currency of stars is also different depending on where they are located. In Europe, soccer players are of great interest to the general public; they are both relative celebrities to soccer aficionados and mainstream celebrities. Not a day goes by without some footballer being featured in the *Sun* for cheating on his wife, getting in a bar fight, or proposing to his model girlfriend (his last game statistics are somewhere in the back of the paper). Whereas in America, most people would recognize only David Beckham or perhaps Ronaldo (who in the summer of 2009 signed the largest soccer contract in history) as mainstream stars. And, as mentioned earlier, Ronaldo's recognition in America can partially be explained by his romantic dalliance with Paris Hilton. Soccer stars aren't as celebrated in America, mainly because soccer isn't as popular a spectator sport in the United States as it is in Europe and England.

Ferguson's move from relative toward mainstream celebrity was predicated on the media's interest and the public responding. This is why his public profile rose simultaneously with his relative rise in academia. All relative celebrity is fluid, but most relative celebrity is vertically fluid: Individuals can move up the ranks in their particular celebrity stratosphere, but they are not increasing their mainstream celebrity. Relative celebrity's exchange rate with mainstream celebrity is horizontal: How interested the public is in one's field of relative celebrity determines if being a luminary of academia, football, or Hollywood has any currency in the world at large. Some types of relative celebrity will simply never be interesting to the wider public. Jervis may reign supreme in Warhammer World, but it is unlikely that his relative celebrity will ever transfer to mainstream stardom, because the popular press and ordinary public will simply never be interested in miniatures battling in space forty thousand years in the future. Thus, no matter the reach of his celebrity in Warhammer World, Jervis's relative-celebrity exchange rate with mainstream celebrity is roughly the same as Iceland's krona with the U.S. dollar.

Conversely, some types of celebrity have an infallibly strong exchange rate with mainstream stardom. If you're a star in Hollywood, you have an almost one-to-one exchange rate of also being a mainstream celebrity. The same holds true for American sports stars. Alex Rodriguez may lose his appeal at some point, but the handsome baseball star is an example of one of the quickest ascents from relative to mainstream celebrity. Baseball players who sign with major franchises almost instantly attain massive media coverage and a huge, diverse fan base interested in all aspects of their persona.[32] Each type of relative celebrity has a different currency with mainstream: Professor Ferguson's relative-celebrity exchange rate with mainstream celebrity may not be as strong as Angelina Jolie's, but it is far and away more valuable than Jervis Johnson's.

We know there are linkages among fame, celebrity, and talent. Some individuals have all three qualities, some possess one or two. We know that famous people (such as Bill Gates) are not necessarily celebrities. Relative celebrity is the converse of this phenomenon, where people who are truly celebrated in their relative worlds are not famous to the world at large. *Fame is global, and most celebrity is local.* Fame is fundamentally about sheer numbers of people who know one's name, while celebrity emerges out of a collective interest in a particular person. Fame is measured by quantity of recognition. Celebrity does not imply that lots of people know about you but instead is indicated by a collective group of people (big or small in number) invested in knowing about you as a person.

Thus, the social phenomenon of celebrity exists every-where, and people all over the place have at least the opportu-nity to become (relative) celebrities by cultivating an interested public. Celebrity can also be at once mainstream and relative. Celebrity is not only malleable and constantly in flux but also operates according to the same principles and emerges from the same conditions regardless of social standing. These unify-ing traits of celebrity explain why we see similarities in how the young high school football star, Jervis from Games Work-shop, M with his three thousand–plus Facebook friends, and Angelina Jolie engage their relative publics, who care about them in similar ways. An analysis of celebrity, then, tells us the story of how people become leaders and stars in their own worlds and in the world at large through very similar mecha-nisms.

4

Inside the Star Machine: Celebrity as Industry

In Hollywood, the golden rule is that gold rules.[1]
—Anonymous movie producer

In Los Angeles, MapQuest is undoubtedly one of the most use-less technologies for predicting the actual time it takes to get anywhere. Mileage means nothing in this city of glittering sprawl. This was the sad reality I was facing as, while driving, I frantically e-mailed Stan Rosenfield's assistant to tell her that yes, I was aware I was to meet Mr. Rosenfield at this precise moment in time, and no, I was nowhere even remotely close to his office. My franticness was partially due to the fact that I was also acutely aware that, as one of the most respected pub-licists in the world, Mr. Rosenfield, who represents George Clooney, Robert De Niro, Danny DeVito, Helen Mirren, and a dozen other elite A-list actors, wasn't usually on the receiving end of tardiness, nor did he have the time for it. My foot had been resting on the brake pedal unmoved for the past ten min-utes while I waited at Wilshire Boulevard and Virgil through an aggressively irritating mix of pedestrians, construction, and sinuous lines of traffic.

At some point I had the chance to hang right and I bombed southwest. As I rounded the bend heading out of Beverly Hills into Century City, I came face-to-face with a massive collec-tion of skyscrapers rivaling the city's downtown financial dis-trict. These were the buildings that housed the thousands of

publicists, agents, managers, media, and other acutely important cogs in the celebrity wheel. Some were heavy hitters like
Rosenfield, others were just getting started, still others would
manage only B- and C-rated stars for their entire career, and
that was just fine. After all, there can be no A-list without a B
and C wistfully trailing behind. These actors would still generate paychecks and have fulfilling careers. The complicated
structure of the celebrity machine is huge and encompasses far
more than just film stars; it produces everyone from supermodels to sports stars to Internet aberrations who want to
take their democratic celebrity and become A-list. The "star
machine" is part and parcel of joining celebrity in all its forms.
"You can be famous, but do you have a career?" One U.K.-
based publicist remarked. "You can be on YouTube and have
twenty million hits—but will twenty million people pay a dollar? Business is what it's all about. You can't pay your grocery
bill with a cutout from a newspaper."

Celebrity is everywhere: We see stars in the tabloids and we
see them on the front page of the BBC website. Entire TV programs, entire channels, even, are devoted to them: TMZ and
E! Entertainment, for example. Reality TV is based on the
premise that an audience will become obsessed with the participants, like they would with any star. Some lawyers and publicists devote their entire careers to protecting (and propagating)
stars' images, whether those individuals have risen through the
ranks of Hollywood or the Internet. Major agencies like Creative Artists Agency and William Morris Endeavor have an
arsenal of thousands of staff devoted to handling stars' (and
aspiring stars') business deals, publication rights, and endorsements. And then there are stardom's various accoutrements:
the hairdressers, clothing stylists, fitness trainers, and so forth
that keep up the physical projection of "star power" that is
essential to capturing and keeping the public's interest.

All of these people work in tandem to max out a star's economic potential, profile, and media interest, and each of these outcomes is predicated on the others. A star can't land a major endorsement without the media creating his or her public profile. Those endorsements may be attained by agents, but lawyers look over the contract and publicists announce the deal to the *Wall Street Journal* and *US Weekly*. And a star doesn't land a makeup deal with L'Oréal or become the face of Armani if she's not working out with trainers and getting skin treatments and great haircuts that get her physical appearance up to snuff for these luxury brands. Celebrity is not conceived of as an industry in the traditional sense, yet when one thinks about all the aspects of creating and maintaining star power, it adds up to an enormous, and surprisingly organized, economic juggernaut with thousands upon thousands of employees, billions of dollars, and thousands of firms, many of whose purpose and livelihood rest solely on the existences of stars.

Yet while the actual celebrities may come and go, Stan Rosenfield and superagent Ari Emanuel are always there. Elliot Mintz chalks up a celebrity's success to possession of "the light," but others more practically say that stars are successful because of an intricate and complicated industrial chain of production that stays in place no matter the ebb and flow of stars. It's almost impossible to capture a complete picture of all the elements of this industry, partially because the concept of celebrity is nebulous and partially because there are so many moving parts essential to creating stardom: brands, endorsements, movie deals, sports contracts, and public profiles. Not to mention that some individuals have a natural charisma or beauty or talent that makes the job that much easier. Some celebrities are almost totally constructed by the handlers and support systems that maintain their image, regulate their interaction with the media, and make sure that they've spent three hours in makeup and wardrobe before they start an interview. "The majority of people we interview are actually rather dull," one producer at a major TV station remarked. "Most of these people are completely lacking in charisma. You think that celebrities have this certain natural spark that makes them a celebrity, but when you talk to them you think, 'Is that all you got?' Top agents are getting these people working, [the industry is] more of a big giant monster that works in unison. There is a whole army of people coming together to sell you the reason why a star is big." People like Rosenfield and Emanuel remain the engineers of the celebrity industry decade after decade, keeping the star machine humming along.

And they keep the industry humming to quite a tune. If celebrity is a business, then New York and Los Angeles are the U.S. headquarters. In these cities, celebrity is a driving force of the economy: In Los Angeles there are almost two thousand firms devoted to handling celebrities, ranging from public relations, like Rosenfield and Associates, to agencies, such as CAA, which represents stars in their movie deals, sports contracts, and endorsements. In total, more than fourteen thousand people in Los Angeles work in these establishments devoted to publicity and representing stars.[2] Overall, in Los Angeles and New York City, almost 110,000 people in each city work broadly in celebrity-related occupations, from publicists to agents, lawyers, photographers, editors of magazines, and so forth.[3] This figure also includes those who prep the stars to actually look the part: the trainers, hairstylists, nutritionists, makeup artists, and skin care specialists who are necessary for transforming stars from ordinary to extraordinary.[4]

These employment numbers translate into real money. Almost $1 billion of New York City's payroll is paid to people working in public relations firms and agencies, and in Los Angeles that figure is $536 million. Media alone generates $3.5 billion in payroll in Los Angeles and $4.9 billion in New

York. Payroll generated by the facets of the support industries devoted to celebrities is approximately $95 million for Los Angeles and $45 million for New York. While not everyone in media or supporting industries deals completely in the business of celebrity, a large number of newspapers, TV programs, and magazines cover celebrity to some degree and thus rely on these individuals to generate new stories. Celebrity-driven occupations themselves—the actors, musicians, athletes—generate a breathtaking amount of salary as well, over $1.5 billion in Los Angeles and $810 million in New York. Drop in the six-figure price points of paparazzi photos, such as the shot of Britney Spears shaving her head (paparazzi agency X17 sold it for $300,000) and Lindsay Lohan passed out intoxicated in her car ($150,000), along with the millions of dollars that particular stars are estimated to contribute to the economy by their sheer existence (by some accounts, Spears apparently generates $110–$120 million annually for the economy).[5] Angelina Jolie and Brad Pitt sold photos of their newborns to *People* for $14 million. Celebrity is big business.[6]

These numbers demonstrate that celebrity is undoubtedly an industry. In places like Los Angeles and New York, celebrity is intrinsic to the success of the cities, powering jobs and cash flow. Think about the dent in employment and tax revenue for these locales if all the stars packed up and headed to Missouri.[7] Similarly, the structure of the mechanism by which the celebrity industry produces stars isn't much different from the financial industry and its assemblage of analysts, market researchers, publicists, and lawyers orbiting a central CEO. And just like in Silicon Valley, where big tech companies find smaller firms to help them build microprocessors or semiconductors, a lot of one's star power is outsourced to experts able to maximize base talent and cultivate media interest.[8]

There are five tiers that make up the celebrity industry.[9]

The first rung is the celebrities and aspiring stars. Whether NFL players, actors, or supermodels, they are the individuals whose existence means that everyone else in the business has a job. It's fair to say that most actors, musicians, and entertainers living in Los Angeles and New York are, at the very least, aspiring stars—that group amounts to almost thirty-five thousand in Los Angeles and twelve thousand in New York.[10] To give a sense of the magnitude of this number, there are over six times more aspiring stars and entertainers in Los Angeles than anywhere else in the United States and one and a half times more in New York.[11] The second tier of people in the celebrity industry work directly for the stars in the form of representing them and creating their public image, a group composed of the agents and publicists. Call these people and businesses "the handlers." Handlers are almost twice as concentrated in Los Angeles and New York than in other metro areas. The third tier of the star machine is the support, ranging from lawyers to couriers to chauffeurs and various attendants. This may seem like a motley crew, but they all have the basic job of making sure things run smoothly, whether finalizing contracts or getting a star to an event on time. Much of the success of stars hinges on their looking like stars, and those who help with this process comprise the fourth tier: "the preppers." As removed as a manicurist may seem from Scarlett Johansson's or Elizabeth Taylor's celebrity, the nail salon, along with the beauty parlor, high-end wardrobe stylist, and nutritionist (who creates perfectly calorie-counted meals), are all part of the necessary prepping process that maxes out a star's physical appearance.

The Media as Message

The fifth and most important tier of the celebrity industry (besides the celebrities themselves) is the media. Everyone in the celebrity business agrees that the media is the raison d'être of the celebrity industry: The media must think you're worth its while.[12] "You need various elements to achieve the elements of celebrity," Rosenfield explained. "One of the things is the media's willingness to cover you." Or as one editor of a celebrity tabloid succinctly put it, "It's crucial that you don't piss off magazines. Because either you will not be reported about at all or reported about in a negative way. And in celebrity, without the coverage, you'll starve."

But this is where the cohesive whole of the industry splits up. Which side of the media you're on determines how you perceive the power dynamic. While handlers, supporters, preppers, and the stars themselves are obviously on the same side of the equation, on the other side stands the media, which ultimately picks some aspiring stars and discards others.[13] Part of the uncertainty of predicting stardom can be explained by the tenuous, antagonistic, yet codependent relationship between the handlers and support elements of the industry and the media. Stars need to be constantly documented to maintain their status and profile, yet publicists (and agents and entertainment lawyers) are desperately trying to protect their stars from damaging information leaking out or from oversaturation in the press. Journalists need to write juicy articles to keep their jobs, but if they write something too scandalous they'll never have access to stars again. Those in media have been bemoaning the tight-lipped and controlled publicity machine since the 1990s, when publicists started demanding to see copy and to sign off on stars' quotes before articles or interviews went to press. Some of these sentiments have resonated since the mid-twentieth-century Hollywood studio system, when stars signed contracts whereby they spoke only to media outlets that the studios had vetted.[14] "Well, we call it 'fine tuning' or 'protecting one's position,'" says Rosenfield, "but if you want to call them 'celebrity covers' [celebrities on the cover of a publication], that's fine with me." Journalists who sidestep this process and write articles that are potentially damaging end up blacklisted from major film openings and other reporting opportunities.[15] The twenty-first-century rise of online media and the frequent use of "unnamed sources" have helped free journalists from hopeless efforts to attempt to deal directly with the A-list. Not to mention that the deluge of oversharing reality TV stars has allowed media to cover other individuals who cravenly desire attention.

Publicists work hard to court good publicity and maintain distance from the bad, creating rather contradictory relationships with media outlets. In the same breath that Rosenfield threatens to sue one tabloid for unsubstantiated reports on the love life of one of his clients, he is more than happy for a *New Yorker* or *GQ* profile of George Clooney. "The powers that be want to control the celebrity that they have created," a TV producer explained. "[It is] extremely controlled. We can't afford to piss anyone off. The publicists are worried about the most unimportant things." And with people like Rosenfield and British publicist extraordinaire Max Clifford handling phone call after phone call from the tabloids, squelching rumors and releasing timely information to media outlets, stars are, theoretically, able to maintain a positive image under the glaring camera lights.

But this positioning is not achieved without draconian measures. According to one report, in the mid-1990s, Pat Kingsley, the grande dame of the Hollywood publicity empire and flack for Tom Cruise (and other film gods and goddesses), demanded that freelance journalists sign agreements promising they wouldn't sell their articles to multiple news outlets. If the writers wouldn't sign, they wouldn't get their interview and might even get permanently taken off the list of all major events associated with her stars.[16] "Simon Cowell pays Max Clifford £20,000 every month," one celebrity reporter told me. "Every major celebrity story that breaks, Max Clifford will have something to do with. [He] has the ears of every media outlet. Who you've got in your corner [your publicist] will show how far you will go in the fight." An exposé of the industry is even more cynical. "In this Puppet Master–controlled planet of celebrity journalism," the journalist Catherine Seipp writes, "the celebrity reveals little except liberal use of the word 'amazing'—the favorite all-purpose adjective these days of people who can't be bothered to think of anything else to say."[17]

But the publicists have a very different perspective. Fueled by the rise of the Internet's 24/7 reportage and the increased popularity of a sneaky tactic called the "write-around," the power dynamic appears to have shifted, or at least that's how publicists perceive the current environment.[18] In recent years, the media started writing what it wanted and the publicists were simply trying to put the fires out. If they couldn't get access, the reporters would merely ask all of the stars' friends, foes, and family to give a quip or two for the article, thus the term "write-around." Sure, Jennifer Aniston was still on the cover of *Elle* and the accompanying interview was likely to have been vetted by her handlers. And, of course, celebrity puff pieces and profiles still existed: in Britain, Katie Price (aka Jordan) was still being paid by *OK!* to do perennial covers with "exclusive" interviews. Celebrity baby albums are sold to *People* and *US Weekly* for millions of dollars. But increasingly, scandal and questionably accurate stories were being written up online and in the weekly tabloids. One editor explained that by simply playing with language and suggestion, a magazine was able to drum up an enticing cover article without doing so much damage that a celebrity or her handlers would bother suing. "Last week's *In Touch* cover reported 'Brad Takes the Kids,'" one celebrity journalist joked. "Then you read inside"—the journalist laughed—"Brad takes the kids . . . to school." "The type of coverage has definitely changed," Rosenfield lamented. "Maybe twenty years ago, if you gave a story to the papers that Andy Garcia was in talks to star in a movie, they'd say, 'When they make the deal let us know.' And now it will be, 'Andy Garcia in Talks,' and it drives us crazy. I remember a situation with Danny DeVito where Paramount wanted to make a movie [*How to Lose a Guy in 10 Days*] and they [media] called us up and I said, 'Well, they're in talks,' and they printed it anyway. And he didn't direct the movie and I can't tell you how many times it was mentioned that he was the director and he wasn't."

That the media is increasingly in control can be partially explained by the changing nature of the industry.[19] With blogs, social-networking sites, and online publications, media needs more content and by extension takes more liberties. Lloyd Grove, former gossip columnist for the *New York Daily News* and current editor-at-large for Tina Brown's *Daily Beast*, explained it simply: "The first thing you have to understand is if you're doing a daily column, you're responsible for filling a page. Say you're charged with [having to write] things that haven't already been written about. You don't have a lot of choice. You're living in a state of constant desperation. [Your column is] a bulletin board for gossip. People stop there. How do you make a decision? Well, what's on offer?" There is also no real incentive to not go straight for the story. Alex Balk, a former editor of *Radar* magazine, described the need for speed that often characterizes online journalism. "If you don't have Britney Spears's story at eight forty-five a.m. when everyone else does, you might as well not do it. The Heath Ledger story [when he was found dead] is a perfect example: We were three minutes ahead of everyone else but because of three minutes we are attributed with breaking it . . . Now if we were wrong and he didn't do it [commit suicide], we would have been wrong and moved on." Ledger, as the autopsy subsequently reported, died of an accidental toxic drug overdose.

This need for nearly real-time media paved the way for a new form of reportage. Enter into the mix the rise of one of the most sensation-seeking and impactful developments in media history: the paparazzi. The paparazzi have been a noted presence since 1962, when Liz Taylor and Richard Burton were famously caught kissing on a yacht, unaware of being watched and photographed. The picture, taken at the height of both actors' celebrity, was shown around the world. Both were married to other people and the photo catalyzed both of their divorces.[20] The paparazzi have been objects of scorn, blamed for the downfall of stars' careers and personal lives. Princess Diana's fatal car accident has been partly attributed to paparazzi hounding: Diana and her boyfriend, Dodi Fayed, were attempting to elude paparazzi as they raced through the streets of Paris and their driver lost control of the car. But, on the whole, the "paps," as they're called in industry jargon, have been on the fringe. To be clear, paparazzi are no ordinary celebrity photographers. You won't catch Annie Leibovitz or Juergen Teller lurking around street corners to take pictures of Britney Spears or Angelina Jolie going about their daily routines. Paparazzi base their entire livelihood on getting the in situ, unposed shots of stars living their lives, and, sometimes, doing terribly damaging things to their reputations.

In the last decade, however, the paparazzi have gone from being annoying to, as one observer put it, "one of the most powerful and lucrative forces driving the American news-gathering industry." Bonnie Fuller is largely attributed with this extraordinary rise. During her tenure as editor of *US Weekly*, Fuller realized that images of stars getting groceries were far more compelling to readers than stars wearing ball gowns.[21] This revelation spawned *US Weekly*'s "Just Like US," a regular montage of candid shots of celebrities. This style of feature has been copied by pretty much every tabloid in the business—both domestically and abroad. Unsurprisingly, it is big business: In 2007, X17, one of the largest paparazzi firms in Los Angeles, generated $12 million in gross revenue, $3 million of that from photos of Britney Spears, who, at the time, was watched by thirty to forty of the firm's paparazzi.[22]

Some stars, like Spears, play the game. Paris Hilton revels in the constant snapping of her visage in real time. Some stars create fake paparazzi shots, staging "candid" shots, such as the image of a pregnant Gwyneth Paltrow with her husband, rock musician Chris Martin. The photograph was actually taken by Paltrow's brother and sold to the media.[23] Conversely, actresses like Keira Knightley and Natalie Portman go to great lengths to avoid being photographed without consent. No one can deny that the paparazzi have extraordinary influence in creating and maintaining celebrity and that they offer a unique form of real-time reportage: Within minutes after they've been shot, photos are posted on the agency's site or by bloggers like Perez Hilton. Brandy Navarre, the cofounder of X17, explained the operation to me. Paparazzi agencies like X17 have licensing agreements with other media outlets that allow them to post videos and photos. X17, like other agencies, acts like a newswire service, except that the agency deals in photos rather than stories. "We work like AP or Reuters," Navarre says. X17 sends its photos to client magazines and TV networks around the world, and if the media outlets are interested, they contact the agency for a price. "We sell each week to all the major celebrity mags (*US Weekly*, *People*, *In Touch*, *Life & Style*, *OK*, etc.)," Navarre explains, "and to the nightly TV programs (*Access Hollywood*, *ET/Insider*, *E! News*, etc.). For particular websites (larger portals like AOL and Yahoo!) we have large subscription deals." Other clients may purchase photos on a once-off basis. While

X17 is unusual in that it also makes money on advertising sales from its website and blog, the licensing business remains the company's top revenue source. For example, the really special footage (read: potentially career-damaging for the star) goes for up to six figures, and these photos are sold to tabloids that buy photos from paparazzi agencies, instead of putting photographers on the street. (X17 will delay posting a photo on its site if the shot looks like it will sell for a lot to another media outlet.) "The sales drive what we do," Navarre says. "We take a picture and it sells for way more than we thought it would. Sometimes we also are proactive: Are we going to say she's going to be the next one? It's to our advantage to build a relationship and build an archive of photos of her. [We are both] reactive and proactive. We did our first post of Robert Pattinson on the blog. People were starting to hear about *Twilight* and we got four hundred comments, and we were like, 'Oh, my God, what is going on?' Four hundred comments is reserved for Britney Spears or Lindsay Lohan. Our website is a big litmus test. So then we put all our troops on Robert Pattinson and he gets bigger every day."

My interview with Navarre was in the summer of 2009. By the fall, Pattinson had become one of the most followed stars in the world. In November, the second part of the *Twilight* Saga (*New Moon*) was released. Despite being panned by critics, on opening day the film brought in an estimated $72.7 million, showing on 8,500 screens at 4,024 theaters and breaking the previous record held by *The Dark Knight*.[24] While there is a cult following of the *Twilight* vampire series, Pattinson is a one-man economic juggernaut for media and in no small part helps drive the record-breaking ticket sales. X17 did its job in creating his celebrity.

With all that print space, all those media outlets, and countless paps at every corner, it seems hard to believe that an aspiring star can't get someone to cover him or her. In Los

Angeles alone, almost thirty thousand people work in media occupations (in New York the number is eighty-three thousand). There are almost two thousand media firms in Los Angeles and almost twice that in New York City. To give a sense of the magnitude of these numbers, Los Angeles's media sector employs almost two and a half times more workers than the architectural field and twice as many employees as the software industry (both formidable industries in Los Angeles).[25] While many news outlets cover topics other than stars, almost all of them devote some ink to celebrity profiles or major scandals. The ubiquitous presence of reportage on stars in the media is demonstrated by the fact that even the *New York Times* covers the topic of celebrity in lead stories, including an in-depth profile of Megan Fox, a front-page story on the teenage pregnancy of Jamie Lynn Spears (sister of Britney), the ups and downs of Tiger Woods in the aftermath of his infidelities, and the fervor around the impending death of reality star Jade Goody, to name a few.

But why does the media fixate on specific celebrities? In some respects it seems so capricious. Balk remarked, "The media throws someone out there and if it sticks you'll hear more about it and if it doesn't then you'll never hear about it again." Even Rosenfield, who holds an impressive track record of representing and cultivating dozens of A-listers, remains mystified. "We tell potential clients, if you could produce it, we would have people lined up around the block. We could charge a million a year and people would find a way to pay it."

For some aspiring stars the problem is fundamentally getting noticed. But for many others the challenge is not lack of coverage but somehow cultivating the right type of public profile. Stars are unlikely to have the capacity or skills to undertake this venture themselves, which is why the star machine exists in the first place. Celebrities have to mind their manners and be (relatively) discreet if they want to be A-listers like the ones Rosenfield represents. People like George Clooney must be a dream to work with. All he does is date good-looking women, attend charity events, and star in decent films. Celebrities like Britney Spears or Amy Winehouse are a different story. Despite employing the best publicists and agents in the business, these young women behave badly on their own time, the media laps it up, and there's rarely anything that can be done. But if a client can resist vomiting in public or avoid getting caught shoplifting, a good publicist can keep a lid on undesirable elements of the star's life and cultivate the magic "light" that his or her client may not naturally possess. "If you sit in my chair, your job is to make recommendations," Rosenfield explained. "I tell all my clients this: We all have one thing in common, we all know the same people. We know the editors, the same journalists, and the same columnists. So you're really hiring us for our judgment. Some of us are better at it than others; some bring different things to the table." When I asked Rosenfield if the star machine could always turn a nobody into a somebody, he shrugged. "It's like I told [George] Clooney: It's a hard question to answer because certain people are going to make it because they're going to make it, but you do need an intelligent team around you. You can only be as good as your client will allow you to be . . . We had an actress come in here and she wanted to change her image. And we said she needs to stop with the nude layouts, [and] wearing clothes that scream, 'I want to get laid.' Needless to say, I didn't get the account. And now, years later, she's in the same position." There is no alternate universe or counterfactual to measure how much the star machine can influence the fate of a particular individual. For now, even if it is sometimes insufficient, engaging the multitier celebrity industry, from the good publicist to the cunning agent to the fabulous haircut, at least provides the potential star with a fighting chance.

The Cost of Doing Business

Here's a figure that will make you stop in your tracks: Jennifer Aniston spent approximately $50,000 on her hair for the London premiere of *Marley & Me*. The breakdown is as follows: She sent her famed hairdresser, Chris McMillan, first-class round-trip from Los Angeles to London (which can cost upward of $10,000). McMillan stayed in the poshest hotels in the city for a week, to a tune of $16,000. And while you might call the above the cost of travel for the jet set, the real indictment is that McMillan's styling costs over $2,000 a day.[26] His bill for an entire week of prepping Aniston's hair was over $15,000, more than some people in America make in an entire year. It's more than the cost of a bachelor's degree at Oxford University, and about the price of an economy car, or a down payment on a three-bedroom house in Harrisburg, Pennsylvania.

Aniston's hair may seem like an anomaly, but to get a decent haircut at McMillan's salon is going to cost at least $200 and goes up to $350 (and that's merely an appointment with one of his staff; he will not be cutting your hair at that price point). Ted Gibson, a New York stylist who has worked on Anne Hathaway's and Angelina Jolie's tresses (with affirming quotes from both of them on his site), charges almost $1,000 for a haircut. Even by New York and Los Angeles standards, that's a lot of cash. The New York professional woman might drop $150 for a haircut at top salon Bumble and Bumble, and for the average American a cut at the local salon or Supercuts isn't going to run more than $50. But let's add in the other parts of Aniston's beauty regime. It is rumored that, per month, she spends $3,000 on personal training and yoga instruction and $3,500 on a private chef and "anticellulite spa treatments" that cost $1,000 per session. In total, some estimates claim Aniston drops almost $20,000 a month on her appearance.[27] She also reportedly bought $34,000 worth of tanning beds (plural) for her home.[28]

These figures may seem like a terrible denunciation of Aniston, but other stars are just the same. Gwyneth Paltrow and Madonna have worked with Tracy Anderson, a fitness guru based in New York. While figures are not disclosed, for some time Anderson was generating most of her income solely from these two clients. In the summer of 2008, Anderson spent the afternoon with Madonna and then in the evening headed to the Hamptons to train Paltrow. Her reputation for getting these two stars into Athenian goddess–like shape has propelled Anderson to open a studio in TriBeCa that charges a $1,500 annual fee on top of the $900 monthly membership cost.[29] Again, returning to reality, even the toniest gyms run the average New Yorker or Angelino only a couple hundred dollars a month: The average Equinox general membership in both New York and Los Angeles ranges from $150 to $200. Typical personal-training sessions at the Equinox in West Hollywood are $85 to $105 an hour and sessions at other locations range from $74 to $150 an hour.[30] Private yoga session rates at the ultratrendy Yogaworks Los Angeles are typically $95 an hour.[31]

Stars also incur "necessary" expenses that normal people do not. The cost of a serious publicist runs from $4,000 to $6,000 a month (and if you're Simon Cowell, a publicist may run you five to six times that amount). Celebrity lawyers don't advertise their fees overtly, but as a proxy, Britney Spears's divorce lawyer charged $700 per hour, while the lawyer for her estranged spouse, Kevin Federline, charged $600 an hour.[32]

Agencies, also known in celebrity parlance as "tenpercenter-ies," charge a standard 10 percent for each deal they make. If you're an A-lister, you're likely to get some clothes and makeup for free, but you still spend pots of money on clothes, jewelry, and accoutrements to keep in vogue. The shopping sprees of stars are regularly documented on blogs and in gossip columns and can go into the six figures. Victoria Beckham is rumored to own more than one hundred Hermès Birkin bags worth over $2 million in total. Her limited-edition "Himalayan" Birkin is worth over $100,000 due to its rare animal skins and materials.[33]

In some respects, it's all relative: If you're Jennifer Aniston and you make $25 million a year, these numbers are likely to seem reasonable. After all, by public estimates, Aniston makes five hundred times more than the average person in the United States.[34] But what if you're not an A-lister or up-and-coming starlet whom every designer and hair stylist wants to groom and associate his or her name with and thus gives you stuff for free? What if you're just a midrange TV personality or an aspiring B-lister toiling away and hoping for a break? What if you've just moved to Los Angeles and signed with a big agency and need to show up at all the parties and auditions and culti-vate a look and buzz about you that make the tabloid reporters and paparazzi take notice, and the studios and brands as well?

Most stars and aspiring stars do not make as much as Aniston and yet they still have to pay the start-up costs. These are a necessary part of doing business regardless of what echelon within the hierarchy the star occupies. To find the jobs, the star still needs the agent who gets the 10 percent cut. To get his or her name out there, the star still has to hire a publicist. And the perfectly toned figure, impeccable makeup, and great hair for the film premieres and gallery openings all add up to a lot of money, even if you've just got the regular membership at the gym and get your hair cut by one of McMillan's staff.

The industry itself is circular: One cannot be a star without bringing in the various people and powers that be that create stardom, yet incorporating them depreciates any economic remuneration one achieves. Nevertheless, the various tiers provide an important function. Don't think for a second that publicists and agents aren't worth their job. One only needs to look at Tom Cruise jumping like a lunatic on Oprah's couch in the aftermath of firing Pat Kingsley (and replacing her with his Scientologist sister—he subsequently replaced his sister with Rogers and Cowan co-chairman Paul Bloch), or at Katie Price drunk and scantily clad after she fired her representative, to see the damage done when a professional isn't there. "I do believe that virtually none of [Cruise's] recent outbursts would have occurred under the watch of his longtime, now-fired publicist Pat Kingsley," the journalist Ken Tucker remarked. "Kingsley, an old-school image-wrangler, would have limited [*Access*] *Hollywood*'s access to these latest, near-Tourettic sound bites—his babblings of 'I care, man, I care,' as he pointed to doubtlessly baffled off-camera soundmen and gaffers. Having protected Cruise from himself for fourteen years, the veteran publicist would have pulled the plug on *Access Hollywood*'s special full-half-hour edition dubbed 'Tom Cruise: Man on a Mission.'"[35] Publicists manage images, scare the media, keep the fires under control, and solve reputation disasters. And no one in Hollywood, the recording industry, or the literary world takes anyone seriously unless there is an agent working the deals for him or her. Having an agent is necessary for being a legitimate part of these worlds. In the 1990s, at the peak of their success, Hollywood agents were rainmakers, landing the "20 and 20" deals, which translated to a $20 million fee and 20 percent of the film's gross for the star. Blockbuster films could result in $100 million paychecks for the film's stars. Or as *Financial Times* writer Matthew Garrahan put it, "They are the deal makers in a town that needs deals like oxygen."[36]

The celebrity industry thrives on its implicit promise to create (and maintain) the ambiguous yet crucial parts of star power; it develops the aspects of a persona that create media buzz and public interest. And the list of players dividing the spoils is endless. "There are plenty of people making money off of stars," explained an insider who requested anonymity. "Agents, publicists, lawyers get the first round. Hair people, makeup people, brand managers . . . ." All in all, it's clear the overhead costs of being a celebrity are high. At the end of the day, the average TV personality or midrange actor likely takes home about as much as a high-end professional such as a lawyer or doctor.

Bollywood and Beyond

There's no question that some relative celebrities engage in similar activities and round up multiple helpers to maintain their stardom. In the most prosaic example, the homecoming queen spends more time and money on her upkeep than the average bookworm, who focuses more on Harvard and less on getting the quarterback's attention. The homecoming queen has her own version of "handlers"—watch any episode of *Gossip Girl* or *90210* for a quick and surprisingly accurate snapshot. These shows are hyperbolic, but they reveal the machinations and intricate networks necessary for producing the high school star—the bratty clique, the gofer that does her bidding, and so forth.

Generally it's fairly hard to quantify the constructs of less formalized versions of celebrity. However, increasingly, even obscure stars are encouraging the development of an industry around them. For example, Internet celebrities are, by their very nature, using the conduit of the web and its message boards, blogs, and online communities to spread their star power, creating a low-cost version of the Hollywood handlers. The rise of companies like ROFLCon, which holds regular events and conferences, is a response to Internet stars attempting to translate their relative stardom into a more mainstream version that could potentially generate a steady income. ROFLCon, for those unaware, is an Internet-derived acronym for "Rolling on the Floor Laughing"—a more in-the-know version of LOL (laughing out loud). ROFLCon's founder, Tim Hwang, a recently graduated Harvard whiz kid, explained that the point of his company was to change the ephemeral and valueless nature of Internet celebrity. As Hwang put it, he wanted to "transcend online celebrity into something more and longer lasting." He pointed to examples of various Internet celebrities such as Tron Guy (discussed in great detail in chapter 7). "Tron Guy became one of the superstars," Hwang said. "There was an appreciation for him as a celebrity. The ephemeral nature of his celebrity of the Internet was only because of the nature of where he initially started [online]." Hwang held the ROFLCon conference in order to figure out if Internet celebrity could be as real and economically viable as Hollywood stardom. "Is the fame here durable?" Hwang asked. "Our thought was yes [it is]."

While Internet celebrity may generate an organizational structure that includes handlers, the Internet stars need something different from those from Hollywood, sports, or popular culture. Hwang explained that physical beauty is far less important to Internet stars, partially because they are not always documented through visual means, but also because beauty is not revered in Internet celebrity as it is in mainstream stardom. "With traditional celebrity, we care about what they look like on the beach etc.," Hwang said. "What makes [Internet celebrity] so interesting is that we are interested in them as they are." And whereas mainstream stardom is localized, Internet celebrities can work from anywhere (Tron Guy came from Missouri). Thus, the need to be located in a particular place (e.g., Los Angeles, New York, London) is not as important as long as they are in the virtual geography of the Internet.

Yet despite the differences for Internet stars, the celebrity industry that emerges around them is, like mainstream celebrity, often about the channels in which to broadcast (and sell) these stars to a wider public and to create as many economic and social platforms for them to become bigger stars. Large mainstream agencies like United Talent Agency are beginning to represent them, as they would any star. "We want them to be known for things other than just what they're known for initially, for being multifaceted," Hwang explained.

Oddly, Bollywood's model of celebrity production is closer to Internet celebrity than to Hollywood. Bollywood does not operate through agents and publicists; the handlers are all but nonexistent. While there is an enormous media and tabloid presence in India, the media is much nicer to the stars and much less invasive, thus limiting some of the revenue that is generated from sheer gossip and scandal. Mark Lorenzen, a professor at the Copenhagen Business School in Denmark and expert on the Indian film industry, explains that Bollywood creates stars through very informal networks. The industry is almost completely organized through very close ties among people who have worked together year after year. "The family-based system tends to govern the whole system," Lorenzen says. "On one hand, [this system] has controlled the negotiations and transaction costs. On the other hand, it has limited Bollywood from becoming really professional like Hollywood. No publishing houses, no conglomerates, no real agents. The stars are represented by their wife or secretary. Everyone knows everyone so you don't really need an agent. Everybody is in the inner circle: There are twenty to twenty-five producers and directors, and in that inner circle maybe one hundred people who know everyone. [A producer] can arrange a breakfast meeting with anyone. [He'll say to an actor], 'How about coffee tomorrow at twelve?' If he [the actor] agrees, it probably means he's going to accept the offer. They know everyone so well that they know who's vegetarian."[37] Additionally, most Indian celebrities are created out of its film industry, and thus models, musicians, and other types of stars common in the West are less prolific. In fact, those who do achieve renown for something outside the film industry are strongly encouraged to become actors in order to perpetuate and maximize their star power. "India has had eleven or twelve Miss Worlds and Miss Universes. There are only like two out of twelve that didn't go into films," Lorenzen explains. "[There's] not even a pretense that it's about talent. It's changing, but until recently it didn't matter whether you were a good actor or not. It all revolves around the star but not the talent of the star."

This system has made life a lot easier for the Indian stars who flit on and off movie sets at a ferocious pace (by Lorenzen's estimate, two to three movies come out of Bollywood per week, and that's not including the other Indian cities that are also producing films). But Lorenzen is quick to point out that the lack of organizational structure also limits the economic potential of the film business. In 2005, Bollywood released 1,041 films, selling 3.6 billion tickets globally, compared to America's 535 films and 2.6 billion tickets. But in terms of moneymaking, Bollywood made $575 million to Hollywood's $23 billion. The lack of agents limits the potential of making greater returns on stars. Agents, after all, are wheeling and dealing with everyone, not just the studios. They are reusing rights, setting up endorsements with advertising agencies, and creating celebrity brands and products with huge companies like Target and Wal-Mart. Publicists help cultivate the celebrity residual that drives much of Western star power. Agents are the ones who can turn that celebrity residual into real money. Bollywood lacks these critical parts of the celebrity industry. And as big an industry as stardom is in Bollywood, financially it could be exponentially bigger.

As frivolous as celebrity may seem at first glance, it is an enormous economic juggernaut. Even those who revile celebrity and celebrities would be impressed by the amount of money the industry and its players give back to the economy. Once again, consider Simon Cowell: Every time one of his shows, *American Idol* or its British equivalent, *X Factor*, picks a winner, that musician goes to the top of the charts, selling millions of albums, which translates into lots of revenue and jobs for people in the recording business. Advertising slots for the *X Factor*'s 2009 finale were £250,000 a pop. ITV, the station that hosted the show, generated £75 million from the season's series.[38] And while Cowell is often demonized for his star-searching empire, he ought not to be: In 2008, he paid almost £22 million in income taxes.[39] That's a lot of cash to Great Britain's government. Cities like Los Angeles, New York, and London are the recipients of massive amounts of jobs and revenue through the intricate structure of the celebrity-making business. While the Internet, Bollywood, and even high schools produce much less monetized forms of the celebrity industry, their fundamental organizational structure isn't so different. The public always wants someone to celebrate, there are a million people who want that spotlight, and the intricate ecosystem of handlers, supporters, and groomers exists everywhere in some shape or form, whether we pay them or not.

5

How to Become a Star: The Celebrity Network

In June 2008, on a hot summer evening, my friend Eric, who had been working tirelessly on Hillary Clinton's presidential campaign, called to say he would be flying into New York City the next day for the senator's speech after the Montana and South Dakota primaries. (This speech would be her last before conceding to Barack Obama.) Eric said that if I wanted to come—the event would take place at Baruch College with a fabulous-sounding after-party at the Gramercy Park Hotel—he would happily get me in. This was an opportunity I couldn't pass up. I canceled my previous plans and the next day at six p.m. I made a beeline for downtown to meet him.

When I arrived, the place was already swarming with people and TV cameras, and there was still a line of supporters all around the block waiting to get in. (The real picture was far removed from the claims journalists made the next day that "barely 300 people showed up" and that the evening was "more like a wake.") I got to the front door where Eric had asked me to wait for him. Of course, with all of the guards, Secret Service, and various Clinton staffers patrolling the front area, I had to make myself look really busy (with the aura of possibly being an important person), which involved frenzied and unnecessary e-mailing on my BlackBerry, thus avoiding all eye contact with people who could ask me to move away from the door or into the line.

Eric arrived just in time, sporting an open-collar white shirt and designer jeans, accompanied by days-old facial hair, looking ever the part of the hipster demographic that had only recently become a politically active and tremendously desired constituency. Slapping a bright yellow band on my wrist, Eric whisked me past some fifteen hundred people who had been waiting in line for hours and were probably going to be told the event was full. After going through a rigorous security check, we went down to the basement where the event was being held and watched the media flurry unfold. Random politicians and high-up staffers were talking to reporters. CNN and Fox News anchors were grooming themselves and talking into their headsets, ready to go at a moment's notice. Socialites and supporters richer than Croesus sashayed about the VIP section, designer handbags and Lilly Pulitzer shift dresses on full display. Shortly before Senator Clinton was to appear on stage, Eric and a few of his staffer friends were busy ensuring I would get a good seat and then, later, get backstage access. Eric worked for her advance team, but more than five hundred media outlets and hundreds of supporters were showing up, so it would be tricky to arrange. Eric, however, was privy to what could only be described as "all-access" buttons, which would allow us backstage and get us into the most privileged parts of the event. These buttons were provided by the Secret Service in very limited batches for staff. And sure enough, Eric produced one from his pocket.

Once the access dilemma had been resolved, we went back to the VIP section (where I had to show my yellow wristband yet again) and awaited the senator's arrival. The staffers were still discussing access and how to get non–advance team fans back to meet the senator. Eric turned to a fellow staffer, a young, pretty blond girl, and asked, "Do you have any of those media passes left? We'll use those for backup." With barely a beat between request and delivery, she proudly reached into her enormous Prada handbag and produced a handful of hot pink passes the size of index cards with Senator Clinton's name emblazoned across the top and MEDIA in boldface on the bottom. Thanks to Eric and his friendly fellow staffers, there I was with backups to backups of access to see one of the most important public figures in the world.

Senator Clinton's speech was impassioned and exhilarating in the way that television can never quite capture. The audience was transfixed while she spoke and erupted into thunderous applause as she finished. Afterward, we went backstage and were introduced to Hillary, Huma Abedin (her right-hand woman), Bill and Chelsea, the former head of the Democratic National Committee and head of the Clinton campaign, Terry McAuliffe, and every other significant member of the presidential campaign. Later that evening all those people (except Senator Clinton, who had to head to Washington, D.C., immediately after the event) attended the after-party at the Gramercy Park Hotel rooftop bar, mingling and chatting for hours with the attendees.

This story makes it seem like access to the senator is easy, but in reality it's impossible. You might think that if you stand in line long enough or keep showing up at the doorstep of important events your chances of befriending stars increases, but it doesn't. Right of entry relies on one very good link. If that link is a legitimate access point (either a celebrity or someone who works closely with stars), then one has a ticket into an exclusive world. Without Eric, my chances of setting foot in the door of the auditorium, let alone meeting Senator Clinton personally and attending her after party, were zero. My success relied solely and totally on my friendship with Eric. But once initial access is granted, the next layer of connections is that much easier. Suddenly, by mingling at the Gramercy Park Hotel, you have all the access in the world to people who have the potential to elevate your profile too. Maybe you want to befriend them, become their boyfriend or girlfriend, or simply request their friendship on Facebook. No matter your net-working goal, by accessing the party, you've never been closer to attaining it. A fundamental quality of celebrity is that celebrities are celebrities because they spend time with other celebrities, reinforcing the belief that they truly are different from you and me. This may be a story about one of the world's biggest political celebrities, but the exclusiveness of the celebrity world can be mirrored in the most ordinary and small-scale ways: High school cliques and college sororities maintain their elite status similarly, except that parties at the Gramercy Park Hotel are replaced with Friday night sleep-overs and private mixers with elite fraternities. By maintaining exclusivity in their social lives, these groups too produce their own relative celebrities. Understanding celebrity requires a knowledge of the social network that produces them. This may be an intellectual exercise for most of us, but in practical terms, those in the business of wanting to become celebrities must first make contact with those who have already achieved this goal.

But who cares? If a clique is that exclusive and that much of a pain to get into, then maybe it's just not worth trying to become a member. In the last few decades, scientists and soci-ologists have devoted much of their lives to answering these questions. Why would anyone want to belong to a group? What are the real outcomes—both benefits and drawbacks—of being a member?

Most of us have friends. Some of us have a lot of friends who aren't close, some of us have a few friends we hold near and dear. If we're lucky, we have lots of friends who are loyal and close and on whom we can depend. On the most basic level, friends form a social network. Some of us have very tight groups of friends who are all friends with one another.[1] Still others have tons of acquaintances who are not necessarily friends but make up a wide and disparate collection of people.

Think of Malcolm Gladwell's famous "connectors" (discussed in *The Tipping Point*), those people with friends on every continent. A lot of us have this type of large and very loosely connected friendship group on our Facebook account. I am "friends" with people I haven't seen in years and also friends with my colleagues at work, my husband, and my best friend, to whom I talk every day. Even before social media websites, social networks formed our basic relationships with people around us.

But friendship isn't the only type of social network. How we get jobs, how disease is spread, how websites become popular, and how people attain upward mobility are all determined by our relations and connections and interactions with other people. Our ability to interact with some people and some groups may provide benefits or may exclude us from other groups. Mean-spirited high school cliques that don't let certain individuals in because they are friends with someone they don't like are the classic example of exclusionary social networks. But in other ways, social networks are useful for meeting people who will introduce us to our future partner or spouse, get us a new job, write us a recommendation for college, and so forth. Studying social networks is a good way of understanding how the world is organized, another lens for interpreting a wide range of phenomena in human society, from why people marry whom they do, to how people become rich, catch a cold, or, in this case, attain celebrity status.[2]

Through the eyes of the media, mainstream celebrities look like beautiful people who are photographed a lot and who are generally sports stars, musicians, actors, or models. But another way to look at celebrities is as a members-only group: Celebrities are celebrities also because they get invited to certain parties and hang out with certain people. They are a part of a very elite invite-only network. Individuals attain celebrity in part by the company they keep and the events they attend—in other words, their social network.

There are benefits to being a part of an exclusive network. While all forms of celebrity exhibit this type of exclusiveness, most (though not all) mainstream celebrities get their foot in the door first by being associated with popular culture industries to some degree. Some of these individuals are genuinely talented actors or musicians, which buys them access to exclusive events. Others may not possess talent but their face and presence are of interest to the popular press and thus they are invited. Their talent or media attention is their entry to the world that would not take notice of them simply as individuals. And this is where the celebrity network is critical. Getting invited to and showing up at the right parties and meeting the right people are only the surface benefits of the celebrity network. If you're an actor or a politician, meeting those important people at those exclusive parties is essential to your career. The *Vanity Fair* Oscar party, for example, is more than just hanging out with other beautiful people. Young actors get the chance to hobnob with influential directors who might remember them down the line and give them a role in a major film.[3] Directors and producers talk shop about movie ideas that might turn into award-winning blockbusters. Even those stars with no talent (the all-residual celebrities) need to be at the events and parties that other celebrities are attending just to define themselves as a part of the exclusive celebrity set (and get themselves photographed). This entitles them to a membership card. For the Paris Hiltons of the world, membership in the exclusive world of celebrity compensates for the lack of an Academy Award or a Grammy. And if you are in show business to show the world your talent, then being a part of the most exclusive and powerful networks offers huge benefits.

Celebrity networks are influential because they are both the means by which celebrity status is perpetuated and they provide access points to important people who can elevate an aspiring star's career. If we could infiltrate this exclusive world, could it tell us something more generally about how people become stars?

A few years back, my Ben-Gurion University colleague Gilad Ravid and I were determined to figure this out. We believed that celebrity status can partially be explained through specific networks of which celebrities are a part. But after establishing that theory we ran into a bit of a basic nonstarter: How does one get into the celebrity network in the first place? And after that, how does someone become a particular type of star?

We knew it would be unlikely that Paris Hilton or Angelina Jolie would fill out weekly surveys on their comings and goings, whom they had lunch with, what they did on Friday night, or whom they met up with for coffee. But we knew that one of the defining differences between celebrities and us is that they spend time with each other, and we spend time with, well, us. That exclusiveness is part and parcel of why it would be almost impossible to document their networks. Most of the point, after all, is that ordinary people can't participate.

Luckily, Gilad is a genius computer scientist and I spend a lot of time reading celebrity magazines. Between the two of us, we figured out a way to access celebrity networks and the exclusiveness of their social lives without asking them a single survey question or trying to talk to Paris Hilton. A definitive aspect of being a celebrity is that your life is fascinating to many other people. And in the case of stars like Paris and Angelina, your life is photographed and documented around the clock, around the world. If many minutes of these celebrities' lives are broadcast to the world in hundreds of media outlets and thousands of photos, wouldn't this be the most obvious way to study their social networks and the things they do that are different from what we do? What parties do celebrities get invited to and which people do they hang out with? What is Paris Hilton doing on Friday night? Well, just a glance at the photos in *US Weekly* or *People* will tell you. So if we look at photographs of celebrities living their lives we'll have a pretty good sense of whom they spend time with and what they do.

For an entire year (March 2006–February 2007), we studied all of the arts and entertainment photos taken by Getty Images, the largest photographic agency in the world. We analyzed some six hundred thousand photos of almost twelve thousand events, recording the 6.5 percent of individuals who appeared in four or more images—the celebrity core, so to speak. We then studied all the events they attended and people they spent time with. So far, we'd figured out a thing or two about the nature of celebrity.[4]

It came as no surprise that celebrities hang out with other celebrities and they go to events that the rest of us aren't invited to. Celebrity tabloids love to breed the fiction that celebrities are "just like us." But they're not. Angelina Jolie goes to parties with George Clooney and Matt Damon, and those "get-togethers" happen to be the *Vanity Fair* Oscar party and the Metropolitan Museum of Art's Costume Institute Ball, as opposed to Aunt Sally's barbeque or Friday night bowling. These differences between celebrities and us are not just anecdotal, they can be statistically measured. Overall, looking at their social lives, we found two very important properties of celebrity networks that distinguish them from "noncelebrity networks."[5] First, there is nothing at all random about celebrity networks: They are connected simply by virtue of being full of celebrities. Second, being a celebrity reinforces itself. In other words, by spending time with other celebrities one gets the opportunity to meet lots of other celebrities and get photographed with even greater frequency, all of which increases one's celebrity all the more. Or as Daniel Boorstin wrote in his famous book *The Image*, "[Celebrities] help make and . . . publicize one another. Being known primarily for their well-knownness, celebrities intensify their celebrity images simply by becoming widely known for relations among themselves."

This may seem obvious, but social network analysts find this celebrity-begets-celebrity phenomenon to be a feature of special types of social networks not present in the average person's social life. In general, studies of human behavior demonstrate that people's interactions are random. Say we took an unbiased, random sample of people who live in Los Angeles and all the places they went during a year and all the people they spent time with. We would likely find that their social network looked quite predictable. Most people are connected because they are genuinely friends. If we look at more loosely linked networks, we can trace most people through regular routine (e.g., where they grab their coffee every morning or where they live or work) and find the same connections. There might be an interloper here and there, a random person we meet at a bar or bookstore and with whom we strike up a conversation. Most of the time, however, people's connections make sense and can be explained by the people they are friends with, their hobbies, job, socioeconomic status, and the places they frequent. My friends are unlikely to be connected to my other acquaintances' friends without my introducing them or unless all of us are working at the same place or are members of the same rock-climbing club.

Celebrities are different. Even those celebrities who are not friends, who are not related by occupation (for example, film stars), who do not live in the same place, who do not attend the same events, tend to be systematically, closely connected to one another despite having no real reason to be so. In a few very short steps, each celebrity can connect to anyone else within the network, even if they don't attend the same parties. Just by virtue of being a celebrity, celebrities tend to be much more closely connected to one another. While most people are connected to everyone else in the world through the well-known "six degrees of separation" (which turns out actually to be true),[6] our analysis of celebrity networks demonstrates that celebrities exhibit just 3.26 degrees of separation from one another.[7]

What this means in real terms is that multi-award-winning actress Kate Winslet, in all her elegance and regal glory, may actually be at the same event where girl-gone-wild Lindsay Lohan is stumbling around in the bathroom and Britney Spears is acting like a crazy person (again). And of course, Kate may say hello to Lindsay and Britney because they know each other by virtue of being at the same exclusive events, even if they have nothing else in common and have never (and will never, to be clear) costarred in a movie or sung a duet. Contrast this with the noncelebrity world: Most people with a predilection for hard partying and bad behavior aren't likely to be running in the same circles as reserved, refined people like my mother. What makes celebrity networks so different from ours is that everyone attends the same events and knows the same people. Additionally, most celebrities' friends tend to be connected to one another, by virtue of ending up at the same parties or being friends with people who end up at events where mutual friends are in attendance. This property can be observed in other tightly knit industries, like finance and publishing, and it can result in career promotions and making friends with important people within these respective industries.[8] But such networks have different purposes from being a celebrity: If one wants to become a celebrity (rather than a CEO or publishing mogul), there is no better network than befriending people who are constantly photographed by the media.

Think about how most of our friendship groups operate: I may have one group of friends that consists of work colleagues and another of college buddies. It's unlikely that these two groups will overlap. But in the celebrity world, people in different social groups are connected. By virtue of the exclusiveness and small number of people in total, there are many individuals who end up crossing multiple social groups, linking disparate groups. This property of celebrity social worlds has a resounding impact on the members' networking capabilities.[9] Because the people they are connected to tend also to be connected to everyone else, they are by default all connected to one another.

Sure, this makes sense when you're looking at Hollywood film star A-listers, who all get invited to the same superexclusive events. But why would a New York socialite have anything to do with a famous Hollywood producer? In reality, they are as far apart as I am from a random lawyer who lives in New York. The tie they share is simply their celebrity status. By virtue of both being high-profile they are a part of the same network that connects both of them to Angelina Jolie, Paris Hilton, and the fashion designer Marc Jacobs. The socialite and the producer may not attend a single event together, but they are more likely than the rest of us to be friends with people who are friends with people who all attend the same events. Many of these people know both the producer and the socialite, and likely the producer and socialite at least know of each other even if they have never met. Despite being utterly different people, with different occupations, located in different parts of the world, members of the celebrity network are closely linked. On some level, celebrities are celebrities because their network defines them as such.[10]

The second important finding, which is correlated to the first, is that within celebrity networks people are much more connected than ordinary people like us. Every time you befriend one celebrity, you gain access to many more. Why is this important? Celebrity networks provide a huge benefit to people who can penetrate them. A popular saying is that the "rich get richer," often accompanied by the statistics that 20 percent of people possess 80 percent of the wealth and that 20 percent of people use 80 percent of health care.[11] This concept, also known as the Pareto Principle or, as Malcolm Gladwell calls it, the "law of the few," demonstrates that a very small number of people get a huge number of benefits and is closely linked to the type of dense networks found among celebrities.[12] In their famous *Science* article studying the World Wide Web, physics professors Albert-László Barabási and Réka Albert observed that these networks exhibit "preferential attachment," which means that being a part of the celebrity network produces exponential benefits as someone within the network becomes increasingly connected.[13] People meet people through their connections with other people. The people within a network that exhibits the property of preferential attachment tend to meet many more people through one connection than they would through everyday networks. I don't have any connections to that Hollywood producer or any of the events he attends. So try as I might, the chance to talk to him about an upcoming role or movie is slim to none. Not so for that directionless New York socialite, who happens to be in the same network as that Hollywood producer, although she may never have gone to film school or even acted. She only has to pick up the phone and call one of her friends, who is friends with that producer, and very likely she'll get him on the phone or be able to grab a quick coffee with him. It is that opportunity that is so important.

What does that mean in terms of celebrity? More media attention, more opportunities for roles in movies, record deals, and modeling campaigns. More access to people you might want to be in touch with. Greater chances to meet very important people who will further your career. And, of course, all of these interactions provide an opportunity to perpetuate one's celebrity. The benefits of these connections are not simply access to more people; there are real advantages to one's career and social status, what sociologists and economists call "positive network externalities": Being a part of a network of celebrities increases the chances of meeting a high-profile partner, landing a major movie role, and getting photographed and featured in popular media outlets, all of which enable one to become a bigger star.[14] The importance of celebrities' interconnectivity is that it enables them to interact if they want to. Each star one becomes "friends" with has a whole Rolodex of contacts that may be useful in attaining these goals. Celebrities need to be able to interact with the most influential people in the film, music, or fashion industries; it's important for their careers and for their ability to nurture and maintain their own celebrity status.

Talent vs. Residual: Getting into the Celebrity Network

For the outsider, the differences among celebrities seem rather academic. But not all celebrities are the same, and not all are celebrities for the same reasons.[15] A basic maxim of stardom is that all celebrity is not created equal. Most of us, for example, have little interest in being Britney Spears, no matter the titanic force of her stardom, which flits across every media source from Perez Hilton to CNN to the *New York Times*. The musician Beyoncé, however, is far more appealing. She doesn't get *that* much media attention (relatively speaking), but when she does it is generally good. She is married to hip-hop mogul and Grammy-winning musician Jay-Z and has won several awards and sold millions of albums in her own right. People around the world idolize her.

Most people would not want to be Lindsay Lohan or Pete Doherty. Despite their stardom, they are not admired. They are celebrities because they are train wrecks—fascinating to watch because they derail into crazy behavior (even if Lohan was once an adorable childhood star with great potential). Most women would rather be George Clooney's girlfriend than Tiger Woods's wife; they'd like to attend parties at Madonna's house but probably wouldn't be so keen on visiting macabre musician Marilyn Manson in his home. In other words, celebrity may be everywhere, but celebrities everywhere are not of the same caliber.

Let's look now at the way people might get into the celebrity network in the first place. We know that celebrity isn't just talent and media exposure, but these might at least increase your chances of becoming a celebrity. There is interplay among three qualities: (1) talent (as measured by top *Billboard* music singles, sports championship games, Oscars and nominations, critics' reviews, and so forth); (2) fame (people knowing who you are, the chances of which are greatly increased by working in highly visible professions like sports or films); and (3) the celebrity residual, that collective obsession with an individual that transcends all tangible qualities or talents. Having a little more talent or a little more residual dramatically changes your network, what events you go to, and whom you have the potential to meet.

If you're talented, how might your talent be measured? Making money for the film studio, attracting other top stars to a movie, and drawing audiences in droves seems like a fair test. The *Forbes* Star Currency index surveyed 157 Hollywood film executives about actors' perceived "bankability" to their studios and ability to attract other stars to join the cast. Based on what studio execs said, *Forbes* ranked more then 1,400 actors. Not surprisingly, the usual suspects are at the top of the pile: Oscar winners and box office sensations like Jolie, Will

Smith, Brad Pitt, Julia Roberts, Matt Damon, and Johnny Depp. The middle rung of actors produces some recognizable names of stars who are primarily TV actors with less successful film careers (Neil Patrick Harris, Jamie-Lynn Sigler, and Lara Flynn Boyle), while the bottom rung (those actors ranked 1,390 to 1,410) are virtually unknown to the general population. Gilad and I looked at these different groups individually to see if their social lives were fundamentally different from one another. We parceled out the top twenty, middle twenty, and bottom twenty ranked stars as proxies for the different stratospheres of stars.

When you look at the networks of these different groups of actors, it turns out that A-list film stars (those top twenty rated by *Forbes*) have absolutely different social networks from the middle-ranked B-listers and the bottom-rung C-listers. A-list status isn't reflected only in box office receipts, awards ceremonies, and reputation among studio execs. A-listers also have a tight and densely connected social network, which allows them to remain the most elite stars on the planet. A-listers attend the most exclusive parties and awards ceremonies, and these events are naturally photographed much more than any other event that might be documented by Getty Images. There's no surprise to this finding: If A-listers are the biggest stars, then, by extension, they are invited to the most prestigious events that then reaffirm their position. Membership in the A-list celebrity network (in which A-listers spend time only with other A-listers at the most exclusive celebrity-studded events) reinforces A-lister status and makes it harder for anyone else (B-list and below) to clamber to the top. If B-list stars are not attending (read: not invited to) A-list events, then their chance to hobnob with the top stars becomes increasingly unlikely.

While A-listers' friends tend to be friends with one another (an important property of a very connected network, or what

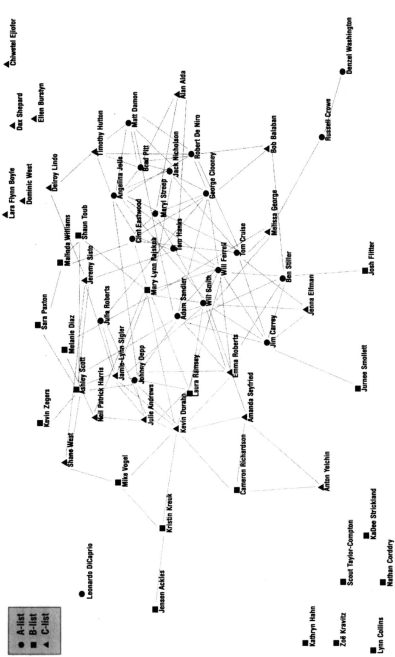

Figure 1. Social Network of A-, B-, and C-List Celebrities

social network analysts call a "clique"), the middle and bottom twenty stars have virtually no special connections with the others in their group. When removed from the entire Getty network and studied in isolation, B-listers and C-listers have hardly any unique ties to one another compared to their relationships within the network as a whole. While being a member of the celebrity network does provide access to other celebrities, only A-listers have their own exclusive inner core within the larger network of celebrities (see Figure 1). So while a B-lister is just a few contacts away from being in touch with a top star (he knows someone who knows someone who is friends with the star), A-listers essentially have no separation from other top stars. In network terms, A-listers are connected to one another by an average of 1.6 degrees of separation, and B- and C-list stars tend to be only slightly more connected to one another (2.5 and 2.22, respectively) than everyone in the entire Getty celebrity network (3.26). To be sure, they are still far more connected to one another than the average person (remember the six degrees of separation), but they are not as closely connected as those within the A-list. As a result, they do not achieve the same network benefits as those on the top rung.[16]

Unquestionably, being a part of the A-list clique is desirable, while being a part of the other groups less so. For a film star, being at the top—getting to the Oscars and the *Vanity Fair* Oscar party and so on—obviously yields greater benefit to one's star power and is an essential part of one's career. Yes, access to those events and to A-list status itself are strongly predicated on being able to generate money for the film studio. So the more Hollywood reveres a star (his perceived "talent"), the greater his chances of penetrating the most elite celebrity networks, which of course helps increase one's overall celebrity status. Thus, being a B-lister isn't a stop on the way to A-list status. B-list stars are viewed as less talented than

A-listers and, as such, B-list stars don't graduate into A-list status. They stay in the middle rung and therefore don't have the same opportunity to maximize their careers. Unless a B-lister lands a leading role that wins her a film award (and thus puts her on the invite list for coveted events) or marries an A-lister (who brings her along to those events), it is unlikely she will be given entrée into the A-list clique. A B-lister must take a quantum leap into A-list status rather than plodding along a linear path, which is why it's often the case that once a B-lister, always a B-lister.

There are, however, other options for the less talented to become just as connected as the exclusive core of the celebrity network. Let us not forget that celebrity rests on the public and the media fixating on some people more than others (the celebrity residual). If you are not particularly talented but the world is talking about you, you can be a celebrity without having to go through the Hollywood exec vetting process. There's no question that some stars who are talked about are talented—we've gone through this in the discussion of the interplay among the celebrity residual, talent, and fame. But besides being incredibly talented, the most obvious and efficient way to be at the core of the celebrity network is to get yourself photographed and written about as much as possible. These are our residual stars. Using Google media hits, we looked at the top twenty most talked about celebrities on blogs, in newspapers, and in other media outlets, and we found that those stars with lots of celebrity residual have a similar social network to Hollywood A-list actors. These most talked about celebrities tend to be connected to lots of people, attend lots of events, and have just as close connections among their friends as A-list Hollywood actors do among themselves.

Unsurprisingly, these residual stars do not have to win Oscars or generate box office receipts, but they do have to put in a huge amount of work to stay at the top. Top residual stars attend almost 80 percent more events than do A-listers. If a star does not have the talent to become a part of the elite, then the best course of action is to get out there and socialize. Socializing a lot doesn't necessarily mean an all-residual celebrity suddenly gets invited to the *Vanity Fair* Oscar party. However, it does mean that an aspiring star gets access to more people and thus increases her chances of being connected to others who may help her career (take a chance on her for a film role, give her a modeling campaign, etc.). If such an opportunity presents itself and she does an excellent job at it (wins an Oscar, becomes the face of a fashion house), that just might be the push she needs to jump from B-list or all-residual to legitimate A-lister.

Celebrity status depends on the individual's networking strategy and ability to penetrate one network versus another. Three principles make celebrity networks unique. First, celebrity reinforces itself by maintaining its collective exclusivity. By extension, celebrities must keep their network tight, so as to maintain both its exclusiveness and desirability. Second, celebrity relies on proximity and close connections to other celebrities. If Celebrity X invites you to the party, you will likely be able to connect to everyone else at the party with very minimal effort. Finally, and most important, these connections are socially and economically meaningful. In *The Warhol Economy*, where I studied the art, fashion, and music industries in New York, I found that a preponderance of those in the creative industries moved to New York primarily for networking purposes. They realized that establishing friendships and connections with high-profile individuals in their industries was essential to their success. Going to parties, gallery openings, and runway shows were the channels to do this. "The social life in New York is very work oriented," Diane von Furstenberg told me. "There is a support system that weaves and creates the social." Fashion designer Daniel Jackson explained, "Informal social networks are probably the most powerful driver, pretty much everyone we work with we have a personal relationship with."[17] By virtue of penetrating the celebrity network you are connected to tons of people who can further your career and status.

The Celebrity Network in Action:
The Social Network of Anna Wintour

For anyone who cares about fashion, the aggressively thin woman with the pageboy bob and enormous dark sunglasses has defined the industry since 1988. With her British accent and pithy retorts, Anna Wintour, editor of American *Vogue* for the last two decades, has made and broken careers with the mere nod of her head. Fashion insiders and reviewers read Wintour's attendance at runway shows like tea leaves. As a public figure, she is known for, among other things, making Zac Posen the darling of Barneys, getting John Galliano his job as creative director of Christian Dior, and being a perennial favorite on PETA's most-hated list for her casual fur wearing. She rarely gives an interview, and is in bed by ten fifteen every night.[18] She is the host of the Metropolitan Museum of Art's annual Costume Institute gala, otherwise known as "the Party of the Year," which is possibly the most concentrated grouping of celebrities in the world.

In 2006, Anna Wintour (also known as "Nuclear Wintour") became a household name. *The Devil Wears Prada*, the novel and blockbuster movie about Miranda Priestly, the ice queen of a top-tier fashion magazine, changed Wintour's profile from relative celebrity for fashion aficionados to world-renowned celebrity likely to be recognized by suburban housewives as well as cargo shorts–wearing engineers like my brother. The book, written by former Wintour assistant Lauren Weisberger, was largely received as the roman à clef of Wintour's reign at *Vogue*. "Besides giving Weisberger her fifteen minutes of fame," Wintour biographer Jerry Oppenheimer remarked, "Anna [was] squarely in the mainstream celebrity pantheon . . . Anna was now known and talked about over Big Macs and fries . . . in Davenport and Dubuque."[19] In all the flurry over the book, Wintour merely commented, "I am looking forward to reading [it]." She personally selects the attire for A-list stars for the Costume Institute gala and once refused to put Oprah Winfrey on the cover of *Vogue* unless she lost weight and Hillary Clinton unless she stopped wearing navy blue pantsuits. Wintour's power in the fashion arena is indisputable. She remains the most influential fashion icon in the world and has access to every celebrity.[20]

Wintour's social life effectively demonstrates the basic principles of celebrity social networks and the various possibilities for attaining celebrity. Once penetrated, her network, like all celebrity networks, enables a person to get to particular people. Between March 2006 and February 2007, Wintour attended sixty-nine events around the world at which she was photographed by Getty. That's actually not a lot compared to our favorite all-residual celebrity, Paris Hilton (who went to 50 percent more events in the same period). Wintour's social life can be categorized as a "fully connected network" or a "clique," which means that all the people who attend events that Wintour attends are likely to attend them together. The members of the network run in a pack, so to speak, even if the pack is made up of separate limos. Figure 2 gives a sense of some of the people in Wintour's network.

Once a person has penetrated Wintour's exclusive circle, there are other networks worth linking into, depending on one's goal. If he or she is at the same party as Wintour, there is much greater potential to access her (and maybe strike up a conversation that leads to friendship). An aspiring fashion

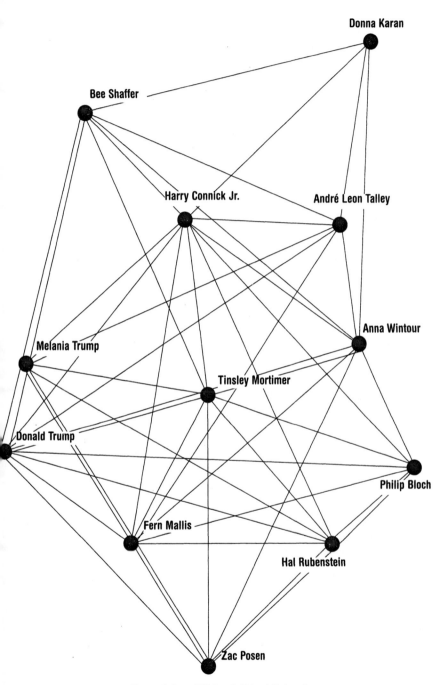

Figure 2. Anna Wintour's Friend Network

designer ought to try to establish a rapport with Wintour that might benefit her career. The rise of fashion houses Proenza Schouler, Rodarte, and Thakoon have been credited to the designers establishing a bond with Wintour.[21] People who go to the same events as Wintour are just one degree of separation away from her, so such a goal is pretty realistic.

If a celebrity or aspiring celebrity simply wants more celebrity friends, his or her best bet is to befriend those in Wintour's circle who are most connected to other celebrities attending these events, such as second in line at *Vogue*, André Leon Talley, rap star Kanye West, or socialite Tinsley Mortimer. These people tend to get photographed with lots of different people. In social-networking terms, these individuals are called "hubs." But just because one has contact with lots of people does not necessarily mean these connections are meaningful for getting a job or an invite to a coveted event. Those who want to get invited to parties and attain a wider net of contacts outside of Wintour's immediate circle (maxing out the "preferential attachment" property of celebrity networks) ought to become friends with those who attend lots of diverse events (not just the ones Wintour attends). Social network analysts call these people "boundary spanners" because they tend to be a part of different social groups and can act as a bridge between diverse members of the network.[22] Within Wintour's circle, examples of boundary spanners are Donald and Melania Trump and burlesque goddess Dita Von Teese. The Trumps are a multi-industry power couple: Donald is a real estate mogul and TV personality and Melania is a former model. Not to mention, they are so powerful and are such celebrities that they are invited to major events simply because of who they are. Von Teese is a model, cult personality, and fashion muse who, like the Trumps, bridges many different industries and social groups.

If a celebrity's basic goal is simply to increase his or her own star wattage, not so much become friends with those in Wintour's network, then the essential connections are with those celebrities who get photographed the most at Wintour events. Harkening back to Boorstin's point that celebrities are celebrities because they spend time and get photographed with one another, an aspiring star must make contact with the biggest stars present at the party. In Wintour's world, these individuals have historically been Katie Holmes, Sienna Miller, and Victoria "Posh" Beckham. But because celebrity status changes at the drop of a dime, the most photographed do so as well.

A Typology of Celebrity

Not all paths to celebrity are equal and, as Wintour's friend network demonstrates, not all celebrity networks offer the same result. Depending on what one wants from celebrity (whether making celebrity friends, becoming a celebrity, or getting access to a particular person), he has to decide which type of celebrity link and network will help him attain his goal. Part of the differences between Paris Hilton's and Anna Wintour's celebrity can be explained by the ratio of the three intermingling qualities a star possesses: talent, fame, and the celebrity residual. The distribution of these attributes in a person influences the type of star he or she becomes. Let's take a look at a few examples.

Some individuals strike the ultimate balance between talent and residual. Stars with consistent talent-based careers like Angelina Jolie or British supermodel Kate Moss perpetuate their elite status by, first, not attending many events and, second, picking those events that reinforce their image. Jolie goes to charity events, a few high-end cultural events (like the art opening for British street artist Banksy), and an award ceremony or two. Moss tends strictly to go to very cool fashion-related events (including, of course, her own Topshop brand launch party). Both Jolie and Moss can afford to be selective. Jolie can easily land another good film role, and Moss is plastered across every billboard or magazine worth a cent. In addition to holding tremendous star power, both are well-known talents in their fields, so they are constantly backing up their celebrity with substance. They rely less on being seen out and about for their celebrity status, because they have a talent that reminds the world they exist.

Additionally, because they have talent, they are able to be more exclusive, which of course increases their prestige. The words "Oh, her again" never emerge out of any paparazzo's mouth when one of these ladies shows up. The all-residual celebrities, however, must plug away at the social scene. They don't have a major fashion advertising campaign splashed on every billboard; they don't have a magazine to edit or a major blockbuster to star in. Since most residual stars do not have a consistent talent with which to broadcast their existence, they need public exposure in order to capture the public's interest and, consequently, to maintain their stardom.

Paris Hilton is nothing if not for the parties she attends. Of every celebrity Gilad and I investigated, she is far and away the most socially promiscuous. She has fewer degrees of separation from other celebrities. Lindsay Lohan may have had promise as a childhood actress, but in recent years she has become all-residual and, like Paris, shows up at any party worth its salt, affording her access to many more people. Most big stars—Tom Cruise, hip-hop musician and actress Queen Latifah, and musician Justin Timberlake—go to twenty or so high-profile events a year that the media covers in great depth and the public has great interest in (the Oscars, major movie premieres, and so forth). They are not, however, attending multiple PlayStation or cell phone launches or clothing boutique openings like all-residual celebrities.

Our look at celebrity networks also indicates that at some point there are diminishing returns to social promiscuity. Despite Paris Hilton's relentless social life, she does not have significantly more access to other celebrities than the more reclusive celebrity does. All of her frolicking makes her only a mere one-third degree of separation closer to others than everyone else, and on average she has the potential to meet a much smaller group of people at a given social event than does any other celebrity. The latter result is explained by the fact that in any exclusive network there are a finite number of people to meet. With each event that Paris attends, she reduces the chances of meeting new people within the network. More generally, one might argue that if Paris did not do all the socializing she does, she would not be nearly the celebrity she has become. Paris's social promiscuity gives her only a marginal leg up, but being just that much more connected is what makes Paris, well, Paris. Meeting just that one extra contact who provides an opportunity can be a game changer for an all-residual star. But it's clear that talent is a far easier (and more certain) way to attain elite status within the celebrity network. The thing going for Paris is that, despite demonstrating no discernible talent, she somehow got into the network in the first place. And she's been exploiting it ever since.

Networking does matter. And celebrities, as their social lives and networks demonstrate, are fundamentally different from you and me. More than talent or even misbehaving and getting written about, their ability to perpetuate their celebrity status is dependent on their ability to remain a part of the celebrity network, which is the way their antics get photographed and written about in the first place and ultimately how we remain fascinated with their lives. Perhaps most important, however, the study of celebrities' social lives tells us that *strategic* networking is the most critical aspect of attaining the type of stardom one desires.

6

Whatever You Do, Don't Go to Vegas: The Geography of Stardom

When I would fly into Los Angeles at night, the city was like a twinkling wonderland. It also held an answer to some fable or dream I was after. I began using it as background, and then I realized how important backgrounds really are. **—Ed Ruscha**

Cory Kennedy became a star at sixteen years old due to the Cobra Snake. Cobra Snake, also known as Mark Hunter, was a photographer documenting the LA party scene. A scruffy young guy (twenty-one when he met Kennedy), Hunter was a bit of a legend for his access to the best of highbrow and low-brow LA nightlife. One night he would be at graffiti star Shepard Fairey's DJ show at La Cita in downtown LA, and another he'd be taking pictures of a fashion runway show. All of these photos were put up on his site, Polaroid Scene, which later became the Cobra Snake.

One night in the summer of 2005, at a music show at El Rey Theatre on Wilshire Boulevard, Hunter met Kennedy, a meeting that would be the watershed moment in Kennedy's life as she knew it. About six months later, Kennedy started interning for Hunter and joining him at all the celebrity events he photographed. But two other things happened: Hunter and Kennedy started dating, and Hunter started posting pictures of Kennedy attending all those events they photographed together. Hunter then noticed something very interesting: When he posted those pictures of Kennedy, his web traffic spiked dramatically. So, naturally, he posted more pictures of her. By the following summer, Kennedy was on the cover of übercool fashion magazine *NYLON* and featured in newspaper articles and profiles in the *New York Times* and *Los Angeles Times* and in various other mainstream media. She appeared in a music video rocking out to Good Charlotte's "Keep Your Hands Off My Girl," which became one of the most widely viewed Internet videos of all time.[1] Kennedy signed on as the face of makeup company Urban Decay and she became friends with all the young starlets from Paris to Lindsay Lohan to Samantha Ronson. She became one of the most popular girls on MySpace (over 20,000 friends) and developed an active Twitter following (some 23,000 followers as I write this).

Along the way, Hunter and Kennedy broke up. These days she spends her time with her new rock star boyfriend (at the time this book was written, she was dating Jamie Reynolds of the indie Brit band Klaxons) and pals around with British socialite celebrity Peaches Geldof. A look at her tweets tells a story of a girl living on a plane traveling from glamorous city to glamorous city to runway shows and parties with the London–LA–New York jet set. Her blog features pictures of the details of her life, including a montage of photos from her attendance at an Easter party thrown by Paris Hilton. (Paris is wearing a faintly ridiculous sequined hot pink bunny outfit, which doesn't really strike the traditional tone of the holiday, but she looks fabulous nonetheless.) Kennedy's MySpace profile features dozens of videos of the various interviews she has given at the Marc Jacobs runway shows, at Betsy Johnson's runway show, at a *NYLON* party, and the list goes on.

In one of these short videos, an overly eager interviewer shoves a microphone in Kennedy's face and asks, "How do you feel about being the 'it' model of the world right now?"

Kennedy's response was not noteworthy. While Paris, despite seeming vapid, is able to entertain with her witty one-liners and the fact that she seems to revel in her gloriously absurd existence, Kennedy's verbal skills are not scintillating. Most of her interviews involve her muttering uninteresting non sequiturs that never quite form a sentence. In that respect, some might argue Cory Kennedy is not actually star material. As one Gawker commentator put it: "Go to school, honey. Go to prom. Assemble a vocabulary." Gawker itself has called Kennedy a variety of cruel names, from "homeless-looking hipster" to "teen fabutard" to "Internetard" to being a part of a coterie of "notable idiots."

Okay, she can't give a good interview, and okay, her insouciance comes with too much effort, but that hasn't stopped Kennedy from maintaining her high-profile existence and hobnobbing with the global in crowd. As long as Kennedy keeps her mouth closed, she certainly looks like any other celebrity. She has nice hair, always tangled in her signature style. She has porcelain skin. She has big, wide eyes and long eyelashes. She dresses somewhat quirkily in the grungy chic that supermodels on their days off cultivate perfectly. Kennedy is as good-looking and stylish as any star, but more important, photographs document Kennedy hanging out front and center with celebrities, including her rock star boyfriend.

Kennedy's star power is fundamentally a function of having physically located herself within the geography of celebrity, or, in common parlance, of being in the right place at the right time. Think of it like this: Pretty people are everywhere. Being a nice dresser doesn't get you on the cover of a fashion magazine. Every actor-cum-waitress can tell you that occupation isn't the sure path either. When we're talking about mainstream celebrity, people become stars by going through the networks and industries in Los Angeles, New York, London, and the other global celebrity hubs before making it around the world. Particular places matter because of the instant nature of current celebrity; everyone who is a part of creating celebrity needs to be in the same tightly constructed geography at the same time and on a fairly consistent basis in order to maintain and document celebrity. Cory Kennedy's celebrity depends on the people and conduits that make her a star.

These mediators, whether publicists, photographers, or journalists, are located primarily in Los Angeles, New York, and London. As Brandy Navarre, one of the cofounders of X17, the largest LA-based paparazzi site, explained to me, celebrities exist because they are written about and photographed consistently. "[X17 is] constructing a story every day. Everyone buys *People* magazine, everyone buys *US Weekly*. They have to be a part of this, in front of our lenses, in order to be a celebrity." Almost four hundred thousand unique visitors from Kansas City to Tokyo may troll X17's website every day for celebrity images, but the lenses generating those photos are in LA.

Take note of this statistic: Of the six hundred thousand–plus photos taken in one year of entertainment and celebrity events by Getty Images, 80 percent are taken in three locales: New York, London, and Los Angeles. Of the 187 places around the world represented in the photo database, London, New York, and Los Angeles are not only the most photographed locales but also the most connected to one another. When my colleague Gilad Ravid and I looked at which places stars attended events we found that they tended to move around among just these three cities. During their annual star-studded events, Cannes, Miami (during Art Basel), and Park City (during the Sundance Film Festival) act as specialized, temporary celebrity centers (see Figure 3). Las Vegas lures some stars off their normal stomping grounds but mainly for parties rather than prestigious industry events. But besides a select few cities no other place is a real player in the geography of stardom. This makes sense: Getty is the largest photographic agency in the world and sells its pictures to big and small media outlets everywhere. It is no surprise that the people who are photographed by Getty are individuals we are aware of, while those who don't get photographed are people we are not. Sure enough, a little over six months after the Cobra Snake started documenting her, Cory Kennedy started showing up in Getty Images photographs taken at LA Fashion Week.

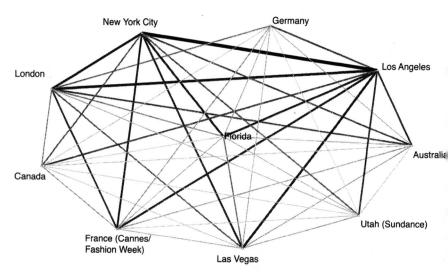

Figure 3. The Geography of Stardom Network

You can't become a global, mainstream celebrity if you don't get yourself to a place where the paparazzi and media outlets have set up shop (and the paparazzi are where the stars are), whether that's in the big global cities or the specialized, temporary celebrity hubs. "If you're not in the thirty-mile zone, then you've kind of opted out," one celebrity journalist explained. "LA, New York, London—that's where you go to show the flag. For the life of me, I can see no other reason to go to Hyde [an LA nightclub]."[2] Hence the circular relationship between the media and celebrity, which calls to mind the response of the famous bank robber Willie Sutton when asked why he robbed banks: "Because that's where the money is."

However, one needs more than being in Los Angeles to become a movie star or in London to be considered part of the global jet-setting elite. If celebrity rests significantly on the photo, then being in front of the flashbulb at the right instant is what counts. Living in New York and Los Angeles, while upping your chances of being "discovered," isn't the same as partying in the same clubs at the same time as Paris Hilton. Paris's presence guarantees a nonzero chance that someone with a camera and a magazine or website will be there taking pictures. Cory Kennedy, trotting along with Hunter to the celebrity events he photographed and then taking her place in front of the camera, was exactly where she needed to be to become a star.

In order to understand precisely where these photographs of stars are taken, my Columbia University colleague Sarah Williams and I studied all of Getty's photos of celebrity events in Los Angeles and New York. We had a few questions: Did all the celebrity industries (e.g., fashion, art, music, film) throw parties in the same places? Were celebrities all hanging out in the same places over and over, or was it completely random? If we observed a concentration of celebrity-studded events in the same place, was it merely a coincidence or had we stumbled across a statistical pattern that documented the physical location where people became stars? Using GIS (geographic information system),[3] which merges cartographic information with database information, we were able to take the data from the photographs' captions (who is in the photo, where it was taken, what event) and attach addresses and longitude and latitude tags (also called "geo-codes") to each of the three hundred thousand total photographs taken in the two cities over a one-year period. We then used those geo-codes to map where each photograph was taken. After mapping the photographs, we analyzed the images and looked for links among art, fashion, music, film, and entertainment events. ·

Our analysis produced robust statistical findings. First, there are a finite number of places where celebrities are photographed. Second, there is nothing random about where these photos are taken; our analysis demonstrated that there is a strong statistical pattern for where celebrity events happen. Further, no one in the celebrity world is acting on his or her own: All the celebrity moments in fashion, film, music, and art occur in the same places, and these places are piled up against one another. In other words, it's not an accident that all the stars are partying, walking down red carpets, or smiling for the camera in the same venues and on the same streets. In Los Angeles, for example, all of Getty's celebrity photographs occur within a very narrow spine along Sunset and Hollywood boulevards between Vine Street and the Beverly Hills Hotel. That's about five miles east to west and a quarter mile north to south (see Figure 4 and Appendix D).

When we look even closer at the photographs, there are literally only four neighborhoods where celebrity events are regularly photographed: Hollywood, Beverly Hills, West Hollywood, and Century City.[4] This geography of stardom does not include the informal, casual shots that photographers for TMZ, X17, *US Weekly*, or Big Pictures take of some celebrity getting a pedicure (Getty covers the "events that matter," so to speak). Not only are these latter photos shot in roughly the same parts of town as Getty's, but also their main purpose is to fill in the narrative of daily life of an already established celebrity. Grabbing coffee at Starbucks in Hollywood is not a way to become a star at the outset, but being on the red carpet at the Oscars, at a best-selling author's book party, or at the TriBeCa Film Festival, or emerging from the Fashion Week

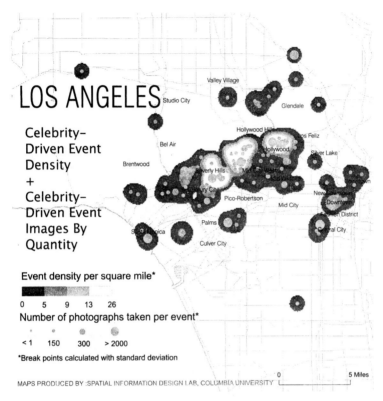

Figure 4. Los Angeles Celebrity-Driven Events

tents at Bryant Park just might be (which means your pedicures and coffee runs to Starbucks may eventually also get photographed by X17 and featured in *US Weekly*).

Plugging into your respective star geography counts. In New York, if you're involved in the music industry and you're not playing at Lincoln Center or Madison Square Garden, your best bet is to be at the nightclubs in Chelsea (see Figure 5). These are the locations that the media covers the most for music-related celebrity-studded events. Luckily, some of these hubs are centers for all types of celebrity, from fashion to art to music and film. For example, the stretch between Holly-

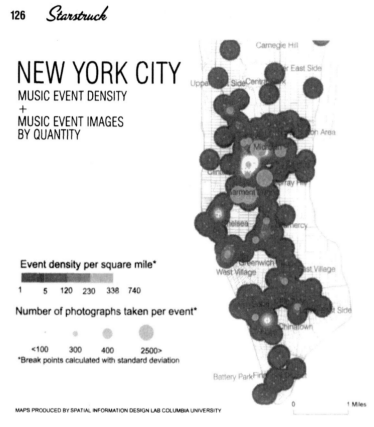

Figure 5. New York City Music Events

wood and Beverly Hills hosts almost all of the important events for the entertainment industries in Los Angeles. As tacky as Times Square may be to New Yorkers, hanging out there will dramatically increase your chance of running into celebrities from music or fashion walking into big events in its environs.

Similarly, there are "places within places" that drive different types of celebrity. In other words, different kinds of people interested in cultivating particular types of star profiles appear at totally different venues and events. Consider the vast chasm between MTV's *Total Request Live* (*TRL*) in Times Square and some hot and exclusive nightclub in Manhattan's hip Lower East Side. Certain celebrities maintain their mystique and cool status by going to "in-the-know" restricted places on the Lower East Side that would be much less appealing to the mainstream celebrity seeking avenues to maximize his or her public recognition. These smaller nodes within the city operate differently from each other in the cultivation of celebrity and are accessed through totally different strategies. *TRL*, one of MTV's most popular daily programs, features a guest star at every show. The program is far more constructed and controlled and requires the "right contacts"—major publicists and agents—and the "right look" that appeals to a mass audience.

Yet, despite all the legwork involved, *TRL* is a more democratic and less exclusive method for distributing information about celebrities. The Lower East Side club may not require a six-month lead time of begging publicists to get their star on the roster, but only the coolest clique of stars and their followers are able to get their foot in the door. In this respect, the LES club affirms the truly elite network of celebrity. Or consider the different types of celebrity—politicians, socialites, the old guard, and the ephemeral—all of which tend to have their own venues to see and be seen. New York's legendary restaurants Michael's and the Four Seasons, while infiltrated by the starlets, are generally the headquarters for the old guard—there is gravitas to these institutions, and the people who frequent them reflect this. The Mayflower is Washington's celebrity institution for politicians, the very hotel where shamed New York governor Eliot Spitzer turned from politician to political celebrity when he got busted for arranging trysts with a prostitute. Contrast these institutions with the flurry of trendy nightclubs, most so short-lived that naming them is gratuitous, as their significance (and chances of remaining open) changes almost monthly. While they are extremely exclusive, they are also interchangeable and occupy temporary positions of stardom, much like their patrons.

Equally, on a larger scale, not all geographies of celebrity are the same. Los Angeles, New York, London—they are different. From the media to the social outings where photos are taken to the types of celebrities these towns produce and attract, the very constitution of celebrity in each of these locales is unique. "The West Coast has been for a long time where a certain kind of fashion that young people want is rooted as well as the proliferation of the paparazzi and the weather," Hollywood PR stalwart Elliot Mintz explained. "In New York City, in the cold, dreary weather, you can't wear those outfits. In Los Angeles, you can. So with all due respect to a picture of Martin Scorsese, in California, all the girls have suntans." This is all by way of saying that being in the right celebrity hub—just like being friends with the right celebrity— is what enables one to cultivate a particular kind of stardom.[5]

A place or an event becomes a celebrity hub because celebrities bother to show up there in the first place. Tom Cruise would likely attend the Academy Awards ceremony, which happens to be in Los Angeles, and serious actors make it a point to attend the Cannes Film Festival, so Cannes and Los Angeles become hot spots. Simply put, the events that celebrities go to are hosted in particular places. Stars are then compelled to go to those places, thus creating a system that creates and reinforces itself—what economists call "endogeneity," whereby each variable in the system predicts the others' behavior.[6] But there is another way to look at these travel choices: Tom Cruise becomes a highly respected star partially *because* he goes to events in those particular places versus attending events in other locales. Consider Cruise's other options: Las Vegas; South Beach, Florida; Ibiza. These are also celebrity hubs. But Tom Cruise is not one of the celebrities who create the reputations of these latter places. Just as on a smaller scale, *Total Request Live* attracts very different stars from the club on the Lower East Side, celebrity geographies are different because the people who frequent them are different. By extension, visiting one city over another may explain how celebrity types emerge. Thus, in order to be a particular type of celebrity, an aspiring star ought to be mimicking a particular travel pattern. As with celebrity networks, there is a strategy buried in a star's geographical choices. Understanding the movements of stars from place to place, where they go and whom they spend time with, tells us a lot about how some people become stars and how one celebrity has a different character from another's.

When my colleague Gilad Ravid and I looked at those six hundred thousand Getty Images photos taken of celebrities around the world in one year, we found that stars exhibit vastly different types of traveling patterns going in and out of celebrity hubs.[7] We know intuitively that stars are fundamentally different from one another. Some launch themselves by being talented and respected by their industry and then are splashed across the tabloids; others are born in the gossip columns and remain there throughout their celebrity lives. Talent is not the same as being "talked about." But how do these stars behave differently? We know that their social networks are different, but do they also hang out in different cities and at different events?

To get at talent, Gilad and I used *Forbes*'s Star Currency, a measure of a star's perceived bankability. Based on a survey of top Hollywood studio executives, *Forbes* allocated each star a composite score from 0 to 10, with number one–ranked Will Smith getting a 10 and Johnny Depp and George Clooney both getting above a 9.8, compared to Paris Hilton, who got a score of 3.21. We compared the talent scores with subjects of gossip, which we measured by searching Google for media and blog mentions. In this area, Paris Hilton is the fourth-ranked star in terms of sheer volume of media mentions (Michael Jackson, Britney Spears, and Madonna ranked first, second, and third). We then studied the A-list, which we defined as the top twenty Star Currency celebrities, to see if they have different types of traveling patterns from everyone else. From the very talented celebrities (those with greater Star Currency), to those residuals who are documented endlessly on blogs and stack up volumes of media mentions, right down to the C-list (those ranked 1,390–1,410 on Star Currency), we found that discrete and unique traveling patterns to and from the celebrity hubs emerge. Going to the right places at the right time is critical in determining celebrity status. Quite simply, if an aspiring celebrity wants to be an A-lister, he or she needs to be making the same global pit stops as other A-listers.

A-list celebrities and residuals tend to make a couple of similar key decisions. First, and unsurprisingly, all celebrities show up in Los Angeles at least some of the time, whether they are residual or the top scorers in Star Currency. Celebrities with lots of Star Currency (read: talent) must show up in Los Angeles like everyone else. Other than making a few cameos, however, top stars keep a relatively low profile in Los Angeles compared to other types of stars (no boutique openings or random parties for Tom Cruise, for example). The rest of the time they are flitting off to other venues for big events and parties, particularly New York and London. Yet visiting these places alone is not a sufficient traveling schedule in itself. Despite the fact that more photos are taken in the Big Three than anywhere else, top stars are traveling to lots of other places, such as Tokyo, Paris, and Germany. Thus we get to a critical juncture: The top talent-driven stars rarely appear at events that do not have a link to the industry, a charity, or a cause they are championing, whereas residuals can be found at virtually any kind of event where photographers are present.

There is a global demand for the top stars at the most prestigious events, which is why they are seen around the world. A-listers keep moving around from place to place more than C-listers and notably more than most other kinds of celebrities. Half of the top twenty ranked in Star Currency are in the top hundred of most-traveled celebrities, which means they are on flights to events around the world more than other celebrities. Because they are so elite, these stars show up primarily at key events like the Academy Awards, the Cannes Film Festival, or London and New York Fashion Week. Top talent-driven stars do not necessarily attend tons of events in Los Angeles. Angelina Jolie showed up at events in LA just five times in one year. Despite being a Hollywood icon, Jack Nicholson was photographed only eleven separate times in Los Angeles. Beyoncé, one of the biggest stars in the world, made just ten appearances in Los Angeles in the same year. Compare these figures to residual stars like Paris Hilton and Lindsay Lohan, who make multiple appearances in LA events, forty-four and twenty-two, respectively. In other words, A-list stars tend to travel far and wide but otherwise scarcely be seen. This makes sense: A-listers are more likely to be at events around the world because of their global celebrity status. B- and C-listers, in contrast, show up disproportionately in Los Angeles. Many of them live in LA (it is, after all, the TV and film capital of the world), and most of the small-scale celebrity events associated with boutique or nightclub openings that a B- and C-lister can get into are located there too.

After studying star travel patterns, Gilad and I wanted to tease out whether showing up in one place over another was positively or negatively associated with a celebrity's Star Currency or media mentions. We looked at where all six hundred thousand photos were taken and ran statistical analyses to study the correlations between where stars go and their rank on Star Currency (talent) and media mentions (a measure of residual).[8] We found that showing up in Los Angeles is not associated with an increase in a celebrity's Star Currency, whereas traveling to exotic locales like Japan or Germany is strongly predictive of increases in star talent-driven power. This can be explained by the fact that Los Angeles is a destination for all stars and therefore is not a unique travel choice. If every other star or aspiring star is passing through Los Angeles, one has to do something different to set oneself apart from the crowd. For example, attending events in Australia seems to be a good move for talent stars and residuals: going to one event is associated with an increase of almost 2,200 media mentions and 0.4 on one's Star Currency score. Going to an event in London correlates with increases in one's Star Currency score by almost 0.5. A New York event is also (though less) important, associated with an increased score of 0.212. These may seem like small increases, but when we're dealing with a range from 0 to 10, an extra half point is a 5 percent increase in Star Currency, no small feat for attending just one extra event in London. And the stars being photographed in London back up these stats: The celebrities most photographed in Great Britain (removing Queen Elizabeth and Prince Charles from our analysis, which, to be fair, slightly skews our results) are Beyoncé, Helen Mirren, and Johnny Depp. All three of these stars are genuine A-listers, and not just because of their celebrity; they are talented and genuinely admired by their public.

For residual celebrities, showing up in London is just as important: One extra visit increases one's coverage on blogs and media by almost 1,250 mentions. The "London effect" isn't surprising. First, Great Britain's influence can partially be explained by the fact that there are fewer events in London than in LA, which means those events are rare and implicitly more exclusive. Second, despite being an island of only sixty million people, Britain is one of the most important celebrity hubs in the world. Media around the globe covers the big Lon-

don celebrity and entertainment scene. But perhaps most critically, unlike the United States with its 1,408 daily newspapers
and endless TV channels, Britain has a far more concentrated
national media. Americans have many more niche and regional media markets: Of those 1,408 dailies, only 395 have
more than fifty thousand subscribers.[9] Contrast this diluted
audience with Great Britain: In England, there are 15 major
dailies (including the tabloids) and 63 regional daily newspapers. Scotland has 12 major dailies and 11 regional daily
newspapers. Further, regardless of their political affiliation,
almost all Brits get a significant proportion of their news from
one centralized source: the BBC. If the BBC reports on an
event, you can bet most Brits have seen the headline online or
on TV or listened to it on their way to work. If you can make
it into London's media montage, then you've immediately
landed a very large and focused audience.

Nonetheless, if you're an A-lister (or an aspiring one), there
is such a thing as too much of a good thing. While showing
face in the top celebrity hubs and a few far-flung cities is
important, repeatedly showing up anywhere tends to at best
have no influence and sometimes is even negatively associated
with Star Currency rank. Being photographed in London for
more than one event in a row reduces Star Currency by 0.1.
Paradoxically, sticking around particular cities is predictive of
an increase in one's residual. Spending more time in Los Angeles and New York is associated with increased Google media
mentions and blog volume by almost 200. Further, showing up
at just one event in Los Angeles is associated with increased
media volume of almost 1,100 mentions, even if it has no association with talent. In other words, it does not behoove Paris
to show up in Los Angeles at forty-four separate events if
she wants to transcend her famous-for-being-famous status,
though it will keep her in the camera's focus. The beneficial
results to the residuals can be explained by the fact that not

only is Los Angeles a huge media hub, but if the A-listers aren't bothering to show up, the media will take photos of whoever is hanging around. Additionally, photographers spend most of their time in Los Angeles (and to a certain extent New York) and so end up capturing a lot of events that aren't necessarily exclusive. But that's no ticket to becoming a legitimate A-lister. While showing up in Los Angeles is a necessary part of being a star, it has a neutral impact on Star Currency score. A-listers stay on the move. Being busy, important, or in demand around the world, or at least pretending to be, is strongly associated with the top stars.

Not everyone can be as gorgeous and talented as Beyoncé or as much of a box office draw as Johnny Depp. As we know already, there are many different types of celebrities. Residual celebrities have their own travel patterns that keep their type of celebrity alive. Never underestimate Paris Hilton's prowess of using her round-the-world travels to max out her all-residual status. Paris recognizes that her celebrity rests on being in the camera's flash as much as possible, which means she needs to be in a lot of places and, simultaneously, in the same place (LA) so that people can constantly record her life as it unfolds. Not having any great talents to fall back on, she can't rely on turning up at the significant events only to disappear from the limelight on other occasions, the way Jolie, Nicholson, and Beyoncé are able to do. So Paris's strategy has to be slightly different. She shows up at the events that count *and* makes sure to be around more generally, which is why Getty gets a shot of her entering an award ceremony or a restaurant opening, and paparazzi agency TMZ catches her leaving a nightclub on a random Wednesday night.

Paris is also on a plane all the time—in fact, significantly more than anyone else. In our study of celebrities' traveling patterns between events, we found that Paris had to get on a plane at least fifty-three times in order to make all the events she went to in one year. And because celebrity is also about generating a collective interest in one's daily life (particularly when there is no talent to push), Paris sticking around LA for extended periods of time is an important way for her to feed tabloid, blog, and general media interest in her general existence. Celebrities like Paris are in a tough position: Getting photographed at various events in the same place definitely bumps up her celebrity residual, but remaining local simultaneously takes away from her Star Currency and thus her ability to be perceived as a talent-driven celebrity. In terms of stardom, there's a real decision to be made: Should Paris toil away at her acting and risk being forgotten, or does she just keep reminding us she exists and remain the ultimate all-residual celebrity?

Paris attends two and a half times as many events around the world as the busiest A-lister (Tom Cruise) and has to travel more to make it to the ninety-five events she appears at in one year. Residual with a touch of B-list star Carmen Electra went to fifty-two events in one year and was photographed 1,149 times by Getty Images. Compare these two celebrities to inveterate A-lister Cruise, who showed up at just thirty-nine events and was photographed 1,446 times, and the seemingly reclusive Angelina Jolie and George Clooney, who attended just twenty-three and twenty-two events, respectively, in the same year. Paris has to maintain her hectic schedule in order to maintain her stardom: While Angelina Jolie attended one Getty-photographed event in London that year, she was photographed 100 times there. When Tom Cruise attended one event in London, his U.K. *Mission: Impossible* film premiere, he was photographed 111 times. Paris, on the other hand, showed up at ten London events and was photographed 173 times. Her ratio of events to coverage is much smaller than Jolie's or Cruise's (17.3 versus 100 and 111), who are in such demand they barely need to show up at anything to generate photographers' flashes. Underneath her seemingly chaotic schedule, Paris's travel patterns reflect a need to remain in the public eye to perpetuate her celebrity.

There is one rule that both A-list and residual celebrities should follow: Don't go to Vegas. Going to an event in Las Vegas not only does not influence your Star Currency, even worse, sticking around has a negative influence. In the year we studied, only two top Star Currency celebrities had been photographed at events in Vegas: Ben Stiller and Adam Sandler. In statistical terms, sticking around Vegas for an extended period is associated with a celebrity's Star Currency score decreasing by almost one-third of a point. Residuals do not follow these rules religiously, even though their media presence is not positively associated with Las Vegas events either. Paris Hilton and Carmen Electra, two of the most photographed residual stars, have been photographed in Vegas numerous times. Outside of Los Angeles and New York, Vegas is these ladies' most documented location. One might argue that spending time in Vegas hasn't hurt Paris, but remember she's counteracting this potentially destructive move with her endless globetrotting. For the residual celebrity, staying in Vegas (as opposed to jetting in and out for one night) is an even worse idea, as it decreases Google media mention volume by almost two thousand mentions. This finding isn't surprising: Las Vegas isn't celebrity central unless Paris is hosting a night at a big club or some celebrity is having a birthday party. If you're in Las Vegas after the party is over and the media long gone, it means you're not in front of a camera or at an important event somewhere else.

Of course, all of these statistics can be explained by the fact that different kinds of celebrities have to behave in different ways. Part of a talent-driven A-lister's strategy is to keep away from the media. If you're an A-lister, you are already in the sights and minds of the powers that be in Hollywood, New York, and London. You've already gotten your invite to the

Vanity Fair Oscar party and Anna Wintour's Costume Institute gala. *Vogue* wants you on the cover because you're beautiful and you've won an Academy Award. In other words, like your networks, you show up in the hubs when you attain maximum impact—and that's it. Your celebrity is perpetuated simply because you are always in the spotlight and on the public's mind for your latest top-ten single or blockbuster movie. We already care about you. If you're an A-lister, being around too much, creating a persona independent of the image the public has of you, can have a negative impact on your career. A Hollywood film development director explained to me that sometimes an actress's celebrity can overshadow her ability to truly become the character in a film. As she put it, "As soon as Lindsay Lohan went from being the cute, seemingly talented actress on *Freaky Friday* to becoming a tabloid [sensation], she dropped off everyone's list in terms of the big producers. If you seem like such a big hot mess in the tabloids, people really don't want to be associated with that."

Even Angelina Jolie, despite seeming to want to live a private life, runs the risk of being overexposed simply because the world is obsessed with her. Manohla Dargis, the *New York Times* film critic, described this danger with regard to Jolie's performance in *A Mighty Heart*. "Like all big movie stars, she can't disappear into her role for long," Dargis wrote. "Rather, she bobs to the surface of our consciousness, recedes, bobs to the surface, recedes. Her celebrity bequeaths the movie its capital 'I' importance." For talented stars whose celebrity is a side effect of their high profile in film, music, fashion, or politics, maintenance of their talent must remain the priority; their celebrity is self-perpetuating as a result of already being in demand.

If you haven't won a major film award or costarred next to Robert De Niro, however, and you want stardom, going out only when the red carpet is particularly plush isn't necessarily a viable option. The whole essence of the celebrity residual is reminding the world of one's existence. The best way to achieve this goal is by maintaining a presence in the celebrity hubs. For the Paris–Carmen–Lindsay–Edie Sedgwicks of the world (and any other aspiring starlet with more residual than talent), there is a real cost to keeping oneself away from the media and the celebrity hubs: The world will indeed forget about you. And thus we can see how stars make what appear to be bad decisions about where they show up: Girl pop bands do gigs in Las Vegas that aren't accompanied by a big celebrity-hosted event. B-listers get paid to show up at tacky events sponsored by vodka brands that might pay the rent but won't earn them a high celebrity profile. Heidi Montag posing for *Playboy* or going to a party at Hugh Hefner's mansion allows her to branch out and capture a whole new audience, drumming up more media attention, and thus expanding her celebrity, but it also rapidly decreases her shot at an invite to the *Vanity Fair* Oscar party with its top film producers and directors. Invitations to the Oscars aren't given out like coupons to Burger King. Even Paris Hilton was denied an invitation, despite her protests that she was a real film star. The options for a residual or B-lister may not be plentiful enough to turn down those extra events in Vegas like *Celebrity Poker* or the hair salon or boutique openings in LA. Even if by some extraordinary luck you land that invite to the Oscars, it will cost you $5,000-plus for dress, hair, makeup, stylist, driver; the list goes on. So those mediocre gigs and appearances at Vegas nightclubs will at least buy your dress if you somehow get the chance at the big time.

If it all seems a bit circular—the way individuals become stars by going to celebrity hubs and these celebrity hubs become what they are because the stars show up—then you're sort of right, but not entirely. Fundamentally, some places possess basic qualities that enable them to become focal points of celebrity.

People don't become in-the-bright-lights stars in Kansas, but it's not simply because Tom Cruise and his ilk don't show up there. Kansas never had a chance to be a major player in the geography of stardom in the first place, because it lacked the necessary ingredients that catalyze success: a collective group of stars; a global media machine; an infrastructure of bars, clubs, and studios that enable the visual footage of celebrities to be captured in a glamorous context; and the surplus of wealth that bankrolls these various activities and places. Some of these attributes arise partially as a result of already being a celebrity hub (more stars move there because stars already live there and thus more media sets up shop), but others are necessary from the get-go for a place to even have a chance.[10]

Let's start with the first element: In order to be a hub in the geography of stardom, a place needs a critical mass of celebrities and a collective group of individuals who socialize publicly and who are generally interesting to a wider public and, just as critically, to the media.[11] How can we explain the concentration of celebrities? Often, they work in industries that are located primarily in one place, which means that to do their job they all have to work and live there as well. In order to be a gainfully employed film star, one has to be in Los Angeles for a good chunk of time. Even if an actor isn't out at the clubs until three a.m., he or she must attend meetings with casting directors and producers located in Los Angeles, and filming often takes place in Hollywood back lots. Politicians may travel around their home state during Congress's recess, but they're expected to show up in D.C. regularly to debate and vote on bills and serve on committees.

However, it's not simply a concentration of similar people. Back in the day, automobile workers all lived and worked in Detroit, but they were not celebrities. Celebrities are not just working in the same industries; the essence of their existence is that they are also very interesting to the media. Hollywood stars easily captivate us: They are attractive, fashionable, and act in movies we want to see, and the media loves to document them. Washington politicians may not be as good-looking or well dressed as George Clooney or Jennifer Aniston, but they also easily command an audience. There is rarely a dull moment inside the Beltway, whether Congress is passing a contentious bill or some senator had an inappropriate relationship with an intern. Conversely, *Star Trek* hobbyists are much less intriguing to a mass audience (even if they are relative celebrities), and most technology geeks in Silicon Valley are certainly uninteresting to mainstream consumers of popular culture and political intrigue.

An active media is the second important ingredient in a celebrity hub. The media needs to care, and the media located in these locales must be globally relevant in order to create megastars.[12] A high-profile socialite in Dublin or Austin may be the talk of her town but rarely crosses over to mainstream stardom because Getty photographers or the *New York Times* or *US Weekly* are not showing up. Finally, there needs to be an infrastructure that lends itself to the cultivation of celebrities and the financial capital to keep opening establishments that are trendy and enticing.[13] Because celebrity rests on the public's obsession with individuals' lives and personae, the media must find ways to obtain this information and capture it visually (what the historian Daniel Boorstin calls the "human pseudo-event"). Having clubs to fall out of, restaurants to glamorously walk into, and film and TV sets for impromptu lunches and romantic tête-à-têtes with costars is important to the media's role in cultivating the celebrity personality. New York, Los Angeles, London, and, to an extent, D.C. all possess these characteristics, but the same basic qualities are necessary for other geographies of stardom too. In the world of country music, Nashville is an essential celebrity hub with the necessary big-hub attributes—just on a much smaller scale. Paris is an essential destination for fashion celebrities but not as important for the celebrity system as a whole.

Once these variables come together, the process of becoming a celebrity hub is set in motion. Economists call this self-reinforcing process "cumulative advantage," but it's as simple as success begets success.[14] Having the basic infrastructure and capital to get the process moving accrues more capital and more people and more infrastructure necessary to perpetuate success, so that over time this dominance as a hub solidifies. We see it in Silicon Valley's reputation as the world's leading technology hub and New York's and London's positions as global financial capitals, and New York's and Paris's domination of the fashion industry. And we see it plain and simple in the geography of stardom.

Celebrity and the "Pseudo-Event"

One spring afternoon in London, my boyfriend (now husband), Richard, and I were strolling along the South Bank of the Thames. The South Bank is a formerly dodgy, now gentrified part of town that has a magnificent view of Westminster and Big Ben and is quickly becoming one of the most desired neighborhoods for the upwardly mobile and trend conscious. En route to lunch, we found ourselves in the midst of a great commotion under way at the Royal Festival Hall, an enormous entertainment venue located on the river. Massive crowds of people had formed a circle around a mysterious presence. Photographers were snapping away. When we investigated, we saw a massive ad hoc backdrop and a woman, some soap star whom Richard sort of recognized, smiling away in a bright red evening gown and far too much makeup. Her poses were obviously forced, and she seemed really uncomfortable. The backdrop indicated it was the BAFTA Television Awards, which are a pretty big deal in England (similar to the Emmys in the United States). Regardless, the little drama unfolding was bizarre. At three o'clock in the afternoon, here was this spectacle of a woman with about five inches of makeup and a tight prom dress smiling away in a gigantic open space along the South Bank, looking like she'd far rather be in sweats on her way to her own weekend lunch. Despite it being BAFTA, the scene seemed cheap and tacky, a far cry from the dazzling affair that it appeared to be in the newspapers and on TV. Yet many events are just like this in real life: quite starkly unspectacular and overly contrived. And rest assured, the photos taken and distributed to blogs and tabloids around the world make the most mundane events appear as the most exciting and sensational places to be.

The construction of a pseudoglamorous event along the South Bank demonstrates exactly how places like London, Los Angeles, and New York remain the big hubs. Celebrity is ultimately constructed by the players involved, and they have every reason to keep the system humming along. Media not only drives celebrity, it also helps establish the places and events that should be deemed important by the public, Boorstin's "human pseudo-event." Boorstin argues that modern culture, particularly the entertainment industries and politics, creates events that have the primary function of producing and feeding advertising and media.[15] The events themselves are not relevant to the public until the media makes them so. In another world, the Oscars could be a subdued and private affair entirely dedicated to the recognition of outstanding performers in the film industry. Instead, with the cooperation of the television stations, newspapers, Motion Picture Association of America, and actors, it is the most high-profile celebrity event in the world. People in Ohio order pizza and throw Oscar parties to watch the event on TV. No one who lives in Los Angeles goes near Sunset Boulevard the entire weekend before the event for fear of drowning in a tsunami of limousines. Sure, the Oscars are important for the film industry, but the public cares about them because the media and the film industries have turned them into a glamorous, prominent event. The media showcases the stars to make them, well, even bigger stars. No wonder everyone wants an invite. The projection of posh glitz and resplendence at these events, whether the Grammys, the Oscars, movie premieres, or the Golden Globes, is necessary because these events drive all the TV, tabloid, and sponsorship revenue streams and maintain the public's interest in particular celebrities. The film industry and the media benefit from making much ado about these events. The public's preoccupation with the event is fundamental to perpetuating the phenomenon of celebrity and its related industries. However, if the powers that be don't create celebrities, then the public has no one to celebrate.

And Getty, TMZ, ABC, and every other photographic and television entity are a part of the construction of the celebrity, not to mention all the clubs and restaurants that play hosts to Oscar after-parties. But consumers of celebrity care about celebrities only because the media makes them exciting and appealing. The marriage of celebrity with the media's high-gloss finishing touch on these events makes them irresistibly enticing. We are drawn in by the reality of the unreality of it all. We like watching the Oscars because the event is filmed in February in the glorious Southern California late afternoon sunlight, when it's cold, dark, and gloomy in most other places. At the Oscars, the people are beautiful and tanned, the dresses magnificent and colorful. There are a lot of very white, straight teeth. The carpet is a deep red and the columned Babylonian-themed Kodak Theater so impressive. The whole affair seems like such a glittering and enchanting backdrop to honor these film icons, the essence of Hollywood celebrity.

However, the red carpet mirage disguises the vast chasm

between what the Kodak Theater looks like on TV and in photos and what it actually is: a suburban mall-like construction in the middle of a seedy section of Hollywood with psychics, wax museums, and strip clubs down the street. The media and the event organizers construct a glamorous image of the Kodak Theater that is completely removed from reality, even going so far as to hide neighboring stores behind curtains.[16] Those who have not been to Los Angeles have no idea that this part of Hollywood is primarily streets of liquor stores, chain stores, and neon lights. The Walk of Fame is a bunch of grungy, faded stars on a littered sidewalk, not a single celebrity in sight. In fact, the most interesting part of Hollywood is the gaggle of tourists standing around confused, with "This is it?" expressions on their faces. The same can be said of Los Angeles's Viper Room, a mile away on Sunset Boulevard, the mythical club where River Phoenix met his death after a drug overdose. A close-up picture of the club with stars falling out in the wee hours of the morning makes it seem like a wild and thrilling place. If you pan the shot out a bit, you'll see a Subway sandwich shop, the Sun Bee Food and Liquor Mart, a dirty sidewalk, and a massive thoroughfare with cars flying by.

And here is where we return to the Cory Kennedy phenomenon. Kennedy's success in cultivating her celebrity is a function of the way the media creates a new breed of celebrity. Kennedy is not simply a new Paris or a new Edie Sedgwick, famous for being famous. (Paris, after all, is a filthy-rich heiress with a sex tape. Sedgwick was a filthy-rich socialite with a drug problem and Andy Warhol's attention. Kennedy comes from much more subdued circumstances.) Kennedy may hang with the celebrity set, but she has not been caught hoovering up cocaine or shoplifting. In another world, Kennedy would have likely lived a very normal life. But all the crucial factors combined to create a perfect channel for her to go from pretty high school girl to international girl-about-town in less than a year.

This is the story that makes celebrity so much a part of our lives today. Because the media is everywhere, with its endless conduits to report on stars, we think stars are everywhere, inhabiting our lives at all times. And we're right. But this phenomenon is not a result of the A-list suddenly being more social or less elitist. Los Angeles, New York, and London remain the stomping grounds for the top celebrities, but these cities have also become destinations for the lesser known and the all-residual celebrities who use the media to cultivate stardom because the media has the ability to turn something ordinary into something glossy and sensational. Simultaneously, the media has chosen to focus on and sometimes create these new forms of stardom, thereby expanding the industry and the revenue generated through celebrity.

The geography of stardom outlines the basic behaviors of celebrities, but that's not the same as providing a map for how to enter A-list territory. Yet by identifying the geographical patterns of top stars, one might have a chance at attaining celebrity status simply by showing up at the right places and being photographed at just the right time. The geography of stardom demonstrates that following stars is a good proxy for tracking the media. And if one can be in step with the media, one does have a real shot at celebrity. When millions upon millions can be made, it's no wonder so many people are motivated to become stars, whether they are talented, all residual, or, like Cory Kennedy, a star utterly different from any form society has seen before.

7

The Economics of the Celebrity Residual

Beckham was wasted on his sport. Most of the money made out of him
in his career probably went to the player himself, his boot company and
other sponsors, who are cleverer than the people who run football
clubs. —**Simon Kuper and Stefan Szymanski,** *Soccernomics*

It seemed like Christmas in July when I landed on the guest list
for Jeff Koons's *Popeye Series* private opening at the Serpentine Gallery (a friend high up in London's art world managed
to finagle an invitation for me). London had, by some extraordinary aberration, been experiencing gorgeous sunny days and
blue skies. In that part of the world, if the rain's not pouring
down, the summer sky remains light until nine p.m., which
makes evenings seemingly last forever. The Serpentine Gallery
is located in the heart of Hyde Park, a public space so glorious
that a summer evening wandering through it is a sublime
pleasure that even Londoners don't take for granted. The Serpentine Gallery is about as innovative and cutting-edge as the
institutionalized art world gets, and attending an opening
there is like scoring a ticket to the Marc Jacobs show at New
York Fashion Week. The Serpentine is one of a few pivotal art
institutions around the world that set the stage for who and
what to care about. And, of course, not to bury the headline,
Jeff Koons is about as iconic and interesting as a living artist
can get. Even if one doesn't like his blend of the banal and the

fantastic, and his sensationalist high-art-meets-hard-core-porn aesthetic, experiencing the Koons phenomenon in person is a rarified experience. Koons's July 2009 opening at the Serpentine was also a first: Despite worldwide acclaim, he had never had a solo exhibition in London, which is pretty surprising given the city's position at the center of the art world and Koons's position as one of the most important artists in history.

The event was swarming with the beautiful people set, paparazzi and cameras out in full force filming ad hoc interviews with celebrity attendees. Koons's artist dinner the night before had been awash with celebrities, from socialites and models to the photographer David Bailey and Koons's art dealer Larry Gagosian, to other art stars like Tracey Emin and the Chapman brothers. All of these details had been splashed on the pages of the London *Evening Standard* and *Vogue* online. On the warm and lovely evening of the opening, Koons stood in the middle of it all, oddly not heckled by the milling fans (I suppose in Celebrity World, celebrities treat one another with equality). A very large and and very tan chiseled man stood next to the rather slight Koons (both men wearing smart suits, no ties), which might also have explained the general lack of frenzy around Koons. Despite his easygoing stance, Koons's Ken doll sidekick was definitely a bodyguard, ready to become intimidating at any minute.

One might think it strange that an artist would need a bodyguard, but Koons's opening was more like a celebrity birthday party than a highbrow art event. The people swirling about were not stuffy art critics stroking their chins and using words like "postmodernity." Instead, the girls were wearing tiny dresses and sky-high stilettos, and the guys were stylishly disheveled. Most art openings are scenes, but Koons's managed to trump even the best of those: More people were outside sipping cocktails than inside the gallery looking at the exhibit. But don't think this demonstrates some lack of appreciation for the art. This heady, glamorous scene is exactly the thing that has made Koons go from artist to art star, leaving broken auction records in his wake. Koons is emblematic of modern celebrity economics: We are always paying a premium for star power.

Jeff Koons is a curious and remarkable person. An American artist who has worked primarily in New York City, by the mid-1980s (when he was in his late twenties), Koons had begun to build quite a name for himself. His method of employing factorylike production techniques is often compared to Andy Warhol's. But that's about where the normal "artist story" ends. In 1988, Koons solidified his position in the art world with his now famous *Michael Jackson and Bubbles*: an enormous statue of Jackson and his chimp done in delicate porcelain and gold plated, resembling a magnified version of those tiny collectible figurines that little old ladies place on side tables next to the jelly bean jar. There is no irony lost in the fact that this faux kitsch depiction of an iconic celebrity is partially what launched Koons's own star status.[1]

In the last two decades, Koons has continued to make outrageous and fun art that has been either reviled or adored by the community, a paradoxically powerful method for success. In 1992, he created *Puppy*, a forty-foot-tall flower sculpture of a . . . puppy. In 2006, Koons showed his five nine-foot-tall metallic *Hanging Heart* sculptures (a part of his *Celebration* series), their vividness and size fully appreciable only in real life. He has done several other pieces in bright metallic colors, including a balloon dog and his enormous *Balloon Flower*.

Koons's *Popeye Series*, exhibited at the Serpentine, is a mixture of sculpture and painting: The sculptures are made of aluminum and have the appearance of children's plastic swimming pool toys. The paintings (an art form he has also practiced throughout his career) depict montages of conflicting images from popular culture: The exhibit as a whole is composed of both the sculptures and silk screen mosaics of semi-naked women, pool toys, and, of course, the cartoon character Popeye. Koons's signature contribution to the art world is taking what seems boring, banal, and pedestrian and making it fantastic by employing large size, outlandish color, and ironic juxtaposition. While some might say Warhol did this too, Koons's creations are far splashier and far bigger: Many of his sculptures tower tens of feet tall.

Koons is possibly the most celebrated living artist, with only the British artist Damien Hirst as his real competition. And his position as *the* art star is reflected in a tangible way: His work appears in every major art institution worth its salt and he is one of the richest living artists, second only to Hirst. To be clear, I mean rich in a global sense, not relative to the average starving artist. In 2001, *Michael Jackson and Bubbles* sold for $5.6 million. Six years later, one of his *Hanging Heart* sculptures sold for $23.4 million at Sotheby's to the celebrated art dealer Larry Gagosian, making it at the time the most expensive piece of art by a living artist. Less than a year later, *Balloon Flower (Magenta/Gold)* sold for $25.7 million.[2]

There are plenty of art critics who think Koons is a snake oil salesman and a trickster, creating works for the "tacky rich," in the words of one commentator. Michael Kimmelman of the *New York Times* called Koons's work "boring," remarking that "the hollowness the artist reveals seems fundamentally his own."[3] But, frankly, when you're Jeff Koons laughing all the way to the bank with a $25 million check, or when star maker Larry Gagosian buys your art like candy and thinks you're a genius and celebrities line up to attend your dinners and openings, who cares? The art devotees who think Koons is making a mockery of them and of art might be right.

Koons himself claims his work means nothing more than what it appears to be on the surface, once commenting, "My work has no aesthetic values."[4]

Koons's 1991 *Made in Heaven* series featured Koons and his then-wife, Ilona Staller (aka Cicciolina, the Hungarian-born porn star who went on to become a member of the Italian parliament), and consisted of graphic close-range depictions of him and Cicciolina having very raunchy sex. It's unnecessary to go into all the details; a pithy description from art critic Kimmelman suffices: "Artificial and cheap in their settings and emotions, they are not fundamentally different from what one might see in *Hustler* magazine, translated almost to the scale of a movie screen." I haven't had the opportunity to see the work in real life, but recently I saw the collection in a book of Koons's work and I admit that one can appreciate Kimmelman's outrage. Koons and Cicciolina were certainly not in the business of discretion, and one would be hard-pressed to call the series high art in the conventional sense. "Cheap" isn't the word I would use to describe the images, but my first glimpse of them was jaw-dropping.

But that is precisely the point. There is a subplot throughout Koons's art career that should not be ignored. Koons is no run-of-the-mill talented artist. His events are attended by the who's who of the art world and the world at large. His work is bought by Hollywood stars. His sculptures break auction house records. Even people who don't care a fig about art know Jeff Koons's name and find his persona interesting and his work accessible. But Koons wants that to be the case; he is not an art star by accident. What drives the critics crazy is that Koons cultivates his celebrity. As one art critic observed, "In an era when artists were not regarded as 'stars,' Koons went to great lengths to cultivate his public persona by employing an image consultant."[5] Consequently, Koons set up a massive ad campaign complete with bikini-clad girls in international art magazines, touting his great success.[6] In interviews and public appearances, he began "referring to himself in the third person."[7] He even held autograph signings. And of course there was the marriage with the porn star/MP, Cicciolina, and its spectacular demise in 1992.

These days, Koons remains a fixture on the gossip circuit, with Koons sightings—from an appearance at the Chanel party to hanging out with rock star Lou Reed—appearing in boldface in the *New York Post*'s Page Six, which dubbed him "bad boy emeritus." His celebrity has inspired a backlash of sorts (possibly one that Koons relishes). "Jeff Koons has provided one last, pathetic gasp of the sort of self-promoting hype and sensationalism that characterized the worst of the decade," Kimmelman remarked, concluding that Koons was "self-destructive," with nowhere to go but down. That was back in 1991, though, before the giant pink flower sold for $25 million.

Despite the criticism, Koons's celebrity is actually part and parcel of his influence in the art world and position in art history. If the market price and Larry Gagosian association are any indication of success, then Koons has blazed to the very top. In a world so subjective and devoid of objective measures of value, Koons has dominated the stage, front and center.[8] As the University of Chicago economist David Galenson found in his study of living artists, those artists who have sold their work for the highest auction prices are also those who end up in art history textbooks. "Art scholars and critics often claim that markets for art are irrational," Galenson writes, "and that the value an artist's work brings at auction is unrelated to the real importance of that artist's work. These claims are wrong . . . Auction outcomes can systematically identify today's greatest living artists."[9] Koons is second only to Damien Hirst in this respect. To be sure, Koons's work is innovative and deserves to be recognized and rewarded. But rewarded is one thing and being paid $25 million for a metal sculpture of a flower is entirely another. Koons's celebrity has reconstructed the art market—even Jasper Johns couldn't compete—and paved the way for Damien Hirst, who first became famous in the 1990s for his dead shark suspended in an enormous fish tank. Renowned art collector Charles Saatchi purchased Hirst's 1990 work *A Thousand Years* (a large sealed glass container with a cow's head and maggots) and then bankrolled him £50,000 to make the shark piece, which Hirst titled *The Physical Impossibility of Death in the Mind of Someone Living*. At the time, the commission price was considered so absurdly high that the *Sun* ran the headline "50,000 for Fish Without Chips."[10] Despite the outcry, the shark became the iconic symbol of 1990s Britart and the rise of the Young British Artists (YBAs) in the global art world.[11] In 2005, the artwork was sold for $8 million to the American hedge fund manager Steven Cohen.[12] In August 2007, Hirst reportedly sold his diamond-encrusted skull, *For the Love of God*, for $100 million (the date of sale has been disputed by critics).[13] "If anyone but Hirst had made this curious object, we would be struck by its vulgarity. It looks like the kind of thing Asprey or Harrods might sell to credulous visitors from the oil states with unlimited amounts of money to spend, little taste, and no knowledge of art," the art critic Richard Dorment commented on the work. "I can imagine it gracing the drawing room of some African dictator or Colombian drug baron. But not just anyone made it—Hirst did. Knowing this, we look at it in a different way."[14] A few months later Hirst went on to break auction house records with his work *Beautiful Inside My Head Forever*, the very same week that Lehman Brothers and the world economy fell apart.

Koons and Hirst exemplify an important part of celebrity: There is money to be made hand over fist if you can cultivate a public interest in yourself that equals or exceeds interest in your work. "Hirst is as much or more known for his lifestyle as for his art," remarks the art historian Julian Stallabrass, "and he takes care to ensure that the two are thoroughly entangled."[15] Certainly talent is important, insofar as we can realistically compare it among artists. But creating a persona that people care about is sine qua non for going from artist to art star. Like any other cultural product that cannot be evaluated with complete objectivity, the value of a particular song, actress, or, in this case, artist comes from the public collectively agreeing on who's hot and who's not. Much of that collective concurrence lies in our relating to that person and being fascinated with him or her: This is the fundamental attribute of celebrity. And, of course, celebrity can be turned into big bucks.

Galenson has devoted much of the last decade to looking at the relationship between art price and an artist's importance, which is well illustrated in the cultivation of people like Hirst and Koons. Galenson explains that Picasso and Marcel Duchamp are the early examples of artists as stars.[16] Rather than limiting their work to commissioned portraits for kings and religious leaders, they began doing portraits of art dealers themselves. Consequently, these artists were able to create a market for their work that circumvented the traditional channels of patronage that artists had to go through to establish their careers.

Part of establishing this new market was creating signature art styles that were synonymous with them as individuals. Picasso's cubism and Duchamp's readymades were so associated with them that the styles became something more like personality traits in the eyes of the public. "The real payoff is that certain artists appear to have personalities that if not trump, certainly complement their work," Galenson remarks. Further, they challenged traditional definitions of "talent": Duchamp's most famous work is a urinal that he flipped 90 degrees and called *Fountain*, submitting it to an art show under the pseudonym R. Mutt. Clever, yes, but how does one measure the skill in it? "Using talent becomes impossible in the 20th century," Galenson explains. "How good a draftsman are they? How good a painter? Well, how do you measure Duchamp's talent? The urinal?" This conundrum, he believes, is precisely the point: In the twentieth-century art world, talent became increasingly ambiguous, and the personalities associated with the artwork became more important. As Galenson put it to me, "See, Picasso created a persona, and Duchamp did even more so. If you're trying to explain a piece of ready-made, you can't explain it simply through the work. You need to explain it by reference to a particular artist."

This inextricable link between personality and art has driven the popularity of many of the great art stars of the twentieth century. Duchamp put a fake name on a urinal and submitted it to an art show that claimed it would accept anything. When it rejected the urinal, Duchamp had essentially proved the show's elitism; in light of this, the piece was as much publicity stunt as artistic creation. The public was as intrigued and perplexed by Duchamp as by the artwork. "Is he serious or is he joking?" Galenson questioned. "Can't he be both? Duchamp always avoided the question. [Yet] as long as the debate goes on, Duchamp is immortal."

Decades later, Andy Warhol took the lessons of Picasso and Duchamp to heart, cultivating public interest in himself and creating art that the public could not interpret without attempting to interpret him. We can't understand Warhol's work without his endless interviews that revealed his "deep superficiality," as he termed it. Artists were not supposed to strive—at least not openly—for fame and money. But not only did Warhol care about money, he had the gall to paint dollar bills. Warhol's strange public behavior made him a figure of interest. He was always odd and unemotional, hung out with socialites and rock stars, and never stepped out of character. (Like Koons, he held autograph signings.) He made silk screens of Campbell soup cans and called them "art." And as with Duchamp, the public and art world asked, "Is he serious or is he joking?"

Jeff Koons fits this model perfectly. We are as fascinated with him as a person as we are with the stuff he puts on art gallery walls, and we cannot separate the two. His persona, which never wavers, is part of his innovation as an artist. Julia Peyton-Jones, director of the Serpentine Gallery, is the genius behind the summer 2009 Koons exhibit. When I spoke with her about the Koons phenomenon, she explained that the worth of an artist and his importance in art history are also based on his larger contribution. The way the world and society view the artist is just as important as his skill as a painter. "I think that the word 'talent' just doesn't come up in that sense," Peyton-Jones explained. "I would never say, 'Jeff Koons is a very talented artist.' One talks about the work and its influence, but talent is implicit. But talent in doing what? What are the constituencies that make someone talented? Talent is not a theme or word that is helpful; it's really about an artist's contribution; it comes down from their work. You can't separate art from its artist."

This contribution is precisely the reason Jeff Koons, whether you like his art or not, has become one of the most important art figures of the twentieth and twenty-first centuries. Koons, his personality, and his impact on the world transcend his art. Jeffrey Deitch, formerly an international art dealer and gallery owner and current director of Los Angeles's Museum of Contemporary Art (who financially supported Koons in the past), explains that talent is essential, but the art star is an individual who becomes bigger than his work. The art star is the person with the colorful personality who bothers to go out to the parties. "There is a whole class of people who 'go out' [and their] profile is much higher than that person who does not," Deitch explains. "Life has become more interesting. We [the public] have more interesting information. Artists who have a consistent image of the way they dress and make provocative statements might be seen in the company of famous people. This will give them higher profile than if they did the same work [but didn't go out]."

Koons's art openings, though they may appear to be thinly disguised parties for celebrities, are all to a very important end: These accoutrements are actually essential to maintaining his place in the art firmament. What Koons has recognized and successfully executed is that the market will pay a premium for his celebrity. Sure, over 99 percent of us cannot afford a Jeff Koons piece. But the less than 1 percent who can are making their purchases based on more than just the art itself. There is a collective buzz about Koons.[17] People line up around the block to get into his exhibitions. His *Michael Jackson and Bubbles* is high art (it's in the Los Angeles County Museum of Art, after all) but has also made it into popular culture. People talk about Koons and his work synonymously. And Koons actively proclaims that he's the artist we should pay attention to. "The seriousness with which a work of art is taken is interrelated to the value that it has," Koons told critic Anthony Haden-Guest. "The market is the greatest critic."[18]

So, by virtue of fame and fortune, is Koons better than all the other living artists who have won awards and been deemed great by the aficionados? Many industry insiders certainly believe art stars like Koons and Damien Hirst are extraordinarily talented: After all, Hirst was awarded the prestigious Turner Prize given annually to a young English artist. Koons is considered a great influence on much of the contemporary conceptual art that came after him, including the work of Hirst and other YBAs. Art experts have a long list of stars who they think are in the same talent league as Koons, but these others have not gotten nearly the press or buzz. Sandy Nairne, director of London's National Portrait Gallery, points to the "Saatchi effect" (of which both Koons and Hirst have been recipients). When Charles Saatchi invests in a particular artist, he influences the broader international market and creates celebrities. Saatchi is good not only at picking talent, he's good at picking artists whose personalities, antics, and lifestyles are interesting to a mainstream public. His artists tend to be real characters, individuals who have more going on than just their art. The same style of picking art stars is attributed to art dealer Larry Gagosian (who has also invested in both Hirst and Koons).

Many artists are deeply respected yet never become main-stream stars. Even artists who do have a wide following and art world recognition may never become known to the wider public. Gerhard Richter is a favorite among art aficionados, he gets major exhibitions, and anyone who knows art knows him. Richter is undoubtedly a full-fledged relative celebrity, an individual obsessed about within his particular world. Despite his talent, however, Richter isn't a flashy art star to a wider public, even if his work is considered some of the best of the twentieth and twenty-first centuries.[19] His most expensive piece of work sold for nearly $15 million, which is a lot of money, to be sure, but $10 million less than a Koons heart and $85 million less than Hirst's skull.[20] "Richter has not created a persona," Galenson explains. "Koons and Hirst wanted to be celebrities and they worked on it." It's impossible to say whether Koons and Hirst are "better" than Richter. As Peyton-Jones put it, "What do we really mean by an art star? Artists who go far beyond the art world? Or do we mean the far greater number of artists who are not known except among the art world? Within the art world, it would not generally be seen that 'talent' is what separates the two: Andy Warhol is a household name and Gerhard Richter is not, but no one in the art world would claim that Warhol is more talented than Richter."

Economists have a term for the Koons and Hirst phenomenon; they call it the "superstar effect." Sherwin Rosen, the economist who first introduced the concept, explains it this way: "Small differences in talent at the top of the distribution will translate into large differences in revenue."[21] But other economists argue that marginal talent is not necessary; just getting more people to pay attention, whether buying one's artwork or following one's name in the tabloids, is what generates the superstar effect. From this perspective, superstars are not significantly more talented, but a substitution of someone else would not produce a better consumer experience. Thus, these superstars are able to generate the masses of consumers, fans, and audiences that aggregately reward them much more than everyone else, even others just as good as them. And such superstar effects are getting greater: The economist Alan Krueger found that in 1981 the top 1 percent of artists took in 26 percent of concert revenue. By 2003, the top 1 percent brought in 56 percent.[22] Are these few individuals really better than everyone else? Even if they are marginally better (taking into account Rosen's theory), are they so much better as to deserve 56 percent of concert revenue? Surely not. Robert Frank and Philip Cook call this the "winner-take-all" society. But what might explain why such a phenomenon occurs? One of the most obvious reasons superstars exist is that cultural goods, whether art or film or sports, require buzz and people talking about them and debating them, going to the movies and baseball games together, and getting excited when a particular song is played on the radio. The Princeton sociologist Paul DiMaggio makes the point that people want to consume cultural goods together because sharing interests enables people to make friends, establish taste, and extend their social networks.[23] Harvard professor of marketing Anita Elberse corroborates this theory with an empirical analysis of music and home video sales. In her critique of Chris Anderson's "long tail" (whereby he argued that in the future the market will be filled with niche demands and suppliers rather than blockbusters), Elberse found that while companies like Amazon and Netflix cultivate niche product demand, people are still buying the same movies and books in droves; blockbusters still exist. Why is this? We are social folks, Elberse argues, and we like to consume and form tastes about art, music, and other cultural goods together.[24]

Part of Koons's and Hirst's success lies in certain social phenomena: We like collective experiences, whether showing up at an art opening in a pack or talking about the show at brunch. People tend to get enjoyment out of sharing cultural experiences, which is why everyone listens to Britney Spears and reads Dan Brown—because they can then talk about the experiences with one another. Economists call these relationships "network externalities": The benefit of consuming something increases with each additional person who also participates.[25] Another explanation for the superstar effect is that it enables us to pick a musician to listen to or book to read with relative ease. The reason we don't go trolling iTunes for another blond pop star to listen to is that Britney Spears is already ranked number one on the chart. There is only a slim chance that the time we would spend looking for a similar type of musician would result in a significantly better musician. Superstars limit our search costs for what to read, watch, listen to, wear, eat, or hang on our walls. Superstars like Hirst and Koons are beneficiaries of the bandwagon effect: We tend to like what everyone else likes and we look for signals that tell us what is "good art" because we are not necessarily sure of our own judgment.[26] Even if we love art, most of us don't have art history degrees or regularly read exhibition reviews. When a collective mass of people are drawn to a particular artist, we tend to assume that we ought to be as well.[27]

Some art critics have publicly disdained the massive fortunes that Koons and Hirst have made due to the superstar and bandwagon effects. In an editorial about Hirst and the celebrity-driven contemporary art market, *Financial Times* arts writer Peter Aspden remarked, "If art is nothing more than a reflection of national values, then . . . what better characterises the 21st century than the lust for celebrity, and the rapid dissemination of triviality?" Aspden went on to point out the similarities between the current art market and the narcissism of the reality TV show *X Factor*, putting Hirst front and center as emblematic of the problem. As Aspden and other art critics have pointed out, Hirst (and Koons, to be sure) is "more highly regarded for his business accomplishments than his artistic endeavors."[28] Hirst's business acumen is so admired it has even been the topic of a London Business School course (much to the chagrin of many art critics and aficionados).[29]

Of course other great artists exist; Koons's and Hirst's star power does not imply that they are the only relevant artists of the day. People like Richter and Kara Walker and Brice Marden certainly create excitement, and when they exhibit at a major museum or gallery, lots of people show up. But having a coterie of art-friendly fans and being revered among art experts isn't the same as having celebrity status with the mainstream public and having the popular press obsess over you for things that transcend your art.[30] Art stars are different from artists because they supply personae to their public. They give it up to the camera and the gossip columns with all the ostentatiousness of Paris Hilton or Britney Spears. Quite simply, Koons, just like Hollywood starlets and M, gives us more to work with.

Consider Tracey Emin, the troubled and provocative British artist. Emin's prominence came only partially out of her talent. In 1997, she was filmed behaving drunk and crazily on a serious Channel 4 program discussing the Turner Prize.[31] Then there was her glorious breakup with fellow artist Billy Childish, whose Stuckism art movement was created in opposition to the YBAs like Emin and Hirst. In 1999, Emin herself was short-listed for the Turner Prize. Although she didn't win, everyone was talking about *My Bed*, which was featured shortly afterward at the Tate. *My Bed* was in fact her bed, unmade and littered with old condoms and underwear.

Emin's signature style is her oversharing of her private life. In *My Bed*, *Everyone I Have Ever Slept With 1963–1995*, and *My Major Retrospective*—to name only a few—she has actively used her personal life to cultivate her art career. And she has succeeded. We are very interested indeed. Despite it being quite literally just her unmade bed, Emin sold *My Bed* for £150,000 to Charles Saatchi, whom, prior to the sale, she publicly disliked. Saatchi has devoted an entire room in his house to displaying the piece of art, which was widely viewed, like Hirst's work, to be sold at an inflated price.[32] "Charles Saatchi has been called a modern-day Medici," one art critic observed. "But had he been living in Florence in its heyday he could have bought four versions of Michelangelo's statue of David for the price he paid for Tracey Emin's dirty bed—even allowing for inflation since 1499."[33] Emin doesn't generate the kind of multimillion-dollar sales that Koons does, but she has managed to consistently sell work in the tens and hundreds of thousands of dollars, almost all of which is inextricably linked to her personal life, including *I Promise to Love You* (a neon heart with those words written in cursive inside) that sold for $200,000 in 2008 and *Fantastic to Feel Beautiful Again* (another neon cursive scrawl of the title) that sold for $70,000 in 2009. Emin now has a new problem: Her credibility as the vulnerable and poor young girl is challenged by her new life as a rich and successful woman. The documentation of Emin's new life of flashing camera lights and copious champagne is not nearly as interesting as her early, pre–art star life. "Emin's celebrity is a problem for her work because it might compromise her authentic primitive self," the art historian Julian Stallabrass writes, "thus her continued mining of her childhood . . . thus her neglect of later events." Emin, however, has a response for those critics who consider her work inauthentic now that she has riches and fame: "People think that because my life has become more comfortable, my work will get insipid, but inside my heart is still in turmoil . . . I still go to bed crying, I still pray to God for a better life, I still curl up in a small fetal shape . . . those feelings never change."[34]

The Economics of the Celebrity Residual

We see the economic impact of celebrity everywhere: art, sports, Hollywood, music, even politics. As Koons and Hirst demonstrate, the celebrity residual pays real economic dividends to those able to cultivate it. Celebrity clearly does not imply talentless. Quite the contrary. Most stars possess some measure of talent, but no one of them is necessarily more talented than his or her peers. And, after all, how do we define and put a value on talent in such subjective industries? Is Koons really $15 million better than Richter? Is Hirst over $75 million better than Koons? The stars of an industry may be very good, but they are disproportionately economically rewarded because of their celebrity. Talent, in other words, buys you only a seat at the poker table. Celebrities don't have to win the most Oscars or make the most touchdowns. In all types of industries where there is an element of ambiguity in how to measure talent there is a chance for money to be made on the celebrity residual.

We pay for the celebrity residual everywhere, but to what extent varies dramatically by industry. In sports, no athlete keeps his day job if he is not really good. Aside from skill, however, some athletes are simply able to capture their audience more than others and they are financially rewarded for their ability to drum up ticket sales and sell merchandise. There are many, many soccer players who have statistics as good as if not better than David Beckham, but those players are not stars. This is not to say Beckham isn't a truly talented player. Anyone who cares about soccer can remember his famous last-minute free kick in a 2001 game in the run-up to the World Cup, and he is known for being a great sportsman, runner-up to the FIFA World Player of the Year award twice. He was also the highest-paid footballer in the world until 2009, getting paid $28 million for the 2003–2004 season.[35] And yet in 2007, past his prime, after a horrible season and in what some might call the sunset of his career as a major soccer player, he signed with the LA Galaxy for $250 million, which included endorsements and advertising fees ($50 million in actual salary).[36] At the time, Beckham's salary was larger than all of the other Major League Soccer salaries *combined* (trailing far behind in second place was Francisco Palencia, who was playing for MLS to the tune of approximately $1 million). Because his contract had an opt-out clause, Beckham left LA Galaxy and went on loan to AC Milan, and in 2009 earned a total of $46 million.[37] These days, Beckham makes two to three times more than any other soccer player in the world, besides Lionel Messi of FC Barcelona and Ronaldinho of AC Milan, who make $37.7 million and $25.5 million, respectively. The only other football star associated with such cash is Cristiano Ronaldo, who in 2009 attained the largest football contract in history. Ronaldo is also a celebrity by anyone's account, with his face splashed across tabloids and an endless gossip column dissection of his wardrobe and dalliances with Paris Hilton.

If stardom and salary were strongly correlated with talent, sports statistics would be a straightforward proxy for income distribution. In terms of soccer stats, the peak of Beckham's considerable talent is many years behind him. He hasn't had a big moment on the field since the 2006 World Cup. "Off the field, Beckham's profile and commercial appeal shows no sign of waning, but on the pitch the past year has seen [him] suffer a series of disappointments," said a CNN commentator in 2009. "It is a far cry from his glory days at Manchester United where he won four English Premier League titles and the Champions League as they memorably won the treble in 1999."[38]

And yet today Beckham is paid pots of money. On the one hand, you could say that he deserves recognition for all of his past effort, but sports is a tough world and nobody gets rewarded just for being a good player three years ago. Sports stars get rewarded for being good players in the present and get benched or dismissed when they drop the ball both literally and figuratively. So it doesn't make sense that Beckham gets paid so much during a time in his life when he's not playing as well as he used to.

Or does it? It depends what Beckham is actually getting paid *for*. Beckham's salary isn't simply about goals or last-minute moves; it's about merchandising and selling seats. When players are bought, their value is measured by both their athletic performance and their ability to bring in spectators. Studying the 2007 season, sports economists found that average MLS ticket sales for games increased from 16,758 to 29,694 when Beckham was on the roster. When Beckham actually played, ticket sales went up to 37,659, demonstrating the influence of Beckham's presence on game attendance.[39] When I ask sports aficionados about the Beckham phenomenon, they always point toward Steven Gerrard, an English footballer who plays midfield (and sometimes second striker) for Liverpool F.C. Gerrard is inarguably a leader in his field and has scooped up awards and championship wins since he arrived on the scene in 1998. To football followers, Gerrard is as good as Beckham was in his prime. He's just not nearly as celebrated. And at a paltry $11.7 million (though considering such a massive figure paltry may sound ridiculous to the average reader), that lack of celebrity shows.

Since the media has become active in cultivating athletes as stars, economic reward comes from more than just playing the game well. The media gloms on to those who are marginally better and creates a personal narrative around these athletes.[40] Beckham's initial talent drew audiences and media attention, but these are not the things that sustain his celebrity. Most people outside of soccer fandom know Beckham as a model and the husband of Victoria Beckham, aka Posh, former member of the Spice Girls. In recent years, Posh has become a force to be reckoned with in the fashion industry, launching her own clothing line and attaining a coveted front-row seat at Fashion Week. Posh's high profile adds fodder to Beckham's star power. Beckham's celebrity appeal is so great that in 2003, when Manchester United coach (now manager) Alex Ferguson threw a boot that "accidentally" hit Beckham in the face, the story was a bigger headline in Britain than the Iraq War. The story was fueled by Posh, who was supposedly leaking stories to the press, including photos of Beckham's beautiful face injured by the boot.[41]

As a former pop star, Posh has every motivation to keep her name in the media, and it has paid off. As Simon Kuper, the sports columnist for the *Financial Times* put it, "[I was there] when Beckham played for England at the World Cup in Tokyo. Like all World Cups, he played terribly. [And yet] the Japanese were totally obsessed." Kuper went on to explain that Beckham's disproportionate appeal is in his star power: He embodies Western glamour, he is fabulously wealthy, and he and his wife sashay around the world with celebrities. Beckham's whole multidimensional life is interesting. When sports stars' personal lives make their way into the headlines, whether by accident or by design, it catalyzes a whole new type of stardom and allows these athletes to resonate with a new and larger fan base.

Consider Alex Rodriguez, or A-Rod, as he's known, one of America's most celebrated baseball players since Babe Ruth. He is the youngest player ever to hit five hundred home runs, breaking the record set by Jimmie Foxx in 1939. A-Rod is fantastic, and he has been handsomely rewarded for this talent, signing with the New York Yankees in 2007 for $275 million, the largest contract in baseball history.[42] The confluence of being a free agent and winning MVP in the same year meant that multiple teams were bidding for A-Rod simultaneously, which of course jacked up the cost of getting him. Several years later, some of those teams might be happy they didn't win the bidding war. In 2006, his postseason batting average was an unimaginably awful .098 (.300 is considered good). In 2007, A-Rod's performance put him at just twenty-fifth place on the list of top ballplayers and yet number one in salary by an incredible margin. He has also been dubbed "the cooler" for having a negative impact on team chemistry and performance when he's around. In 2008, he didn't make it to the top five for RBIs, home runs, or batting average. A-Rod's disappointing performance in the "clutch" (the high-stakes critical part of a game or series) is widely debated and criticized. And in 2009, A-Rod admitted he had used banned substances just a few years earlier. In the clubhouse, according to former Yankees manager Joe Torre in *The Yankee Years*, A-Rod began to be teased as A-Fraud.

This is not to say that A-Rod is a bad ballplayer. Many would argue that despite his mishaps he is still one of the best and generally outperforms other players during the season. But so much better than all the other ballplayers that he deserves the attention and salary that are awarded to him? Is he $86 million better than Yankees player Derek Jeter, who, in

2009, broke the Yankees' record for number of hits? Jeter's record (2,722 hits) trumps Lou Gehrig's record made over sixty years ago. Jeter has led the Yankees to five World Series titles, is captain of the team, and has been on the All-Star team ten times. He is widely considered one of the best ballplayers of his generation and noted for his extreme professionalism.[43] Jeter also has a ten-year contract with the Yankees, but his is for $189 million.[44] In fact, in 2009, A-Rod's $275 million contract was worth over $150 million more than over half of the highest contracts ever awarded. His contract was $100 million more than every other baseball contract ever awarded other than to Jeter, newcomer Mark Teixeira (Yankees), and Rodriguez's previous $252 million contract with the Texas Rangers.

Is A-Rod so good that he deserves to be paid over $100 million more than 99 percent of all other ballplayers?[45] If he's that good, then the Yankees should never lose another game as long as they have him, which as it turns out is not the case. The Yankees had very disappointing seasons from 2004 to 2008, ironically commencing the same year the team acquired A-Rod.[46] And while in 2009 A-Rod's postseason game started picking up in the play-offs as the Yankees went on to win the World Series, his performance was primarily viewed as a welcome departure from his usual tepid postseason.[47] But still he could not be considered the dominant force on the Yankees' field: Every position is filled by an All-Star player (Hideki Matsui won the 2009 MVP award and Mariano Rivera was a close second). I'm no sports economist, but I'll speculate that as good as A-Rod may be, he's not talented enough to justify tens of millions of dollars over every other baseball player, particularly if the team isn't *always* winning with him on board.

But, like Beckham's, A-Rod's contribution isn't based strictly on talent; it's based on merchandising, network programming, and ticket sales. On February 16, 2004, when the

Yankees announced their acquisition of Rodriguez, the team sold 22,000 tickets, 8,000 more than on an average day. Traffic to the Yankees' website jumped to 2.5 million hits— that's five times the number of hits on the same day the year before. That week, Manhattan sports stores reported a deluge of demand for merchandise with Rodriguez's famous No. 13 emblazoned somewhere on the product.[48] Besides the buzz around the Rodriguez trade due to how good he is as a player (what sports economists call "performance value"), Rodriguez has "marquee value"—the value of his persona and celebrity on the baseball team's revenue. Sports analyst Vince Gennaro estimates that Rodriguez's marquee value will increase the value of YES Network (Yankees Entertainment and Sports Network, the station that runs Yankees games) by anywhere from $50 to $100 million over just ten years. Gennaro approximates that Rodriguez's marquee value alone should generate $145 million over the duration of the ballplayer's contract. Overall, Rodriguez will generate $450 million in "marginal product revenue" or, in simple terms, value to the Yankees franchise.[49]

Marquee value can be attained only by A-Rod's fans following him, and his celebrity persona both on the field and off. Eight thousand extra ticket sales can't be explained entirely by die-hard baseball fans. While A-Rod's batting average is modest (brought down by his postseason calamities), his Google hits are out of the ballpark.[50] It certainly doesn't hurt that Rodriguez dated Madonna and the actress Kate Hudson. Even though Madonna came after the salary, it was pretty clear early on that Rodriguez had more than just baseball skills; he was able to capture an audience outside baseball and cultivate a collective interest in his persona. In 2009, he had well over five times more Google hits than Jason Giambi, who ranked second by this measure. And if you look at the peaks in A-Rod's Google hits over time, they do not occur after a good game. From 2004 to 2008, A-Rod's number one Google hit peak was his divorce, which occurred in the aftermath of his widely speculated upon affair with Madonna (which the *New York Post* splashed across its front page day after day during that summer). In 2008, the number one search term in Google for Rodriguez other than just his name was "Alex Rodriguez Madonna."

Despite being less of a leading soccer player these days, Beckham is still one of the most Google-searched sports topics in the world. Gerrard, though actually one of the world's best footballers, is miles behind Beckham in public interest, which is reflected in his relative lack of Google hits. According to Google Trends, from 2004 to 2009, Gerrard got just 12 percent of the media coverage that Beckham attained.

What, then, are sports teams paying for when they hire Alex Rodriguez or David Beckham?[51] Besides sheer talent, teams are paying for the celebrity that increases merchandising and ticket sales. In economic terms, A-Rod's celebrity residual brings a quantifiable increase in spectators who buy tickets and hot dogs and Bud Light simply because he's playing. The disproportionate reward system that they benefit from is a product of their enormous fan base. Beckham and A-Rod were celebrities before their high-profile contracts, but the contracts and increased media attention increased their star power, thus begetting even more economic opportunities as they became increasingly celebrated by a wider audience.[52]

In Hollywood we see the economics of the residual at work even more strongly, particularly because talent is more ambiguously measured. Take a look at Jennifer Aniston and Kate Winslet and how much they get paid versus our best proxy for talent, how many film awards they accrue. Aniston has no Oscars or Oscar nominations, two Golden Globe nominations for films, and no wins. For her 2008 film *Marley & Me*, Aniston got $8 million up front and she earns about

$25 million a year, which includes her endorsements and the enormous amount of back end revenue she attains from box office receipts. Back end means that if Aniston's films make a lot of money at theaters or in DVD sales, it is written into her contract that she will get a percentage of the profits. For *Marley & Me*, Aniston pulled in approximately twice her initial salary in back end.[53] Contrast Winslet, who at thirty-three became the youngest film actress to be nominated for six Oscars, has won one Oscar, has been nominated for six BAFTA awards and won two of them, and has been nominated for seven Golden Globes and won one in 2009 (admittedly she had the advantage of being nominated *twice* that year in the same category). While Winslet also gets paid between $6 and $10 million per film, her back end and endorsements are significantly less. In 2009, Aniston was eighth on the *Forbes* ranking of the most powerful stars (defined as a combination of media and Internet presence and overall earnings). Winslet didn't even make the top 100. If star power were about talent, Jennifer Aniston would not be getting paid over two and a half times as much as Kate Winslet, with her four major awards to Aniston's zero. Aniston is not a bad actress, but she is certainly no better than Winslet, and yet she is economically rewarded for something that has clearly nothing to do with pure acting talent. Not to mention, most of her films are almost universally panned by critics.

But in celebrity economics, other stats matter more than film awards: from April 2008 to 2010, Kate Winslet was mentioned 476 times in *US Weekly*, and since 1998, 230 times overall in *People*. Aniston, on the other hand, was mentioned more than 1,000 times in *US Weekly* during that time and more than 1,300 times in *People* (since 1995). Aniston has been featured on *People*'s cover 25 times compared to Winslet's two.[54] According to *OK!* magazine's former features editor, when Jennifer Aniston graces their cover, the magazine sees a spike in sales of 120,000 copies. In 2008, Aniston was the cover story for four of the top-ten-selling issues of *OK!*

Winslet burnishes her studio's reputation by winning awards, but Aniston is the fan favorite as demonstrated by her mentions in the tabloids (five times more than Winslet) and her ability to sell magazines. To be clear, Aniston's covers aren't about her latest movies. Aniston is "splitting up with John Mayer," "dating British hunk," "secretly texting with Brad." Aniston's presence in films brings in audiences simply because they like her, and ultimately that increases a studio's bottom line. Jennifer Aniston is rewarded for this star power, her residual. *Marley & Me* (2008) made almost $400 million worldwide in box office receipts. If Aniston is getting back end revenue on $400 million, no matter how small the percentage, that's a lot of cash. Winslet's *The Reader* (2008), despite a cornucopia of film awards and nominations, brought in $135 million. *The Reader*'s box office receipts are impressive but just a third of what Aniston's movie brought in. *Marley* was not a hit with the critics, nor did it possess a profound and emotive story line like *The Reader*. Unquestionably, the pairing of Aniston with Owen Wilson and the light story line revolving around a cute dog helped make the movie accessible to a wide audience, whereas *The Reader*'s solemn plot surrounding Nazism and a relationship between an older woman and a teenage boy would be a deterrent to some filmgoers. Not to mention, the book *Marley & Me* was a runaway best seller, selling millions of copies. But *The Reader* was hailed as a remarkable movie and *Marley* was universally panned. This debate is academic: Aniston's fans in Kansas aren't swayed by what a *New York Times* critic says. For them, a movie with their favorite star is enough motivation to go to the cinema on a Friday night, no matter how much it's lacking Oscar credibility. And at the end of the day, each ticket purchased is what keeps a studio in business. But does Aniston explain the success of *Marley & Me*? "It's a matter of much debate," one film executive explained. "Truth be told, no one's quite sure if Aniston's a movie star or not." One could argue quite easily that movies starring Aniston have flopped as much as they have succeeded. *Love Happens* made only $22.9 million domestically and *Management* didn't even break a million in the domestic box office (*Marley & Me* made $145 million and *The Break-Up* made $119 million domestically). The films starring Aniston alone bombed, while those that have been financially successful had top costars (Vince Vaughn in *The Break-Up* and Wilson in *Marley*). But as long as Aniston's influence on a movie's success remains ambiguous, she can command a high salary.[55] As one studio executive explained to me, film stars' agents often try to up the value of the contract by purporting that the actor's star power will increase the success of the film. (Studios at least try to remain unconvinced in order to keep the salaries down.)[56]

If you believe Anita Elberse, a star is worth approximately $3 million in box office revenue. Elberse studied twelve hundred film-casting announcements and observed the influence of new information about a film (e.g., Matt Damon starring in the latest *Bourne* film or Julia Roberts joining *Ocean's Eleven*) on the Hollywood Stock Exchange, an online prediction market that looks at a film's expected revenue based on casting and financial decisions. Elberse found that the stars' biggest impact is their ability to draw other stars to act in the film and to drum up financial backing for production. Stars do not, however, increase a studio's valuation. Stars certainly obtain more value from their paycheck than the studios get in ticket sales. Elberse notes that stars are unable to generate substantial additional film revenue individually; the real revenue generation is produced through hiring a cast of stars. If a studio's goal is to just increase shareholder value rather than revenue, hiring just "ordinary talent" suffices.[57] By just these measures, studios are paying way too much in the belief that the intangible celebrity residual will draw audiences, a mistake often called "the curse of the superstar."[58] "There is insufficient reason to support the hypothesis that stars add more value than they capture," Elberse concludes.

The Difference Across Industries

There is almost always a celebrity premium that the market is willing to pay, but the balance of how much paid for celebrity versus talent varies depending on the industry. In sports, no one hires a bad ballplayer and keeps him around, no matter how much the tabloids love him. Nick Hornby famously wrote in *Fever Pitch*, "One of the great things about sport is its cruel clarity: there is no such thing, for example, as a bad one-hundred-metre runner, or a hopeless centre-half who got lucky; in sport, you get found out. Nor is there such a thing as an unknown genius striker starving in a garret somewhere." As one sports agent put it, baseball players can work the social life of New York and Los Angeles and become local celebrities, but "if on field performance is not spectacular, they will have their fifteen minutes but won't become international stars."

As counterintuitive as it may seem, sports and art are birds of a feather, while Hollywood has its own breed of residual economics. Because the individuals in the former two rise from within the community, there is a vetting process such that even though many stars in art and sports attain disproportionate celebrity vis-à-vis their talent, they do not get paid for celebrity *without* being really talented. We may think art is subjective, but within the art community certain criteria of excellence are set; distinctions and awards highlight those perceived as the most talented.[59] As much of a stuntman and prankster that Hirst might be viewed as by his naysayers, he did after all win a Turner Prize. With regard to sports, journalist Simon Kuper explains that despite all the ridicule Beckham faced for being more star than talent, he was still ultimately one of the very good footballers of his generation. He needed the talent to attain the celebrity. "That's the sine qua non," as Kuper puts it. "Sports stars have to be good. They wouldn't have been stars if they hadn't been good on the field."

As such, in sports, talent and celebrity (while not on balance) are at least related. Athletes first must pass through the lowly ranks of local teams before they are paid attention to by mainstream fans. Think about the process by which Rodriguez even ended up with the potential to be photographed by the paparazzi and gossiped about on Page Six. Rodriguez has been playing baseball since high school. He then went on to play for the Seattle Mariners from 1996 to 2000. He transferred to the Texas Rangers in 2001 and played with them until 2003. It wasn't until 2004, when Rodriguez was traded to the New York Yankees and exploded onto the New York social scene, that he was catapulted from very good baseball player Alex Rodriguez to Madonna-dating, stripper-cavorting, wife-divorcing, Kate Hudson–heartbreaking A-Rod. But by this point, Rodriguez had been playing ball for well over a decade. Only after each small move up the food chain did he accrue enough industry credibility to gain a position with the Yankees and for the outside world to take notice.

Art stars, like sports stars, are disproportionately rewarded for their celebrity, but they are still fundamentally created through standards set by the people within their fields. Jeffrey Deitch explained that the art community must support an artist in the first place before that individual has a chance to be relevant to a mainstream public. "[An art star] starts out as something very real," Deitch remarked. "It is more community based. There is a whole network of respect [within the art community]." Koons, Deitch noted, was long followed in the art world and appraised through the industry's institutions, from the museums to the galleries to the magazines, before he did an interview with the *Financial Times*.

But celebrity in Hollywood is different. Hollywood stars can end up being paid entirely for their celebrity residual. The very people the mass public views as stars are often remarkably different from those the industry reveres.[60] Stardom and talent are not necessarily mutually exclusive in Hollywood, but one does not beget the other, and a star can draw a steady income based on his or her residual without being perceived as an industry talent. When I talk to people in Hollywood about celebrity, they almost always point to how divorced it is from real talent and from the real stars within the industry. So much of star power in Hollywood is fundamentally about one's appeal to the media. The increased emphasis on the personae of stars over their talent is a function of the rise in media coverage and the changing nature of subject matter the media reports on. The media sells magazines and TV programs based on whom their audiences are interested in knowing about, regardless of industry vetting standards.

Similarly, in politics, a lifelong senator can toil away at legislation for many decades and still some young brilliant whippersnapper can end up resonating with the public, which in turn makes him the star, or in the case of Barack Obama, the president of the United States. No one would say that Sarah Palin deserved her political celebrity because of all her hard work or astute comprehension of foreign policy. In fact, most believe she attained stardom despite her lack of those attributes. But Palin is attractive and accessible, and the GOP jumped on the bandwagon. Sarah Palin decided to forgo realizing her star power in the political realm and instead cashed in her residual and is laughing her way to the bank, endlessly blabbing on talk shows about her best-selling book that dishes on her experiences on the campaign trail. Palin has reportedly made $12 million since she stepped down from the Alaskan govenorship.[61]

The economics of the celebrity residual demonstrates that we do pay for more than talent alone; we pay for the persona and the buzz. In this respect, Koons's and Hirst's art is probably worth exactly what it goes for on the market, if you include all the things we're paying for beyond talent. Because these artists have also defined a particular moment in art (like their predecessors Warhol and Duchamp), buying their work is an investment. "The critical question is, 'Has Koons been influential?' And the answer is yes," Galenson explains. "And that is what makes you important in the long run; that's what makes you a part of the canon." As the director of the Serpentine remarked, "One goes to exhibitions of artists because they have something to say which is of interest. They are making a contribution that is intriguing in a wide variety of ways, across a whole range of different criteria . . . You could argue that Hirst's production and entrepreneurial endeavors were also the very substance of his very talent: The incredible tour de force was an encapsulation of everything that made Damien Hirst who he is."

"It's Gotta Be the Shoes": The Basics of Celebrity Economics

In the beginning, he was just "the kid from North Carolina." Michael Jordan was good, scoring the winning shot for UNC–Chapel Hill in the 1982 NCAA Championship basketball game. But there were others Nike could have considered to be the face of its basketball merchandise. The talented and larger-than-life personality, Auburn University player Charles Barkley, was a more obvious choice. Jordan, the gangly and subdued shooting guard who, at the time, wasn't even considered much of a scorer, was just the number three draft pick for the NBA. Why not hire the top draft? Yet, one January afternoon in 1984 at a Nike corporate meeting, that skinny number three draft was announced as the next face of Nike. The mastermind behind the plan, John Paul "Sonny" Vaccaro, put his job on the line, insistent that Jordan was the man, with no real explanation besides instinct, by all accounts.[62]

The details behind the deal are as follows: Nike desperately wanted to get its foot in the door of basketball merchandise. Because Converse had a monopoly on the big NBA players like Magic Johnson, it would be impossible to break into the market without Nike creating its own stars. The game plan was to get young draft picks to become big endorsers. Of course, this was a gamble: These rookies had no professional experience, the transition from NCAA to NBA is huge, and no one knew if they would successfully make it. But the sports company had no other options if it wanted to create a new market for its merchandise, and it took a gamble on Jordan. It was probably the smartest decision that Nike ever made. The skeptical Nike executives, and even Vaccaro himself, could never have anticipated in 1984 that they would not just create a star but that the star would, within fewer than fifteen years, turn Nike from a $900 million company into a $9.19 billion company.[63]

Any doubts the executives had were banished pretty quickly. Jordan signed with the Chicago Bulls and was on the cover of *Sports Illustrated* a little over a month after his NBA career commenced. Later that season he was crowned Rookie of the Year. Throughout his almost twenty-year career, Jordan won five MVPs, fourteen NBA All-Star Game performances, and three MVP All-Star awards, among many other honors and awards. He holds the NBA record for highest scoring average (both regular and playoff season), and he has been on the cover of *Sports Illustrated* almost fifty times, trumping even Muhammad Ali's record. By many accounts, Michael Jordan is considered the greatest basketball player of the twentieth century.

Jordan is also the most definitive example of turning a celebrity residual into a concrete lucrative product and, in his case, an actual brand. We know that we pay a premium for the celebrity residual. Often, this payment is affiliated with the star's actual field: For Aniston, her celebrity is in the form of extra back end on box office receipts. For Koons and Hirst, it's the price their work sells for as a result of the buzz surrounding them as people. To be clear, Michael Jordan was notably rewarded for his star power on the court; when he returned to the Chicago Bulls in 1996 he was the highest-paid NBA player, earning $30 million a year.[64] But the other thing that Jordan's story demonstrates is that star power can be turned into a commodity. Jordan didn't just scoop up extra on his paycheck as a result of his celebrity residual; he actually created an entire market of things from endorsements to actual products with the Jordan brand. Jordan recognized that his star power could be applied to products that far transcended basketball. It all started with the now famous Air Jordan basketball sneaker. In stride with Nike's strategy to build a product line around one player, the company created the shoe in 1985. While it was not aesthetically elegant, it resonated with Jordan's fans: It was red and black, the colors of the Chicago Bulls. Almost overnight, the shoe became a sensation. When the NBA commissioner banned it because it violated the league's color codes, the sneaker, and all of the merchandise associated with Jordan, flew off the shelves with even greater velocity. "It was like election night. Like, who's buying what?" Sonny Vaccaro recalled. "Oh, my God, they sold 100 pair of shoes in Pittsburgh, yesterday. They sold 400 pair of shoes in New York City. That's the way it was like. An election day count."[65] The frenzy for Jordan's line at Nike was overwhelming, and the company responded by making more and more of the merchandise, which only fueled more demand. In their first year, Air Jordans sold $130 million worth of shoes for the company. By 1990, Jordan products made $200 million annually for Nike.[66] One sports commentator reported that "at one point, there was a run on the world's supply of red-colored thread."[67] He wasn't joking. For a moment, there literally wasn't enough red thread in the world to match demand for Jordan's Nike product line.

Jordan's line made Nike's entry into basketball merchandising an unimaginable success. His clothes still sell, and limited editions of the Air Jordans sell on eBay for $750 (a twenty-pair collection of vintage Air Jordans was being auctioned for $20,000). The obsession with Air Jordans was a magical brew of Jordan's phenomenal on-court performance and Nike's aggressive marketing to portray the shoe as cool. In one famous Nike commercial, film director Spike Lee explains Jordan's talent by simply saying, "It's gotta be the shoes."

Jordan didn't stop with Nike. He endorsed numerous products, from Wheaties to Gatorade to McDonald's.[68] By one estimate, in 1993, Jordan was making more than $32 million in product endorsements.[69] In fact, when the media announced that Jordan would return to the NBA in 1995 after a two-year hiatus, one study measured that his homecoming amounted to a $1 billion impact on the market. McDonald's alone gained $192 million in sales from Jordan's announcement. As the researchers concluded, "At an average price of $3 for a Value Meal, this $192 million in incremental sales translates into about 64 million additional Value Meal sales."[70] All in all, during his basketball career, Michael Jordan generated almost $10 billion for the world economy.[71]

He has been called "Air Jordan" and "His Airness," but Michael Jordan should also be called one of the savviest businessmen on the planet. He employed a three-pronged strategy that is fundamental to celebrity economics: He was paid on the court for both his talent and his ability to sell tickets; he used his star power to endorse multiple companies that would pay him millions to associate with their products; and finally, he took his celebrity and made his own products: cologne, steakhouses, and of course his signature Nike line.

How to Be "The Face of . . ."

Once upon a time, celebrities were a product of the Hollywood studio system or a sports franchise, in the sense that they would draw crowds to their movies (or games) and readership to their magazine interviews. But celebrities still had a finite number of revenue streams. Now, however, there are lots of options for increasing celebrity and revenue.

The beginning of this chapter examined the first strategy: how the celebrity residual enables some individuals to be paid more for doing the same thing as others like them (whether that's playing basketball, selling art, or acting). But endorsements and celebrity brands enable stars to actually build a market for themselves outside their field. Many celebrities, if they can keep their image intact, can do endorsements. Jordan, by virtue of being an enormous star, was given the opportunity to do many, many endorsements. Marketing executives call this "borrowed equity": The star's value to his public (read: his celebrity residual) can be transferred over to whatever product he claims to use. It is estimated that at least a quarter of all U.S. ads involve a celebrity endorsement.[72] And it's no surprise: Bringing in a celebrity to represent a product can mean enormous additional revenue for the company. In 1997, PepsiCo attributed its 2 percent rise in market share to signing on the Spice Girls to do ads.[73] That may seem like a small percentage, but a 2 percent increase in the global market share of soft drinks is millions upon millions of dollars.

As a function of their global megastardom, some celebrities are able to penetrate markets far away from their immediate base, even breaking into non-Western markets. But these stars are few and far between. At any given time in the world, there may be a handful of individuals whose celebrity status is that far-reaching. These stars are usually major athletes (European football and American baseball) or Hollywood actors, particularly those who have been in action films.[74] Doing ads abroad is a clever means of making money without U.S. or U.K. brand dilution. Most people in the United States have no way of knowing that Brad Pitt advertised coffee in Japan (he did) or Madonna endorsed liquor there (she did).

However, it's a popular misconception that breaking into the U.S. market means a star can automatically show up in a Chinese living room during TV hour. Most stars are not interesting to people outside of their immediate market. Just like American slapstick comedy doesn't sell well in France (barring rare exceptions like Woody Allen and Jerry Lewis), most foreign markets are interested in their own celebrities and not the girls starring in U.S. reality TV shows. The relative nature of even mainstream stars means that most stars have a limited (but profitable) opportunity to be domestic endorsers but are unlikely to reach an Asian consumer base. As one marketing executive put it, "Many Chinese do not know who Jude Law is, and he is not the type of guy Chinese males aspire to."[75] China, Japan, and South Korea do tend to feature celebrities in advertisements (up to 50 percent of all commercials in China feature a star); however, most of them are homegrown.[76]

Celebrity as Brand

Recently, I was at the West Hollywood Target store stocking up on various unnecessary necessities. I was heading toward cosmetics and then on to the diet soda aisle when I spied a wardrobe item worthy of purchase: the Hannah Montana sweatshirt. This purple fitted number, with a hint of being more a crop top than proper outerwear, had Hannah Montana written in cursive all over it. I had to have it. There was the minor problem that I had found it in the children's section, which resulted in me frantically rummaging like a bag lady through the few remaining sweatshirts hanging up, looking for the largest child size ("fits 10–12 year olds").

As the star character of an eponymous Emmy-nominated Disney show, Hannah Montana is a normal girl by day, rock star by night. Montana is played by Miley Cyrus (the daughter of nineties country music sensation Billy Ray Cyrus). Using both her fictional and real identities, Cyrus produces music, movies, and a clothing line, all of which have been breathtakingly successful with the tween and teen set: she has top ten music singles, has sold millions of albums, and has starred in several movies. She also has the Hannah Montana line of hand cream, shower gel, and 2-in-1 shampoo, not to mention the Hannah Montana Disney clothing line, which she helped design. In collaboration with couture designer Max Azria, Cyrus designed a line for Wal-Mart.[77] In 2008, at sixteen years old, Cyrus's estimated worth was pegged at $25 million.[78]

Miley Cyrus demonstrates the most profitable element of celebrity economics: the translation of celebrity into products directly branded with the star's name. Unlike endorsements, whereby stars simply say they like a particular lip gloss or breakfast cereal or sneaker, brand creation allows stars to make products based solely on their identity.[79] Again, being a star is a basic criterion for this strategy to succeed. Michael Jordan did this many times over. The supermodel Kate Moss signed a £3 million deal with the retailer Topshop to design her own line.[80] Victoria Beckham shed her Posh Spice persona and started a highly praised clothing line, the Victoria Beckham Collection. But the ability of these stars to commodify their celebrity does not rest solely on the decision to design clothing or sell shampoo. Being a star is necessary, but the translation of stardom into product popularity is far more complicated.

If anyone knows how to create a link between star and product, it's Charles Garland. Garland is a media mogul who developed Britain's *Pop Idol* (which turned into *The X Factor*) and America's *So You Think You Can Dance*, and built up 19 Entertainment with Simon Fuller, which was eventually sold to CKX for £100 million. Currently the head of Crystal Entertainment, Garland has advised celebrities from the Beckhams to Madonna on how to manage their brand and create a market for products affiliated with them. Garland maintains that the only way stars can build brands is if consumers actually believe in what they are producing. "If you are coherent and consistent, then your brand is quite powerful," he says. Stars should develop a "multiplatform message."

If you're Miley Cyrus, those platforms consist of clothes, beauty products, even stationery. Part of creating a successful brand is determining what audiences most admire about the celebrity. "[You] can't make something from nothing," Garland explained. If you're Miley Cyrus, that something is being accessibly pretty and fashionable and having great hair; all of her products align with her persona. Madonna was once a major musician who could make pots of money on her albums, but her music sales are down. In order to continue to make money, she needs to find another aspect of her identity that can be commodified. (Though with hundreds of millions in the bank, she could stop at any time.) That natural next step could be, Garland suggests, capitalizing on her seemingly eternal youth. What better way to monetize her appearance than to open up fitness clubs or create a line of skin care products? In other words, we buy celebrity products if they are plausible extensions of the stars. If those products allow us to be more like them, the stars and the products are all the more successful. Kate Moss got her gig with Topshop not because she's a supermodel, but because she's one of the greatest style icons of the last hundred years. If she designs clothes, those who buy them hope that a little bit of Moss's magic chic will rub off on them.

The Failure of Celebrity Brands

What we wouldn't buy is Madonna Cupcakes or Kate Moss Organic Veggies. Madonna is known for her draconian fitness regime and diet. Kate Moss is regularly spotted emerging from nightclubs in the wee hours of the morning, a far cry from a poster child for healthy living. If stars push products that are unconnected to our sense of them as people, they are not likely to succeed.[81] Stars must operate under the principle of what marketers call "matchup"; we have to believe they use the product they are endorsing or have created, and we have to believe that they have the taste to choose the best products.

If you're a megastar, the means to wealth through branding and endorsements seems fairly straightforward. But of course on a not so infrequent basis, executives make bad decisions or stars flop gloriously in their entrepreneurial endeavors. How could that be? A lot of research has been undertaken on this phenomenon, because if marketing executives could figure out how celebrity brands fail, they would never hire a star without economic potential again, or match the wrong star to a product. Paris Hilton's watch collection (which you are unlikely to be aware of) or Lindsay Lohan's attempt to be creative director at the fashion company Ungaro (which was such a disaster that she was nearly in tears as she took her postshow walk down the runway)[82] are just two examples of the market failure of celebrity brands. Ringo Starr couldn't sell wine coolers for Sun Country Classic.[83] John Wayne couldn't sell Datril, a painkiller. Some endorsement failures can be explained by what I've just discussed: If we don't believe them, we won't buy their products. "[John] Wayne had nothing to do with the product, and sales of the analgesic languished," remarked one marketing scholar, "a classic mismatch . . . between star and product."[84] "Consumers are not stupid," Garland summarized. "They won't be bluffed."

But star products and endorsements also fail because a star is doing too many of them. Consumers reach a critical tipping point of oversaturation. In multiple academic studies, researchers have concluded that if a star endorses more than four products at the same time, his or her credibility as someone to trust in influencing buying choices declines dramatically.[85] Consumers feel that these multiendorsing stars lack expertise (how could they be experts in everything?) and they are likely endorsing only for the paycheck (which is probably accurate). Oversaturation results in consumers having negative associations with both the star and the product itself.

There is a final way a celebrity brand can fail. There's no delicate way to put it: When O. J. Simpson was accused of murdering his wife, Hertz had a huge problem. Simpson was, at the time, the spokesman for the car company and it wasn't such a leap to assume that potential renters would not be positively disposed toward a man whose only possible chance of innocence hung on the fact that a leather glove didn't fit. Hertz quickly ended the contract. The "O.J. risk," as it has been called in some advertising circles, has catalyzed companies to put in a "good behavior" clause in contracts in case a star acts in a way that could harm the brand. When Kate Moss was caught on camera snorting cocaine, companies from Chanel to Burberry dropped her unceremoniously for fear that her druggie lifestyle would be a liability to their brand. (When it turned out that the scandal increased her iconic status and profile, they rehired her.)

In November 2009, world-renowned golfer Tiger Woods was involved in a mysterious car accident mere feet away from his home in Florida, and his wife, golf club in hand, had smashed one of the car's windows. It emerged that the accident occurred after the two had an argument about Woods's supposed infidelities, and in the following weeks, Woods, the highest-paid athlete and celebrity endorser of all time, was found to have had more than a dozen extramarital affairs including a porn star, a pancake waitress, and a lingerie model. While Nike stood by their man (likely with great hopes that the scandal would just go away and the company could continue to make money on the Woods brand), the stories were too breathtakingly deviant for most of Woods's clean-cut brands to handle. "When the *National Enquirer* catches Tiger Woods philandering and his furious wife pursues him down his driveway . . . causing him to crash his Cadillac Escalade, it isn't just a big newsbreak: it is an oilstrike," wrote John Cassidy in the *New Yorker*.[86] From a consulting firm (Accenture) to sports drinks (Gatorade), endorsements dropped like flies. Prior to the scandal, Woods's lifetime endorsement deals were approximated at $6 billion. Since the revelations surrounding his personal life, Woods's management company, IMG, has lost $4.6 million in fees. It is estimated that Woods has lost between $23 million and $30 million since the scandal broke.[87] "The problem isn't a question of morals, exactly," James Surowiecki writes. "It's that a huge gap has opened up between Woods's advertising persona and his public image."[88]

Celebrity, a seemingly intangible quality, translates into real money and lots of it. And while it's not economically irrational that stars get paid more than nonstars, what's fascinating is that stars get paid *that* much more. Economists call this phenomenon "winner-take-all" or the "superstar" model of income distribution. Quite simply, the people at the top reap all the rewards. We see this principle operate across politics, art, music, and so forth. When Britney Spears's song hits number one, more people listen to it because it is number one, which perpetuates its position. She's then a big enough star to start her own perfume line. Those with a large celebrity residual produce real profit for all entities involved. The way they cash in may be different, the way the various industries reward this residual slightly different, but it comes down to the same thing: Ultimately, the economics of the celebrity residual exist everywhere.

8

The Democratic Celebrity

The Great Gatsby is as much as anything a novel about appearances, about Gatsby remaking himself from J. Gatz to the Great Gatsby by putting on the right clothes, by living in the right mansion. —**Neal Gabler**

How many celebrities will truly achieve greatness? A handful. There are very few people who are radically different. There are six billion people on the planet, most of whom are totally ordinary. —**Matthew Freud**

I met Max Clifford on a summer Friday afternoon in London. His office is tucked away on cobblestone alley off Bond Street, the illustrious address of hedge fund managers, oil tycoons, and the well-heeled jet set and celebrity elite. This was a fitting locale for Clifford, Britain's most celebrated and hated public relations guru, or "p.r. agent in the raw," as one profile described him.[1]

My visit happened to be on June 26, 2009, the day after Michael Jackson died of cardiac arrest. I called Clifford's assistant earlier that morning just to see if he was still available, thinking that the media would undoubtedly be hounding its celebrity guru for his twopence on one of the biggest celebrities of all time. But Clifford is a man of his word, whether you like what he says or not, and he kept his appointment with me.

Clifford's conversation, often delivered in perfect sound bites, further enhances his almost caricature-like public persona. The week before I met him, I was at a dinner party with friends who were disgusted that I was meeting Clifford. To them, and many Brits, Clifford represents everything that is wrong with the modern-day media and the cult of celebrity: the kiss-and-tell scandal-saturated newspapers and the paying off of aspiring stars who sell their privacy to the media. As one commentator put it, "Clifford has the instinct of the natural bully to imagine himself on the moral high ground even when standing knee-deep in the sewer."[2] And there is truth to that observation. Clifford is undoubtedly responsible for a not insignificant chunk of the tittle-tattle and scandal that keep newspapers and tabloids going. Right there in the center of the frenzy of gossip splashed across the *Sun*, the *Daily Mail*, and the *News of the World* is Clifford, "pulling the levers and pressing the buttons like a sweating disk jockey," as another described him.[3]

Clifford has represented soccer star David Beckham's supposed mistress, Rebecca Loos, as well as mistresses of high-level Parliament members, scorned lovers, reality TV stars, along with a bevy of A-listers. He represents these diverse clients with an intense righteousness and seemingly steadfast loyalty. In one scandal, Clifford represented Lady Buck, a Spanish rags-to-riches socialite who was having an affair with the British defense minister, Sir Peter Harding. She sold her tale for six figures and Harding resigned from his position. Yet despite Buck's obvious money grabbing and general exploitation of her private life, Clifford maintained the conviction that she was the wronged one. During the height of the scandal, Clifford was heard having a phone conversation with Buck, thundering into the receiver, "They're coming out and saying the most terrible things about you and you're just supposed to say nothing?"[4]

Clifford contends that most of the time his job consists of keeping stories *out* of the news, though that's not apparent from the dozens upon dozens of framed front-page U.K. newspaper stories on his office walls: "Jude Cheats on Sienna" (Hollywood actors Jude Law and Sienna Miller), "Beckham's Secret Affair," "Branson's Feud with Elton over Diana" (media and transportation mogul Richard Branson, Elton John, and Princess Diana). And perhaps Clifford's most famous coup: "Freddie Starr Ate My Hamster," the March 13, 1986, headline of the *Sun*, which detailed comedian Starr eating his girlfriend's hamster between two slices of bread after she refused to make him a sandwich. The story remains unverified, but as Clifford is quick to observe, it nevertheless made Starr a star, which is the ultimate endgame, after all.

Despite the scandals and frenzy that a Clifford headline may catalyze, Clifford himself appears calm and pleasant. With his perfect white smile, bouffant silver hair, and golden tan, he looks more suited to the palm trees and celebrity of Los Angeles than the capricious cool weather of London. And for all the deserved and undeserved vitriol spewed his way, Max Clifford represents people he thinks deserve to be heard, which is the mantra he repeats no matter whom he is representing. That Friday afternoon, no doubt like any other Friday afternoon, attractive women with shiny, perfectly groomed hair were sashaying about the office. One in particular was dressed in something only a semantic shade away from a cocktail dress, accompanied by sky-high bright red stilettos. The office was serene and under control, with Wimbledon playing quietly on a TV discreetly mounted on the wall along with a giant silk screen portrait of reality TV star Jade Goody, painted in Warhol's famous Marilyn style.

Jade Goody was Clifford's most recent high-profile rescue. Goody was a problematic Horatio Alger type who went from working class to *Big Brother* to Bentley-driving multimillionaire. Along the way, Goody was both celebrated for her "everywoman" persona and reviled for racism and bad language and her uneducated ways. In the end, she died a saint. The evolution of her status occurred over a period of about six years. Following her initial stint on *Big Brother* in 2002, she became a fixture of the British gossip and tabloid press. While she did not win, the show launched her public presence and celebrity brand, resulting in a perfume, an autobiography, a column in a celebrity glossy magazine, and yet more reality TV shows culminating in *Celebrity Big Brother* in 2007. This latter endeavor brought on a slew of additional business opportunities, another perfume, and another (updated) autobiography.

However, Goody's celebrity was often closer to notoriety. During her time on *Celebrity Big Brother*, she sparked international debates because of racial slurs (she called a fellow contestant of Indian ethnicity a "papadum"). In her earlier reality TV performances she mistook Cambridge, the famous university town, for a London borough. Goody was never your traditional platinum blond, size-two starlet. Nevertheless, the Brits were obsessed with her. She appeared genuine, outrageous, and, despite her missteps, appealing and accessible due to her lack of pretense or preciousness. She came from working-class roots, the daughter of a drug-addicted father who overdosed and died. She grew up to become a dental nurse and bore two children out of wedlock. "Jade Goody was the first person in the modern reality TV era who people identified with in a major way," said Mark Frith, former editor of *heat*. The publication went from failing men's magazine to leading celebrity glossy all by putting the *Big Brother* stars like Jade Goody on its covers.[5]

Unfortunately, Goody's story became, as often happens in the celebrity world, paradoxically more tragic and more celebrated. In the summer of 2008, she was diagnosed with cervical cancer, and within six months it had metastasized and became terminal. Despite her sometimes appalling public behavior and unsavory racist remarks, there was an over-whelming outpouring of sincere sympathy from both the media and the general public. Goody's short life (she died at age twenty-seven) would always have been mourned, but by the time she died she had rectified her image, had become an international news story, and had made millions of dollars by selling her story to the tabloids. Each day the *Sun* reported on her impending death: the spread of cancer, her rushed marriage, her last wishes, and so forth. We knew as much about her death as that of a close loved one. "I've lived my whole adult life talking about my life," she said on her deathbed. "I've lived in front of the cameras. And maybe I'll die in front of them."[6]

In the center of it all was Clifford, whom Goody employed shortly after her diagnosis to do her wheeling and dealing. He sold her story to the press, brokered the deal with the *Sun*, and was, by many accounts, responsible for her transformation from trash-talking B-lister to legitimate poster child of strength and perseverance in her losing battle with cancer. So much had Clifford repaired her reputation in the year since her diagnosis that the increase in cervical cancer screenings after her death was dubbed the "Jade Goody effect."[7] Her story's profits gave Goody's children a trust fund and made Clifford an even richer man. By his own account, Clifford conducted interviews on her behalf and scripted her responses. "Because I was doing 98 percent of her interviews, I knew what she wanted to say. [I would tell her,] 'No, love, you don't mean that, you mean this.'" Clifford's machinations worked brilliantly and helped transform her into a celebrity whose death prompted even Prime Minister Gordon Brown to make a public acknowledgment of her life and influence on British society.

Goody's story is remarkable for a number of reasons. Even in the midst of tragedy, it is another spectacular example of Clifford's sphinxlike celebrity mastermind. There is also real reason to wonder why we as viewers and readers were so grotesquely interested in Goody's last days. After all, Clifford was able to get a deal with the *Sun* and *OK!* only because their readers were interested in the first place. We were engrossed by Goody from the get-go and she was able to capitalize on our interest all along the way. Clifford wouldn't have taken her on if she hadn't been worth selling to the media, and if we, as her public, didn't find her inherently compelling.

Since her first *Big Brother* stint in 2002, Jade Goody attained a public presence as prolific and ubiquitous as any other celebrity. But why? Goody was not beautiful, she was not brilliant, she did not come from aristocracy or wealth. Her father wasn't famous. *Goody was utterly ordinary.* Unlike Warhammer World's Jervis or the clever academic who ends up with his own TV series, Goody was no relative celebrity to an adoring, albeit small, fan base. Despite her complete ordinariness, Goody became a mainstream, everyone-knows-your-name star who was featured in the gossip columns next to Kate Moss and Victoria Beckham. However, Goody's celebrity was not a function of being an icon of perfection, of her notable beauty or eccentricity, or of her talent. Nor was her celebrity a function of being "just like us." Instead, Goody represented a demagogic impulse of the media, someone that both the press and Goody's audience championed precisely because she was contrary to the conventional archetype of stardom. She was slightly chunky, had a nice smile without being beautiful, was uneducated, and misspoke regularly. Hers was not a rags-to-riches story like Sean Connery's or Jennifer Lopez's, who, despite the odds, were able to get a foot in the door to demonstrate their extraordinary talent to Hollywood. No, Goody had no obvious or unique talent. In all of her documented life, she portrayed the aspects of human fallibility and imperfection. When she became a star, Goody remained herself. "Jade was a natural exhibitionist," Clifford explained, "and she happened to be in the right show at the right time. It was her honesty and vulnerability and not knowing the capital of a country and that was part of her appeal. That's what it was with Jade."

Jade Goody's celebrity rested entirely on the fantasy that any one of us could become a star too.[8] Although she did not possess any ostensible star qualities, Goody acquired the fancy car, the mansion, the wealth, and the high-profile life of someone society would deem remarkable. Goody demonstrated that mainstream, all-encompassing celebrity can be bestowed upon a person who is no more remarkable than the viewers and fans who pay attention to her. She represented the rise of a new class of celebrity, never more present than in today's society: the democratic celebrity. "Ordinary people have never been more visible in the media," the Australian media critic Graeme Turner remarked, "nor have their own utterances ever been reproduced with the faithfulness, respect and accuracy they are today."[9] Goody is not an exceptional case: Dozens of democratic stars exist, and their star power is unique to modern society.[10] As the *Sunday Times* television critic A. A. Gill observed, "The democracy of dream-achievement provoked the leitmotif of the decade: the culture and triumph of amateurism . . . the feeling that people without experience, expert knowledge, skill, learning or aptitude had something extra, something special to offer."[11]

There are three principles underpinning democratic stardom. First, the celebrity of these stars relies on their fans identifying with them rather than adoring them. Goody is revered for her ordinariness in the extraordinary world of celebrity. Second, like all forms of celebrity, democratic celebrities run the gamut of talent-driven to all-residual. They may be discovered on *American Idol* for their beautiful voices or simply famous for being famous, like Goody. Third, democratic stars circumvent the normal vetting process, and that is part of their appeal. The development of technology, the rise of reality TV shows (and their great popularity), and the use of social media to perpetuate all forms of celebrity have reduced barriers to entry unlike at any other point in history. Reality TV stars, popular bloggers, MySpace and Facebook members who have thousands of friends, in another era would not have had the conduits to become mainstream stars. New forms of media and publicity allow individuals to become celebrities without being rejected by an elite Hollywood agent telling them they don't have what it takes. Consider thirteen-year-old blogger Tavi Gevinson, who stunned the fashion world when she started blogging eloquently at age eleven about high-end designers. By 2009, her blog, Style Rookie, which has attracted over four million viewers, got her front-row seats at fashion runway shows and mentions in *Vogue*, *Elle*, and the *New York Times*, among countless other publications. In the summer of 2009, she appeared on the cover of *Pop* magazine, designed by Damien Hirst. Tavi started her blog on her own and we made her a star by reading it; it was irrelevant whether Creative Artists Agency or any other gatekeeper to stardom thought she was good enough, because we did. Tavi, like Goody, beat the system.

American Idol and the Making of a Star

But democratic celebrity does not imply that these individuals have nothing to offer; rather, they now have new opportunities to attain mainstream celebrity. There is perhaps no more vivid example of democratic stardom than *American Idol*, which has managed to enthrall American viewers for nine seasons straight, with a viewership peaking at thirty million. The show is hosted by Ryan Seacrest and features a coterie of telegenic stars who act as "judges," including several rotating, attractive females, and Simon Cowell, who also hosts Britain's similar star-making shows, *Pop Idol* and *Britain's Got Talent*. (Cowell, who announced in the spring of 2010 that he would be leaving *American Idol*, also happens to be represented by Max Clifford.) Since 2002, *American Idol* has given people the belief that their perfectly pitched singing in the shower really could result in a Grammy and hundreds of thousands of record sales—if they could just get on the show. *American Idol* makes the promise of such reward explicit in its subtitle: *The Search for a Superstar*.

In its nine seasons, the show has gone on to produce legitimate stars, voted in by both the judges and television viewers who can call in and text their votes. Jennifer Hudson, a season-three contestant, won a Grammy as well as an Oscar for best supporting actress for her role in *Dreamgirls*. She was featured on the cover of *Vogue* and hangs out with any A-lister of her choosing. Chris Daughtry, the fourth-place finalist on the fifth season, landed a record deal with RCA with his rock band, Daughtry. The band's first album sold more than one million copies in just five weeks, making it the fastest-selling rock debut album of all time. Kelly Clarkson and Carrie Underwood, both *American Idol* first-place winners, have gone on to become multimillion record sellers and popular topics of conversation in various celebrity tabloids. Clarkson has reached number one both on the U.K. and U.S. singles charts, selling more than twenty million albums worldwide. She is one of the top two hundred album sellers in music history. At seventeen years old, Fantasia Barrino was a single teenage mom without a job. She won season three of *American Idol* and has since played a leading role in Broadway's *The Color Purple* and has been nominated for eight Grammy Awards. The list of *American Idol* participants who have become mainstream stars goes on.[12] Even those who do not become megastars reap the benefits of making it onto the show. Including performance fees and royalties from merchandise sales, a winner makes at least $1 million in the year or two after their participation on the show. But any contestant in the top five makes around $100,000 and often three or four times more if they land a record deal.[13] *American Idol* is one of the most compelling shows in television history precisely because it achieves exactly what it sets out to do: making stars out of seemingly ordinary people.

One might say that Kelly Clarkson is more extraordinary than ordinary, and she's got infinitely more star power than Jade Goody. Without *American Idol*, however, Clarkson never would have become a superstar, just as Fantasia would have remained a mom with a child out of wedlock instead of a Broadway actress and Grammy-nominated musician.

Part of the *American Idol* method of success is telling the stories of the contestants' lives, enabling viewers to identify with them as ordinary people who have been given a chance to become a star. The viewers' participation in the selection process is essential to democratic celebrity. "*American Idol* is very interesting in terms of reality versus appearance because it's predicated on the idea when you look at the people who have succeeded . . . These are people who never, never, never would have made it through the normal course of the recording industry," said the author and media commentator Neal Gabler. "Kelly Clarkson . . . who had that big, powerful voice but not the drop dead good looks that everybody in the recording industry now seems to have, was made a star by the audience. The audience said, 'This is real . . . Kelly Clarkson, Ruben Studdard, Clay Aiken, they're real, they belong to me, and I will make them stars.' "[14]

Inarguably, despite the democratic principles underlying the show, *American Idol* has created its own system of selecting individuals to become stars. While Clarkson got a chance that she would not have been given if she had simply showed up at the doors of record companies in Los Angeles or New York, she still had to go through a rigorous audition process with the show's judges and be the favorite of a tough audience that voted for her over the other contestants. *American Idol* is not a free-for-all. But then again, no form of celebrity is. After all, even Tavi the fashion blogger and M the endless Facebook updater are vetted and chosen by their respective audiences. Not all participants succeed, and some mediums are better than others at creating stars. Shows like *American Idol* produce more stars than the average hastily put together reality TV program, or any random person starting a blog.

At the outset, it is doubtful that the producers of the early reality shows (*Big Brother*, MTV's *The Real World*) anticipated the extent to which their programs would create celebrities out of otherwise ordinary people. Because these programs did cultivate such a fan base and a longer-term celebrity career for some of the participants, a deluge of reality programs have been broadcasted in their wake. The more successful reality shows have structured marketing campaigns and are often advertised heavily, and most producers aim to cultivate a following around the participants. Despite having some of the qualities of Hollywood or the music industry, the premise for these programs remains democratic: Unless specified (e.g., *Celebrity Big Brother*), the participants are ultimately selected from the wider populace. Calls are not placed to Creative Artists Agency; auditions with Hollywood directors are not held. In its tasteless, tacky, clever, and impressive forms, most reality TV still aims to be an entry point that provides a chance at stardom to those who would not likely have one through the more elite channels of celebrity.[15]

Creating Our Own Stars

Whatever its stripe, celebrity fundamentally relies on the choices that we as fans and audience members make about individuals. We choose to care about Jennifer Aniston's love life and choose not to care much about Cate Blanchett's. But democratic celebrity is more than just the audience deciding to buy the celebrity glossy featuring one star over another. What we want from our democratic celebrities (at least at the outset) is unlike what we want from Hollywood A-list stars. First, we identify with (rather than idolize) these celebrities. "Viewers are invited to imagine 'it could be me or someone I know,'" remarks the media scholar Henry Jenkins.[16] Second, we delight and participate in the democratic star's ability to buck the system. Whereas buying a magazine or going to the movies costs anywhere from $4 to $15, watching someone on TV, following him or her on Twitter, reading a blog, or downloading a YouTube video costs very little if anything at all. Therefore, when we elect to follow democratic celebrities, we make choices without any real constraints, and thus these stars are better reflections of our preferences.[17] We read one person's blog over another; we watch the YouTube video we want to; we phone in our favorite *American Idol* contestant. Sure, someone has to make it onto *American Idol* for us to vote for him or her, and, yes, there is a constant barrage of marketing and publicity associated with the more commercial versions of democratic celebrity. Ultimately, however, we are able to participate in the outcome if we are so inclined, which is not an option with the latest boy band single or blockbuster from Hollywood. Unlike the classic Hollywood studio system that created its own stars and foisted them upon us, we create the democratic star ourselves if we choose to be involved in the process. Democratic celebrity relies on our empathy or sympathy with the stars as individuals. We might vote for Fantasia because we get a glimpse of her hardship and struggles, and we want to help determine her success.[18]

American Idol is just one of many reality TV shows and other democratic channels through which the ordinary becomes extraordinary. VH1 attained its highest viewership ever in 2006 (increasing by 15 percent from 2005), and much of this success was attributed to the launch of *Celebrity Rehab* (the plotline is all in the title) and *Fantasia for Real*, which is former *American Idol* winner Fantasia Barrino's reality TV program. Starting in 2004, *Project Runway*, Bravo's reality show that helps turn one aspiring young fashion designer into a legitimate fashion star, was the highest-rated program in the channel's twenty-seven-year history (starting in 2009, the show began broadcasting on Lifetime). *Dancing with the Stars*'s finale brought ABC more than twenty million viewers, and of course *American Idol* continues to bring in viewers by the tens of millions. According to one estimate, there may be one thousand reality show contestants on TV at any moment, with at least twenty networks offering approximately four reality programs and at least two hours of programming per week (this latter figure doubling in size during the summer season).[19] Reality TV is only one form of this type of stardom, all of which rests on the ability to create what the media scholar Mark Andrejevic has called "mass individuation" and "the democratization of publicity as celebrity." [20] In other words, each one of these hundreds of people who attain fame through reality TV, Twitter, or various other social media seems fundamentally unique and worthy of celebrity, despite being one of many. Our love for democratic stars rests partially on the premise that their uniqueness is not that different from our own.

The Mechanics of the Democratic Star

On June 16, 2006, an unknown girl in a small Midwestern town became a global sensation when she posted home videos of herself and her friends on YouTube. Her alias was lonely-girl15 (real name Bree), and the videos documenting her life were innocuous and dull. Yet upward of fifteen million viewers kept watching her. She was homeschooled, her parents apparently strict and religious, and she was not exceptionally funny or bright. Yet for some reason, whether because of her quaint charm or middle-American wholesome good looks, or perhaps just because there was a morbid fascination with exactly how dull (and lonely) her life was, lonelygirl15's videos made her an international phenomenon. Her videos were some of the most watched on YouTube, and viewers eagerly awaited the next update on her unexciting, no-need-to-be-updated life. "She is a high school girl with swooping eyebrows, boy problems, and a webcam willing to listen," *Wired* magazine wrote. "The room behind her could be anywhere in America—there's a pink floral-print bedspread, a half-dozen stuffed animals, and a framed picture of a rose on the wall."[21] So why did viewers care? Why did they keep watching?

By early September, viewers were suspicious that perhaps lonelygirl15 was a fake. Or as *New York* magazine put it, "Along the way, people have started questioning whether she even exists, and for good reason: She's just a little *too* charming, her videos a little *too* well edited, and her story a little *too* neatly laid out."[22] These suspicions ultimately resulted in several viewers setting up a sting operation through making contact with lonelygirl15 on her MySpace page. Using IP address–tracking software, they were able to trace her e-mails from her MySpace page to Creative Artists Agency in Beverly Hills. Concurrently, it was also discovered that lonelygirl15 had a U.S. federal trademark 78957059, which was filed on

August 22, 2006. In this filing, it stated that lonelygirl15 had been used in interstate commerce since May 24, 2006. It turned out that lonelygirl15 was actually Jessica Rose, a New Zealand–born actress living in Los Angeles, and her creators were Ramesh Flinders, a filmmaker and screenwriter from outside Los Angeles, and Miles Beckett, a medical school dropout turned filmmaker. The videos were being filmed in Flinders's bedroom. The story that lonelygirl15 was a fraud broke at 1:41 a.m. on September 12. Every major newspaper from the *New York Times* to the *Los Angeles Times* and thousands of blogs covered it that day. Two days later, Jessica Rose, aka lonelygirl15, made a surprise visit to Jay Leno's *The Tonight Show*. She didn't seem so lonely anymore.

At the time, it seemed the sky was the limit for Rose. The media was agog over this new type of star that could emerge from YouTube without the constraints of the Hollywood star machine. And so what if she had a little help from some pros at CAA? The bottom line was that Rose had made the big time, appeared on Jay Leno, an opportunity even A-listers covet, and succeeded without having to navigate the conventional channels. In 2007, *Forbes* ranked her the number one web celebrity, *Maxim* covered her, and she won a few awards for her Internet stardom. However, three years later most people don't know Jessica Rose. She has not been featured in any major blockbusters and she does not grace the covers of magazines. In 2007, she appeared in a Lindsay Lohan film, *I Know Who Killed Me*, and a few smaller films as well as on web outlets that haven't received much press. Rose's life doesn't seem very different from what it was the week before her story broke. Despite her best efforts, there were no big results from Rose's Internet celebrity. And herein lies the paradox of the democratic star: While it ostensibly seems much easier to get one's foot in the door, keeping oneself in the limelight is much harder. Hollywood is difficult to break into, but Hollywood stardom has a longer life span. If everyone has a chance to attain celebrity through democratic stardom, keeping people interested over time becomes that much harder. As the economist Tyler Cowen remarked, "It's never a secure position, precisely because entry is easy."[23]

In its early stages (before agents are hired and Perez Hilton is blogging about you), democratic celebrity is different in how it is maintained. Hollywood, sports, and political celebrity have their own built-in vetting processes. Hollywood agents and directors choose who to represent or star in their films. Scouts and agents make the big choices about who gets to play professionally. The Republicans and the Democrats hold party conferences and fund-raisers that either build more support for an already selected candidate or test the temperature for potential stars. If Creative Artists Agency picks a young starlet and does her bidding, she may or may not get parts, but someone is working around the clock to procure her a media profile, invites to events where she will be seen, auditions, and so forth.[24] But YouTube stars and bloggers do it all themselves.[25] The democratic star does not have a structured star machine to rely on; he does not have agents and handlers to help him perpetuate his star power. He can't afford to wait for his nonexistent publicist to put out a press release. Thus, as much as M bemuses me with his endless status updates about his magazine and his trips back and forth between the coasts, he is doing his job perfectly. I am reminded of his existence and how important and busy he is. Jennifer Aniston, on the other hand, has her agent to groom and perpetuate her star power.

Jay Maynard, aka Tron Guy, is a perfect example of the intense but fleeting nature of democratic stardom. Maynard, a computer programmer and denizen of Fairmont, Minnesota (population 11,000), went from geek to Internet celebrity after pictures of him in a luminescent costume inspired by the Disney science-fiction movie *Tron* showed up all over the Internet.

Maynard actually never intended on becoming a celebrity but capitalized on his star power when it came around. "I think everyone wants to become famous kind of idly. I never expected to become famous," he said. "What happened was that I submitted a story to Slashdot [a technology news website]. It was a follow-up to other stories about other *Tron* fan costumes . . . I thought maybe a couple of people would be interested . . . The story just spread across the Internet instantly . . . People were making pretty seriously derogatory comments. Like 'that guy in spandex.' They didn't think that anybody that was my shape should ever put on tights. I knew darn well going in that I wasn't shaped like Bruce Boxleitner, the guy who plays Tron." But that latter point was irrelevant. Soon, Maynard ended up on the Jimmy Kimmel show and an episode of *South Park*, and was a headliner for the Internet celebrity conference ROFLCon. Once Maynard's celebrity status was established, he worked his own media machine to perpetuate his star power. As he told me, "I make a policy of never turning down an interview request. Part of this is because it's my chance to show there's more to me than just a fat guy in spandex."

For about a year and a half, Maynard experienced acute celebrity, requests for interviews, and a constant media profile. Maynard started a website (www.tronguy.net) and a LiveJournal. And his *Tron* photo shoots continued. But like most Internet celebrity, public interest slacked off without a structured system to perpetuate Maynard's public persona. For Maynard, this result was inevitable: "I honestly believe you cannot get Internet fame seeking it out. Those who have tried have universally failed."

If you look at the statistics, the way Maynard's celebrity played out is to be expected. When I spoke to YouTube executives about the rise of Internet celebrity, they explained the immense difficulty in perpetuating stardom, despite the website's egalitarian mantra. In the fall of 2009, more than twenty hours of content were uploaded every minute on YouTube, a 60 percent increase in just a year and a half. Considering that most uploads are an average of one minute each, you get a sense of how hard it is to stay on top. As one YouTube executive put it, "You are up against a sea of competition." And this is another aspect of how democratic celebrity plays out: The sheer number of contestants all vying for the same place makes democratic stardom much harder to sustain than conventional Hollywood or sports celebrity. Uploading a video to YouTube might take five minutes and no one needs an agent to do it, but the only YouTube celebrities who make it in the long term are those who have viewers who "subscribe" to see their videos regularly, or those whose video is featured on the YouTube home page. He continued, "Hollywood is push celebrity, while YouTube is pull. Users troll the web and find what they care about or not. We give them the tools, but then they have to find [what they want to watch] themselves."

The paradox of democratic star power is that, yes, everyone has a shot at it, but no one is given special status.[26] Hollywood anoints a very finite number of people to become stars, but it backs up this selection through financial and time investment and an intricate network of publicists, agents, and media devoted to the creation of one particular star, making his or her chances of success much higher. In the world of democratic celebrity, there is always another compulsive blogger to take your place. And as viewers we barely notice the difference among them all. Given that the democratic star is up against twenty hours of content uploaded every minute on YouTube, the strategy must always be oversaturation.

In this respect, *American Idol* is unique as a form of democratic celebrity. While its premise (picking unknowns from the masses) is fundamentally democratic, once selected, its contestants are initiated into the *American Idol* star-making machine, which includes adverts, media blitz, and prime-time broadcasting. Also, all the winners and many of the top contestants are offered record contracts in the postseason. Thus, it is no surprise that the stars of *American Idol* have a longer shelf life than most other democratic stars, even if the audience is initially drawn to these stars because they identify with them and because the contestants challenge the conventional stardom frameworks. *American Idol* actively brands and seeks profits from its contenders and does this through contracts binding the contestants to the show for up to seven years, giving *American Idol* the right to use their images for promotional purposes.[27] There is the *American Idol* brand (which has even been a featured Dreyer's ice cream flavor), but also marketing, licensing fees, and royalties from the sale of music performances by its contestants, all of which adds up to hundreds of millions of dollars.[28] *American Idol* is therefore invested in perpetuating its contestants' careers, even if just a season ago these stars were nobodies.

The Dark Side of Democratic Celebrity

There is reason for pause before we revel in Twitter and reality TV celebrity as fairer versions of star power. The traditional star machine of agents, publicists, and magazine editors is discriminatory, but these professionals perform a very important function: They vet the celebrities and in many ways test their fortitude along the trajectory of stardom. The barrage of agents, producers, directors, and media can regulate and control the process by which one becomes a star. Without these gatekeepers, the rise to celebrity can be destructive for some individuals who go from zero to hero in under two weeks and cannot handle the pressure of being a newfound celebrity.

Most Hollywood celebrities value their position; they also

have an entourage of people equipped with media and publicity skills to smooth their path to stardom. Publicists and agents help protect a celebrity by screening unwise offers. They work full-time dealing with the media demands. They make the decisions about what media outlets a star will talk to, squelch rumors, and deal with all entities that want something from the star they represent (whether cosmetic contracts, interviews, or movie deals). Democratic stars may hire a publicist once they have become famous, but they usually have to become celebrities before anyone invests in them. The established system by which stars are selected, handled, and represented works by both providing expertise to its fledgling stars and protecting them. Although entry and acceptance into this star machine involve a far more difficult and formal process, the Hollywood mechanism appears more merciful and works to defend its celebrities against the meteoric rise and fall that many democratic stars face. At least since the Greek tragedies, society has relished watching the rise and inevitable fall of its heroes, but reality TV has established a recurring mechanism to create stars out of nothing only to watch them combust into nothing again. As Peter Bazalgette, the TV mogul and producer of the U.K. *Big Brother*, put it, "We've always had people who are famous for being famous. There is nothing new about the public wishing to put people on a pedestal, then knock them down again. The difference now is that it has been realized."[29]

A recent example of this process is *Britain's Got Talent* star Susan Boyle, who in the spring of 2009 went from an average woman from a small town in Scotland singing in her local church to international sensation in three minutes. Her awkwardness and frumpiness were painfully clear on her first audition for the show (which is almost identical in format to *American Idol*, with Simon Cowell as a judge on this program as well). Cowell made no attempts to hide his amusement and disdain. He asked her what she wanted to be and she said, "A professional singer." Cowell replied with a smirk: "Why do you think that's never happened?" to which Boyle said, "I've never been given the chance before," and then opened her mouth to sing a breathtakingly beautiful version of *Les Misérables*'s "I Dreamed a Dream." More than one hundred million people around the world watched the video of her performance on various media sites. In that moment, her winning *Britain's Got Talent* seemed all but a fait accompli, with one judge, Piers Morgan, remarking after he voted for her to remain on the show, "That's the biggest yes I've ever given anybody." Boyle was euphoric, dancing onstage after she was voted onto the next round.

In the following months, though, Boyle's personal life was scrutinized, ridiculed, and obsessed over: She lived in her family's state-supported housing in a small village with her cat, Pebbles. She had been greatly devoted to her mother, who had passed away a few years earlier. She seemed kind, if odd and rather overwhelmed, but willing to ham it up for the cameras. In the endless media frenzy, however, Boyle seemed unable to handle the pressure and invasiveness. She swore at the media, she locked herself up. And while she went on to make it to the final, she lost to a young dance group called Diversity. Boyle had a breakdown and was ultimately checked into a mental health facility. In the days after Boyle's hospitalization, the media went wild. She was seen as a freak show by some, the encapsulation of the "American dream" by others, and also a candid reminder never to judge by appearance alone. But there was an underlying current of disapproval directed at *Britain's Got Talent*: They did not shelter Boyle, they did not protect her, and some went as far as to say the show exploited her. Mary Beard, a professor at Cambridge, railed against the show in a London *Times* op-ed: "Susan Boyle is a vulnerable and exploited middle-aged woman. She is not a star in the making, being given a lucky break thanks to *BGT*."[30] In a commentary for the BBC, the psychologist Glen Wilson remarked, "Most reality TV is in some respects exploitative, but *Britain's Got Talent* seemed to me to be particularly so."[31] Even Cowell later expressed regret for how the show handled Boyle's obviously deteriorating capacity to deal with her newfound celebrity. In an op-ed in the *Daily Mail* he wrote, "Looking back on it all, it has become clear to me that we didn't handle the situation with Susan as well as we could have."[32]

Unquestionably, Boyle was unsteady and vulnerable, and no one was there to help her handle celebrity that she could not have foreseen in a million years. And yet, her celebrity continued. Her debut album, released in November 2009, was Amazon's largest presale in history. According to *Billboard*, her version of "I Dreamed a Dream" debuted as the largest sale in history for a female vocalist. Despite Boyle's success, however, there were still rumblings of her being on the verge of a breakdown. What this story makes clear is that there can be a sinister aspect to democratic celebrity. It can happen too quickly, it can be overwhelming, and very often the people who experience such a sudden rise have no framework within which to navigate their newfound stardom. There is no system in place to check the potential invasiveness of the media. The lack of handlers also means that there is less control over the development and outcome of any situation in which these stars might be involved. Hollywood publicists stamp out rumors and are experts in dealing with scandals; they act as mouthpieces and have connections with reporters and gossip columnists who can spin a story a particular way. Some publicists might know Oprah personally and be able to arrange a spot on her show for a star to defend himself or herself. Max Clifford guides his stars through tricky interviews and screens every media call.

Without the experts around, however, anything is possible.

A case in point is the reality TV show gone awry, *Jon & Kate Plus 8*, which initially aired in 2008 as the story of a happy couple living in a Pennsylvania suburb with their very large family. Then Kate was accused of having an affair with her bodyguard (both denied it vehemently), and Jon was accused of having several affairs, sneaking out of the house, and partying with college girls. The disintegration of their marriage was happening in real time on TV. TLC, the cable network that aired the show, experienced a record viewership of almost ten million. The celebrity print media jumped on board too. From March to October 2009, Jon and Kate were on the cover of the big celebrity tabloids more than fifty times, trumping every other star's coverage. When Jon graced the cover of *In Touch* with a tell-all exclusive, the magazine sold nearly one million copies. Other tabloids reported similar figures associated with Jon and Kate on their covers.[33] When the couple's marriage fell apart, TLC comically changed the show's name to *Kate Plus 8* to reflect the impending divorce. Jon challenged this decision, and the show has since been canceled. The unraveling and attendant public spectacle can hardly be terrific for the couple or their children. Inquiries were made into whether Pennsylvania child labor laws had been violated.[34] (The charges have since been dropped.) What is clear about democratic celebrity is that, while it is free and easy to attain, it often exploits people who would be better off away from the spotlight.[35] " 'Reality' grew to mean a particular type of closely choreographed and edited ultra-reality—a hyperventilating, tearful, exhibitionist spectacle initially hailed as the democratization of television," the British newspaper columnist A. A. Gill commented. "Or, alternatively, as the lunatics taking over the asylum."[36]

The PR guru Matthew Freud told me, "Sigmund Freud, my great-grandfather, was one of the first to achieve fame while alive. And my father [Sir Clement Freud] was quite famous, on thirty million televisions every night. That was a very weird thing to grow up with. With television, fame moved closer to our orbit. Now everyone is famous—that guy was an X Factor star, that guy won the lottery . . . People who we aspired to be like, we suddenly became." The ultimate problem is that democratic stars are "just like us." The everywoman turned celebrity may not be ready for stardom or able to manage its accompanying crush of attention both positive and negative. "The less connected the achievement of celebrity was to some training," Graeme Turner writes, "the more arbitrary it was— the less equipped the person concerned was to handle the inevitable discovery that fame had nothing to do with them and that it could disappear overnight."[37] Further, it is their ordinariness that both attracts and repels us and can cause democratic stars to crash and burn. Freud elaborated: "Suddenly it became apparent that these people weren't exceptional. No matter how dull you are, you can be famous. Then the media builds them up and then gives them a sucker punch. So it's not surprising that these unexceptional people are, in fact, unexceptional. Exceptional and celebrity, there used to be a correlation between the two. The last cycle of reality TV stars were unspeakably ordinary. Susan Boyle being a small footnote." Or as Max Clifford explained, "More and more in the last ten years, they [the media] take ordinary members of the public, they become famous for five or ten minutes, sometimes fifteen minutes. Tabloids feed off of them, they feed off of the tabloid newspapers in the short term. Very few celebrities go on . . . very few last more than five or ten minutes. Media has to keep creating new celebrities, to go through the motion of creating them, ridiculing them and then forgetting them." This dynamic illustrates the cruelest aspect of democratic celebrity: experiencing stardom only to have it taken away. Clifford continued: "Celebrity is like a drug. The more you get, the more you want. And fame is just as deadly as any."

9

The Future of Celebrity

The ideas for this book came to life over the course of a Midtown Manhattan lunch with my friend and long-term mentor, Harvey Molotch. Harvey, a New York University sociologist, has been my academic hero since my graduate school days. As we gazed down on Central Park South, I told him about my new research project: a critical analysis of celebrity.

Celebrity permeates society and generates billions of dollars. It destroys some individuals, elevates others to mythical status, and sometimes manages to do both to a person at the same time. Yet celebrity is not examined seriously, nor are its contributions to the shape of modern society and culture judged to be significant. Many people think celebrity merely means tabloids and drug-addled beautiful people. Commentators wax on about the simultaneous demise of society and rise of reality TV stars. They deride celebrity as silly and a waste of time and ink.

But any social scientist will tell you that something that consumes the public dialogue with such fervor, dominates the airwaves, and involves so many people and so much money ought to be looked at more closely. Something extraordinary is happening in society today. Yes, celebrity has always existed. Beginning in the twenty-first century, however, celebrity truly became present *everywhere*. Celebrity emerged as an exaggerated nexus for virtually everything that defines contemporary society: conspicuous consumption, voyeurism, narcissism, information overload, and oversharing. Celebrity also became a focal point to discuss the issues that society wrestled with more generally: infidelity, addictions, loneliness, sexuality, and so forth.[1] There is almost no way of escaping celebrity's hold on television, newspapers, and people's conversations. We are starstruck. Did Obama win the presidency because of his extraordinary political talent? Yes. Do we now obsess about him like we do about Angelina Jolie? Yes. What is it about those people that society just can't stop talking about? Are they more beautiful? More intelligent? Is it simply charisma or looking great at the Oscars? The qualities these individuals possess are often far from unique.

"Aunt Tillie," Harvey said. "My aunt Tillie was our family's celebrity." Tillie was tall, slender, wore beautiful clothing, and didn't do a day of work in her married life. While ostensibly she was a homemaker, Tillie had a housekeeper in attendance seven days a week. Tillie's living room had a blue carpet that never looked anything other than plush and rich. If she had anything in the room replaced, it was done unceremoniously so that the carpets and the room appeared ageless and impervious to wear. She also knew how to dance the cha-cha. "Aunt Tillie was stunning and had beautiful taste," Harvey said. "I think that was the primary conversation [about her], but probably people talked about how handsome her home was . . . In the younger days, the cigarette lighters in her living room always worked, even though she didn't smoke. I think they were Ronson in silver plate. Post-Ronson, she was early onto clear plastic candy dishes . . . and the candy dishes always had candy in them." People loved the coffee cake Aunt Tillie brought to the family gatherings and attributed its tastiness to her, even though, as it turned out, the dessert was purchased from the local fancy bakery. In Harvey's family, Aunt Tillie was talked about and revered in a way that no one else was; the qualities of her persona and its accoutrements were known and obsessed about in great detail. "My mother liked her a lot," Harvey explained, "but resented, I think, her accomplishments in taste and my grandmother's [Tillie's mother-in-law] evident celebration of Tillie compared to my mother."

Harvey could recall everything about Tillie, even decades after her star had dimmed. Through her impeccably maintained home and her signature coffee cake she projected an image of herself as an effortless homemaker who still managed to look beautiful and dance well. It didn't matter to the family that she had help in maintaining this image. "I think part of her stardom was that [the cake] was not 'store-bought,' " Harvey explained, "but rather made by 'a lady.' " Tillie created star power in a way not unlike today's celebrities and aspiring ones.

Celebrities exist everywhere, at every level. Mainstream celebrities, who emerge from Hollywood, sports, fashion, and politics, are the types we all know. Relative celebrities, like Jervis, Tillie, and the high school quarterback, exist in all our lives even if we don't label them as such. Democratic celebrity is a truly unique twenty-first-century type of stardom that has emerged from the deluge of new forms of media and entertainment. Each type of celebrity has its talent-based individuals (the high school quarterback, the Oscar winner, Susan Boyle) and its all-residual stars (Paris, Jade Goody). The common theme emerging in all forms of stardom is the way the public cares about the stars for reasons that transcend their contribution to the world.

Economically, celebrity is no frivolous matter. The industry generates billions of dollars and thousands of jobs. Individuals like Britney Spears and Michael Jordan are single-handedly responsible for an economic impact of hundreds of millions of dollars. But even smaller forms of celebrity—whether on YouTube or Twitter, or in subcultures like Games Workshop, *Star Trek*, or graffiti—make money. These niche markets have their own celebrities who generate revenues through brands, particular products, speaking fees, videos, and tweets and blogs that draw advertisers. Not to mention the thousands of people who have jobs at tabloids, agencies, online social media sites, or TV stations devoted to reporting on these individuals, or the stylists, trainers, or any number of other types of workers who groom celebrities to look like celebrities.

More significant, celebrity is a social phenomenon that tells us about how the world is organized. Societies contain hierarchies and categories, and celebrities fit within the upper echelon of our social structures.[2] They, like characters in literature, film, or television, operate as a point of reference for human behavior. We can compare ourselves to these individuals and either aspire to be like them, or breathe a sigh of relief when we recognize we are not like them at all.[3] Celebrities exist only because we want them to. Not unlike the great Houdini tricks of old where the audience could be tricked only if they attended the show in the first place, celebrity is defined as much by its spectators as by its protagonists. The media invests in people as celebrities only as long as those watching are willing to continue to watch, that is, maintain their celebrity status. Fans are the underestimated but critical ingredient in the success of popular culture enterprises. They are both consumers and active participants in the triumph of *American Idol*, YouTube, and other new media forms.[4] Fans essentially create the celebrities they obsess about. If we want to know why celebrity holds such a prominent position in media and society, then we need to examine ourselves.

Some stars are simply special. They are emblematic of the sociologist Max Weber's famous "charismatic authority," a term he defined as "a certain quality of an individual personality, by virtue of which he is set apart from ordinary men and treated as endowed with supernatural, superhuman, or at least specifically exceptional powers or qualities."[5] Some celebrities are genuinely charismatic, or seem to possess a natural je ne sais quoi. People who knew Barack Obama before he became president have said that even as a junior senator from Chicago, he was very attractive as an individual—people were drawn to him. I recall the first time I met Senator Hillary Clinton during my internship with her office. I was captivated by the way she spoke, what she said, and the way she smiled. There was something about her that was magnetic. Similar things have been said about Bill Clinton, John F. Kennedy, and Tony Blair. Yes, these individuals are attractive and articulate, but those attributes apply to many people who are not stars. And not all Hollywood actors, supermodels, or athletes possess these qualities: Those who work closely with stars are the first to point out how much of their supposedly magnetic personality is orchestrated through camera lights and angles, well-applied makeup, and scripted interview questions.

Celebrities *may* be inherently special and extraordinary, but they are not necessarily so. What defines stars is that they engage in social behaviors that are fundamentally different from those of nonstars. The mechanisms they use to interact with the world are different from those used by the majority of society. This is not to say that all individuals who participate in these behaviors become stars. Quite the contrary: As ubiquitous as celebrities appear to be, only some who aspire to this position attain it. Celebrity cannot, however, be anointed to someone unless he engages in the mechanics that allow him to generate a public. Celebrities tend to get themselves in the media and in venues that allow information about them to be conveyed to their public. This happens in mainstream celebrity through the requisite "geographies of stardom," but even the homecoming queen makes it a point to show up to the Friday night high school football games just as Aunt Tillie never missed a family reunion or event to which she could bring her famous coffee cake. Attending events in high-profile places is how stars perpetuate their presence.

Stars also penetrate networks of people who will uphold their status—this is where the A-list, the clique of popular high school girls, and the most revered graffiti artists (who in the 1980s hung out along designated parts of the New York subway system) all behave similarly. They cultivate elite networks of individuals just like themselves as a visual reinforcement of their elite status. Sociologists have found almost identical networking structures in elite populations ranging from financiers to scientists.[6] UCLA professors Lynne Zucker and Michael Darby discovered that the location of "star scientists" in the biotechnology industry tends to be predictive of concentrations of successful commercial ventures and invention.[7] Star networking and geographical concentration are not simply for the hell of it; both behaviors produce important positive side effects for their industries. In Hollywood, stars influence movies and ticket sales; in science, star presence catalyzes innovation.

Most important, celebrities project an image of themselves and their lives onto the public that we can aspire to, identify with, envy, or simply find fascinating. For some stars, particularly those in popular culture industries, such overexposure is a necessary cost of doing business. But many celebrities, particularly those emerging from all-residual channels, are driven to attain a public profile for reasons that are not entirely healthy or congruent with who they really are as people. I had an acquaintance (a relative celebrity) who had the most amazing MySpace page. The photos she uploaded were either black-and-white or gritty Polaroids. She made funny faces while still looking very pretty. In the images she was always in a Marc Jacobs dress, standing by a Brooklyn diner or posing outside a nightclub at three a.m. Her hobbies and interests sections of her MySpace page listed only obscure poetry I had never heard of and books by Bret Easton Ellis and David Foster Wallace. She listed quotes from Woody Allen and Sid Vicious. To her hundreds of MySpace friends, my friend seemed to have the most fabulous life ever.

But in reality she worked in a bookstore and lived with her father in a conventional middle-class suburb. She had an eating disorder. Her romantic life was in utter chaos. She was deeply unhappy, and none of her various psychiatrists and therapists could find an antidepressant that would work for her. Yet every Friday night she headed down to the Lower East Side or Williamsburg and hung out at rock shows with one of her boyfriends (and sometimes me). We would go to gallery openings and hip restaurants and underground clubs. And even if we spent most of the night talking about how lonely or disconnected she felt, her Polaroid was always present, clicking away and creating a life that seemed to the rest of the world as if it were nothing short of sublime. It never mattered what actually happened that Friday night; by Monday morning her MySpace page told a story of another unbelievably exciting, edgy weekend.[8] And her friends left comment after comment remarking on how cute, cool, or beautiful she looked in her photos. The dichotomy between the celebrity visage she maintained and the reality of her life is not unlike many tragic stories that we see splashed across major news outlets, whether Heath Ledger's accidental overdose, Kurt Cobain's suicide, or Britney Spears's roller coaster ride.

Celebrities and the forms in which they emerge are a reflection of the zeitgeist and are similarly ephemeral and short-lived. Friendster gave way to MySpace, which lost out to Facebook (and some new social-networking site is surely just round the corner). Celebrity gossip sites TMZ and Perez Hilton are now being overtaken by Yahoo! omg!; reality TV shows lose viewership because a newer reality program has captured audiences' interest; and nightclubs that host star-studded parties eventually shut their doors because a more coveted venue opens up down the street.

In his clever *New Yorker* essay, "The Iron Laws of Stardom," the Harvard professor Louis Menand points out that most stars have three years of true stardom at best. Perhaps the time frame is not this exact, though Menand does a thorough job of sourcing data that demonstrates the three-year pattern. (Before one challenges with the obvious example, Menand argues that the Beatles did not violate his rule but instead attained *two consecutive* three-year periods.) This is not to say that individuals do not remain famous or revered, but the desire for people to know all the things about an individual—the residual—has a surprisingly short shelf life. Menand writes, "Stardom is the condition in which the star penetrates reality so thoroughly that you feel you can no more run away from it than you can run away from oxygen. Then suddenly there is a different oxygen." Or, as Harvey put it to me, "I left home and then was somewhat out of the loop. For the younger people, like myself, the grandeur of Tillie's accomplishments receded because we became parts of different cultures and, for a few of us, went on to bigger worlds. The Waldorf, Tillie's living room was not."

Increasingly, that time span between the rise and evaporation of celebrity is getting shorter. The gale-force winds of technology and new media sites have made it almost impossible for a celebrity to remain relevant to his or her fan base without leaking more and more information to the public sphere. Yes, there are stars who will always have another major blockbuster to act in or ad campaign to plaster their face across, which will help maintain their existence in the camera's flash. But those celebrities who rely completely on cultivating their public persona to maintain their celebrity must provide an almost constant newsfeed reporting on their lives. The public is not interested in what happened to a celebrity two weeks ago; the public is interested in what happened to him or her two hours ago. Individuals with public profiles are then challenged with the choice of oversharing or losing the media's attention. For those in mainstream and democratic celebrity, the cost of discretion is the loss of stardom.

The transformation of celebrity is not dissimilar from changes happening within other realms of society and the economy—including labor mobility, inequality, and capital flows—that are reactions to twenty-first-century revolutions: globalization, technology, oversaturated and rapid-fire media, and so forth. The journalist Thomas Friedman has warned the United States to pay attention to Indian innovators or it will lose its supreme position. Martin Jacques, an academic and the former editor of *Marxism Today*, argues that China will overtake Western hegemony and dominance.[9] Their arguments are not a million miles from the broader point that technology and globalization have created lower barriers to entry, which in turn have enabled people (whether Indian entrepreneurs or YouTube exhibitionists) to compete on a larger scale and distribute information about their ideas or personae to a global audience.

Similarly, the "world is flat" when it comes to software competition, commerce, and the celebrity industry. The latter is no longer dominated by Hollywood; billions of dollars are being made by Bollywood and reality TV stars who will never visit Los Angeles and will still reap economic rewards for their celebrity. Through globalization and technology, celebrity has emerged as the defining example of cultural multipolarity. It has no central economic or social headquarters; the Internet, Hollywood, Bollywood, and reality TV are all viable and self-sufficient versions of mainstream celebrity. These nodes of celebrity may overlap, but there is no necessity that they do so.

So much of the transformation and future of celebrity will be a function of its present and future relationship to the media. Celebrity, as a social phenomenon and economic juggernaut, hinges essentially on the public's awareness of and consequential interest in particular individuals. As such, celebrity and celebrities will rely on new forms of media in addition to the old guard of newspapers and tabloids, in a process that the media scholar Henry Jenkins calls "convergence culture," whereby different media systems coexist and can act as substitutes for one another. Ultimately the news-feeds, whether print or online, are all just information. How will *People* or *HELLO!* sustain weekly publications in the face of online news sources such as omg! or Perez Hilton, which give the public real-time updates on stars' lives? Like the *New York Times* and other print publications, glossy weeklies will have to rely on a contingent of the population that enjoys the tactile experience of reading news on paper rather than on a computer screen, BlackBerry, Kindle, or iPad. But their numbers are dwindling.

New media forms have enabled viewers to become participants rather than merely adoring fans—what Jenkins calls "participatory culture." *American Idol* allows its viewers to dictate the outcome of the show and bloggers and tweeters are only as popular and influential as those who read their updates allow them to be. All-residual celebrities have always existed, but no one would ever characterize Paris Hilton or Edie Sedgwick as conventional. Reality TV and social media have given truly ordinary people a sparkling veneer. Celebrity has never been just about talent, but it has also never been so clearly just about celebrity residual as it is in contemporary society. As the historian Leo Braudy remarked, "Fame, which used to be connected to honor, and bestowed by achievement, has now become so separated from either that it exists in a category of its own, frequently valueless and often unrelated to anything resembling actual accomplishment."[10]

How long will this last? Over the long term will society again seek out those individuals who are truly talented? At some point will fans demand something more solid to admire than a star's carefully cultivated persona? If in fact society begins to demand some form of talent (or at least true uniqueness of character) as a requisite for stardom, what will happen to our democratic media forms? Will new media forms start to operate more like traditional forms (that is, operate based on profitability)? Will Twitter require a minimum number of followers for an individual to keep an account open? Will YouTube remove videos that don't make a base count of views? Will blog sites require a head count of unique page visits for a member's blog to remain on the web?

Given that having additional tweeters or bloggers is essentially costless, it would seem unlikely that these forms of media will become more elite in their membership criteria. Perhaps, however, as YouTube has done by creating a subscriber option to watch some of its online personalities, other social media sites will find ways for users to sift through all of the noise to find those contributors with a critical mass of followers. Already YouTube is looking for ways to sort content based on a user's video-watching history so that users link to videos that seem to align with their interests. Media sites may also begin to charge for use, creating another self-selection mechanism for both aspiring stars and those who follow them. Monetizing the democratic celebrity will force both fans and stars to decide whether they really want to participate in the process. Would you pay ten dollars a month to keep your Twitter account open? Would you pay one dollar a month to follow a particular person? The commodification of democratic stardom will mean it is no longer really democratic. Even *Ameri-*

can Idol, which maintains a front of offering a chance for anyone to become a superstar, requires fans to text or call in votes (which benefits telephone companies and charges fans). The show also slaps its brand on anything it can. As such, its stars must really demonstrate they can capture the audience's interest. *American Idol* winners may have come from humble origins and may have never had a shot with a recording studio without the show's help, but when they start singing, it's apparent that the finalists of the show are not just ordinary people.

And what of the increased narcissism that goes hand in hand with celebrity culture? Not all stars on the big screen or in our small towns are egomaniacs, to be sure. But celebrity has become so associated with wealth, media exposure, and obsession that large contingents of the population want to attain it simply on its own, divorced from any achievement. For many sociologists and psychologists, this is a very problematic trend. The University of Southern California professors Drew Pinsky and Mark Young found that celebrities are disproportionately more likely than civilians to exhibit the traits of clinical narcissism.[11] The human development scholar Orville Brim notes that four million American adults list fame as their number one life goal and 2 percent of individuals are "consumed" by their desire to be a star.[12]

Contemporary society can be defined by its "look at me" culture, which is visible on Facebook as much as in Hollywood. Recent studies have found that increasing numbers of adolescents in the general population are rating high on the Narcissistic Personality Inventory (NPI). The studies' results noted a marked upswing in high NPI scores in 2002, which uncannily correlates with the rise of social media sites.[13] What are the ramifications of a culture of people addicted to sharing so much—too much, perhaps—about themselves? Would these individuals be narcissists if not for the rise of social media that enables that part of their personality to develop? "Whether the sites are a breeding ground for narcissists or just a watering hole," *Scientific American* writer David DiSalvo muses, "it is hard not to think of the spectacular rise of social networking as part and parcel of the culture of entitlement."[14]

Then there's the simple fact that when we're tweeting and updating Facebook, we're not studying for exams or working hard at our jobs (most Facebook activity and trolling celebrity websites happens at work).[15] Some celebrities do need to be in the public eye. Their public genuinely wants to know about their lives, and part of their appeal as authors, actors, or politicians may rest in their oversharing. But what about the all-residual relative celebrities? Would the girl cultivating her Facebook celebrity devote that time and effort to something more meaningful—like writing a book or going to law school? Or perhaps cultivating her relative celebrity is actually maximizing her potential; maybe she wouldn't have become a lawyer or author anyway.

But with 400 million Facebook users worldwide, 2.5 million unique monthly visitors to PerezHilton.com, and 10 million unique monthly visitors to TMZ, we need to ask ourselves what we're doing in following celebrities.[16] We're the very ones who sustain Houdini's trick. According to Compete.com, U.S. Facebook membership alone had reached 132 million by December 2009.[17] Users spend over fifty-five minutes a day on the site, and 35 million users worldwide update their status *every day*.[18] Mark Zuckerberg, founder of Facebook, doesn't see an end to these numbers: "Next year, Facebook users will share twice as much information as they share this year, and next year, they will be sharing twice as much as they did the year before."[19] One has to wonder why we care so much about people who for all intents and purposes could be fictional characters for how little impact they have on our real worlds. Current news—that is, stories about politics or world events—actually does have an impact on our lives (big and small) and, if nothing else, matters to the world at large and to the broader scope of how history is written. It's not surprising that we care about what's happening in the Sudan or China's economic policy or the latest Senate bill passed (or endlessly filibustered); such events may have direct influence on our future. Even if the 2010 Haiti earthquake or the 2004 Indian Ocean tsunami did not affect us directly, they are tragedies of such magnitude, and from these natural disasters emerge such important stories about the human condition, that our fascination with and investment in their outcome are unsurprising. But why we care about Jennifer Aniston's coffee order or Sienna Miller's relationship with a married man or our friend's trivial yet incessantly updated Facebook status—well, that's something entirely different. In fact, let's be honest, on the whole many of us care far more about Aniston's latte than the thousands being brutally murdered in the Sudan. It's a terrifying reality of contemporary culture, made worse by the fact that we have the tools and resources for anyone to know about the atrocities and important events going on around the world and yet we still are consumed with the banality of other people's lives. This observation is not to say we shouldn't be somewhat interested in others, but not to such a degree that it distracts us from critical things going on in society.

This book describes the mechanics of how celebrity works, but despite all of the variables involved in creating stars, our participation is the essential mechanism. Celebrity ultimately hinges on whether we decide to pay attention or not. Some of our increased attention and the acute nature of current celebrity culture can be explained by the restructuring of society into more loosely knit connections, and some can be explained by the rise of instant and easily accessible information brought forth via new technology and media. While our fascination with celebrities may ebb and flow, it will not disappear; our curiosity in other people and the personal narrative of their lives has always existed, whether M, Aunt Tillie, Princess Diana, or Paris Hilton. There is a paradoxical element to our interest too: Obsessing about people we think are beautiful, interesting, charismatic, or curious is a pleasant and seemingly harmless way to pass the time. In a world filled with strife and anxiety, celebrity is a sugar-coated outlet of distraction. Yet with all the dreams made and broken, the places and networks necessary for producing stars, and the billions of dollars and thousands of jobs dependent on celebrities' existence, celebrity as an economic system and social phenomenon is not so ephemeral and superficial after all.

Appendix A: Bureau of Labor Statistics Data by Occupation and Payroll (2008); Census Data (County Business Patterns) by Establishment (2007)

Table 1. Occupational Employment Statistics, Number of Employees[a]

	Celeb-driven	Handler	Media	Prep	Support	Tot. Celeb.
LA	34,800	5,320	64,850	678	1,310	106,958
NYC	12,020	7,980	88,190	293	500	108,983

a. Per note 2 to chapter 4, I incorporate only a percentage of total support and prep workers, establishments, and payroll figures in my analysis of the celebrity industry, as not all individuals working in these jobs are working directly with celebrities (1.9 percent in Los Angeles and 0.4 percent in New York City). These charts reflect the approximated numbers of support and prep workers, establishments, and payroll figures associated with the celebrity industry. There is no meaningful way to gauge how many support and prep establishments deal with celebrities, as firms range in size and resources. Approximated employment numbers are a conservative estimate due to the nature of the data—for example, one cannot know with certainty which manicurists and fitness trainers work with stars versus ordinary folks.

Table 2. County Business Pattern Industry Data, Number of Establishments

	Celeb-driven	Handler	Media	Prep	Support	Tot. Celeb.
LA	974	1,915	1,946	4,316	10,993	20,144
NYC	1,296	2,648	3,562	12,461	16,812	36,779

Table 3. Bureau of Labor Statistics, Payroll (in dollars)

	Celeb-driven	Handler	Media	Prep	Support	Tot. Celeb.
LA	1,541,451,444	536,621,000	3,526,262,600	1,099,856,400	5,002,608,100	11,706,799,544
NYC	810,150,784	950,788,500	4,896,616,400	2,532,564,200	11,339,303,200	20,529,423,084

Table 4. Industry Codes Incorporated in Celebrity Industry Analysis

Industry Code	Type[b]	Industry Code Description
51111	M	Newspaper Publishers
51112	M	Periodical Publishers
51611	M	Internet Publishing and Broadcasting
54111	S	Offices of Lawyers
54181	S	Advertising Agencies
54182	H	Public Relations Agencies
54183	M	Media Buying Agencies
54184	M	Media Representatives
54191	S	Marketing Research and Public Opinion Polling
54192	M	Photographic Services
71111	E	Theater Companies and Dinner Theaters
71113	E	Musical Groups and Artists
71119	E	Other Performng Arts Companies
71131	H	Promoters of Performing Arts, Sports, and Similar Events with Facilities
71132	H	Promoters of Performing Arts, Sports, and Similar Events Without Facilities
71141	H	Agents and Managers for Artists, Athletes, Entertainers, and Other Public Figures
71151	E	Independent Artists, Writers, and Performers
71394	P	Fitness and Recreational Sports Centers

| 81211 | P | Hair, Nail, and Skin Care Services |
| 81219 | P | Other Personal Care Services |

b. M = Media, S = Support, H = Handlers, E = Entertainment/Celebrity-Driven, P = Prep

Table 5. Occupational Employment Statistics: Occupational Codes Included in Celebrity Industry Analysis

OCC Code	Type^c	OCC Title
11-2031	H	Public Relations Managers
13-1011	H	Agents and Business Managers of Artists, Performers, and Athletes
19-3022	S	Survery Researchers
23-1011	S	Lawyers
27-2011	E	Actors
27-2021	E	Athletes and Sports Competitors
27-2042	E	Musicians and Singers
27-2099	E	Entertainers and Performers, Sports and Related Workers, All Other
27-3011	M	Radio and Television Announcers
27-3012	M	Public Address System and Other Announcers
27-3021	M	Broadcast News Analysts
27-3022	M	Reporters and Correspondents
27-3031	M	Public Relations Specialists
27-3041	M	Editors
27-3043	M	Writers and Authors
27-3099	M	Media and Communication Workers, All Other
27-4011	M	Audio and Video Equipment Technicians
27-4012	M	Broadcast Technicians
27-4013	M	Radio Operators
27-4014	M	Sound Engineering Technicians
27-4021	M	Photographers
27-4031	M	Camera Operators, Television, Video, and Motion Picture
27-4032	M	Film and Video Editors
27-4099	M	Media and Communication Equipment Workers, All Other

29-1029	P	Dentists, All Other Specialists
29-1031	P	Dieticians and Nutritionists
39-3092	P	Costume Attendants
39-3093	P	Locker Room, Coatroom, and Dressing Room Attendants
39-3099	P	Entertainment Attendants and Related Workers, All Other
39-5012	P	Hairdressers, Hairstylists, and Cosmetologists
39-5091	P	Makeup Artists, Theatrical and Performance
39-5092	P	Manicurists and Pedicurists
39-5093	P	Shampooers
39-5094	P	Skin Care Specialists
39-9031	P	Fitness Trainers and Aerobics Instructors
43-4111	M	Interviewers, Except Eligibility and Loan
43-5021	S	Couriers and Messengers
51-5023	S	Printing Machine Operators
51-6051	P	Sewers, Hand
51-6052	P	Tailors, Dressmakers, and Custom Sewers
51-9071	P	Jewelers and Precious Stone and Metal Workers
51-9131	M	Photographic Process Workers
51-9132	M	Photographic Processing Machine Operators
53-3041	S	Taxi Drivers and Chauffeurs
53-6021	S	Parking Lot Attendants

c. H = Handlers, S = Support, E = Entertainment/Celebrity-Driven, M = Media

Appendix B: Social Network Analysis Results

Table 1. General Properties of the Getty Images Celebrity Network

	Full Network	More than 4 Photographs
Nodes	66,100	6,754
Edges	2,705,937	798,636
Density	0.0006	0.0175
Average degree	75.74	236.49

Table 2. CPL and CC for Celebrity Network and Random Network

	CPL	CC
Getty Image celebrity network	2.55	0.45
Random network (average of three computer simulation generated networks)	2.1	0.02
Theoretical random network	–	0
Theoretical random bipartite network[a]	–	0.1
Ratio of celebrity network to theoretical random bipartite network	1.21	4.5

a. Mark E. J. Newman, Steven H. Strogatz, and Duncan J. Watts, "Random Graphs with Arbitrary Degree Distributions and Their Applications," *Physical Review* 64, no. 2 (2001).

The Getty network is a small world, which means that individuals can reach one another through a few steps. Small-world networks are characterized by measuring the clustering coefficient (CC) and the characteristic path length (CPL) and comparing these results to a random network. The CPL measures the number of nodes between any two nodes within a network, also known as "degrees of separation." The CC measures how many of a node's contacts are connected to one another. Most random networks have a short CPL, but the CC of random networks is low. Small worlds, however, have both short CPL and very high CC compared to a random network. In our network, n, number of nodes, is 6,754; k, average degree, is 0.1605. The requirement stated by the hypothesis is, therefore, that $Q(CPL) \approx 1$ and $Q(CC) > 1$, where Q is the ratio of the metrics between the studied network and random network (Uzzi et al., 2007). In our network, $Q(CPL) = 1.21$ and $Q(CC) = 4.5$. See Jerrold W. Grossman, "The Evolution of the Mathematical Research Collaboration Graph," 2003, www.oakland.edu/~grossman/eddie.pdf; Stefan Bornholdt and Heinz Georg Schuster, eds., *Handbook of Graphs and Networks* (Weinheim, Germany: Wiley-VCH, 2003); Uzzi, Amaral, and Reed-Tsochas, "Small-World Networks and Management Science Research"; Stanley Wasserman and Katherine Faust, *Social Network Analysis* (New York: Cambridge University Press, 1994); Watts and Strogatz, "Collective Dynamics of 'Small-World' Networks."

Table 3. Social Network Analysis Comparison of Talent vs. Media-Driven Celebrities

	Top 20 Star Currency	Top 20 Media Volume
Minimum Star Currency rank	1	2
Maximum Star Currency rank	20	645
Stars (tried to select)	20	12
Stars in the group	20	20
Links	63	60
Density	0.33	0.32
Average degree	3.15	3
Components	3	2
Inclusiveness	0.95	0.95
Transitivity	0.64	0.57

Clustering coefficient	0.61	0.71
Mean distance	1.61	1.77
Diameter	4	3
Connectedness	0.72	0.9
Efficiency	0.58	0.69

Stars Included in Top 20 (A-list), Middle 20 (B-list), and Bottom 20 (C-List), *Forbes* Star Currency, 2009

TOP 20

Will Smith, Johnny Depp, Leonardo DiCaprio, Angelina Jolie, Brad Pitt, Tom Hanks, George Clooney, Denzel Washington, Matt Damon, Jack Nicholson, Julia Roberts, Adam Sandler, Tom Cruise, Russell Crowe, Will Ferrell, Meryl Streep, Robert De Niro, Ben Stiller, Jim Carrey, Clint Eastwood

MIDDLE 20

Neil Patrick Harris, Emma Roberts, Amanda Seyfried, Jeremy Sisto, Jenna Elfman, Dominic West, Vanessa L. Williams, Lara Flynn Boyle, Chiwetel Ejiofor, Anton Yelchin, Kevin Dillon, Delroy Lindo, Alan Alda, Ellen Burstyn, Melissa George, Timothy Hutton, Dax Shepard, Jamie-Lynn Sigler, Shane West, Julie Andrews, Bob Balaban

BOTTOM 20

William Adams, Scout Taylor-Compton, Clancy Brown, Sara Paxton, Joanne Whalley, Ashley Scott, Kevin Zigers, Gil Bellows, Jurnee Smollett, Karen Allen, Brady Corbet, Laura Ramsey, Melonie Diaz, Mary Lynn Rajskub, Odette Yustman, Cameron Richardson, Busy Philipps, Nathan Corddry, Lynn Collins, Kathryn Hahn, Josh Flitter, Zoë Kravitz, Alexie Gilmore, Mike Vogel, Jensen Ackles, Kristin Kreuk, Nate Hartley, DeRay Davis, Juno Temple, Malinda Williams, Ryan Pinkston, KaDee Strickland, Shaun Toub, Justina Machado, Sasha Alexander

Table 4. Top 20 Individuals by Google Blog Coverage

Rank	Name	Volume	Star Currency Rank
1	Michael Jackson	952,568	–
2	Britney Spears	125,704	–
3	Madonna	81,507	–
4	Paris Hilton	77,913	645
5	Beyoncé	64,557	210
6	Lindsay Lohan	62,513	153
7	Angelina Jolie	52,161	2
8	Brad Pitt	44,591	2
9	Jessica Simpson	44,259	462
10	Tom Cruise	42,770	13
11	Justin Timberlake	42,427	180
12	Anna Nicole Smith	38,027	–
13	Jennifer Aniston	37,577	55
14	Johnny Depp	37,550	2
15	Mariah Carey	36,195	–
16	Kanye West	35,786	–
17	Jessica Alba	34,689	108
18	Christina Aguilera	33,760	–
19	Miley Cyrus	33,064	177
20	Kim Kardashian	32,609	–

Appendix C: Multivariate Regression Results for Star Currency and Media Volume

Table 1. Model Summary: Star Currency Score				
Model	R	R Square	Adjusted R Square	Standard Error of Estimate
1	.509[a]	.259	.242	1.66378
2	.509[b]	.259	.243	1.66279
3	.509[c]	.259	.243	1.66181
4	.509[d]	.259	.244	1.66083
5	.509[e]	.259	.245	1.65986
6	.509[f]	.259	.246	1.65906
7	.509[g]	.259	.247	1.65834
8	.508[h]	.258	.247	1.65820
9	.507[i]	.257	.246	1.65851
10	.506[j]	.256	.246	1.65883
11	.504[k]	.254	.246	1.65952
12	.503[l]	.253	.245	1.66043
13	.501[m]	.251	.244	1.66103

a. Predictors (independent variables): (Constant), otherh, NYh, NVs, AUSh, GBRs, FRAh, FLh, DEUh, CAh, JPNs, GBRh, DEUs, NVh, NYs, JPNh, FLs, FRAs, AUSs, others, CAs

b. Predictors: (Constant), otherh, NYh, NVs, AUSh, GBRs, FRAh, FLh, DEUh, CAh, GBRh, DEUs, NVh, NYs, JPNh, FLs, FRAs, AUSs, others, CAs

c. Predictors: (Constant), otherh, NYh, NVs, AUSh, GBRs, FLh, DEUh, CAh, GBRh, DEUs, NVh, NYs, JPNh, FLs, FRAs, AUSs, others, CAs

d. Predictors: (Constant), otherh, NYh, AUSh, GBRs, FLh, DEUh, CAh, GBRh, DEUs, NVh, NYs, JPNh, FLs, FRAs, AUSs, others, CAs

e. Predictors: (Constant), otherh, AUSh, GBRs, FLh, DEUh, CAh, GBRh, DEUs, NVh, NYs, JPNh, FLs, FRAs, AUSs, others, CAs

f. Predictors: (Constant), otherh, AUSh, GBRs, FLh, DEUh, CAh, GBRh, DEUs, NVh, NYs, JPNh, FRAs, AUSs, others, CAs

g. Predictors: (Constant), otherh, AUSh, GBRs, FLh, CAh, GBRh, DEUs, NVh, NYs, JPNh, FRAs, AUSs, others, CAs

h. Predictors: (Constant), AUSh, GBRs, FLh, CAh, GBRh, DEUs, NVh, NYs, JPNh, FRAs, AUSs, others, CAs

i. Predictors: (Constant), AUSh, GBRs, CAh, GBRh, DEUs, NVh, NYs, JPNh, FRAs, AUSs, others, CAs

j. Predictors: (Constant), AUSh, GBRs, CAh, GBRh, DEUs, NVh, NYs, JPNh, AUSs, others, CAs

k. Predictors: (Constant), GBRs, CAh, GBRh, DEUs, NVh, NYs, JPNh, AUSs, others, CAs

l. Predictors: (Constant), GBRs, GBRh, DEUs, NVh, NYs, JPNh, AUSs, others, CAs

m. Predictors: (Constant), GBRs, GBRh, DEUs, NVh, NYs, JPNh, AUSs, others

Table 2. Star Currency Model Results

Coefficients[a]

Model	Unstandardized Coefficients B	Std. Error	Standardized Coefficients Beta	t	Sig.
13 (Constant)	3.204	.086	–	37.306	.000
NYs	.212	.047	.144	4.544	.000
GBRs	.432	.085	.184	5.073	.000
AUSs	.364	.147	.076	2.475	.014
DEUs	.415	.189	.069	2.202	.028
others	.380	.046	.273	8.206	.000
GBRh	–.099	.053	–.066	–1.870	.062
NVh	–.272	.151	–.054	–1.800	.072
JPNh	1.696	.442	.116	3.841	.000

a. Dependent variable: Star Currency score

Table 3. Model Summary: Google Media Volume

Model	R	R Square	Adjusted R Square	Standard Error of Estimate
1	.606ª	.367	.352	5350.311
2	.606ᵇ	.367	.353	5347.156
3	.606ᶜ	.367	.353	5344.050
4	.605ᵈ	.366	.354	5342.997
5	.605ᵉ	.366	.354	5342.174
6	.604ᶠ	.365	.354	5341.702
7	.604ᵍ	.364	.354	5341.737
8	.603ʰ	.364	.354	5341.670
9	.603ⁱ	.363	.354	5339.923
10	.602ʲ	.362	.354	5340.718

a. Predictors (independent variables): (Constant), otherh, NYh, NVs, AUSh, GBRs, FRAh, FLh, DEUh, CAh, JPNs, GBRh, DEUs, NVh, NYs, JPNh, FLs, FRAs, AUSs, others, CAs

b. Predictors: (Constant), otherh, NYh, NVs, AUSh, GBRs, FLh, DEUh, CAh, JPNs, GBRh, DEUs, NVh, NYs, JPNh, FLs, FRAs, AUSs, others, CAs

c. Predictors: (Constant), otherh, NYh, NVs, AUSh, GBRs, FLh, DEUh, CAh, JPNs, DEUs, NVh, NYs, JPNh, FLs, FRAs, AUSs, others, CAs

d. Predictors: (Constant), otherh, NYh, NVs, AUSh, GBRs, DEUh, CAh, JPNs, DEUs, NVh, NYs, JPNh, FLs, FRAs, AUSs, others, CAs

e. Predictors: (Constant), otherh, NYh, NVs, AUSh, GBRs, DEUh, CAh, JPNs, DEUs, NVh, NYs, JPNh, FLs, AUSs, others, CAs

f. Predictors: (Constant), otherh, NYh, AUSh, GBRs, DEUh, CAh, JPNs, DEUs, NVh, NYs, JPNh, FLs, AUSs, others, CAs

g. Predictors: (Constant), otherh, NYh, AUSh, GBRs, DEUh, CAh, JPNs, DEUs, NVh, JPNh, FLs, AUSs, others, CAs

h. Predictors: (Constant), otherh, NYh, AUSh, GBRs, CAh, JPNs, DEUs, NVh, JPNh, FLs, AUSs, others, CAs

i. Predictors: (Constant), otherh, NYh, AUSh, GBRs, CAh, JPNs, NVh, JPNh, FLs, AUSs, others, CAs

j. Predictors: (Constant), NYh, AUSh, GBRs, CAh, JPNs, NVh, JPNh, FLs, AUSs, others, CAs

Table 4. Google Media Volume Results

Coefficients[a]

Model	Unstandardized Coefficients		Standardized Coefficients		
	B	Std. Error	Beta	t	Sig.
10 (Constant)	−1324.156	321.455		-4.119	.000
CAs	1096.034	157.059	.252	6.978	.000
GBRs	1227.955	232.123	.150	5.290	.000
JPNs	2428.748	1066.364	.073	2.278	.023
AUSs	2170.539	603.282	.131	3.598	.000
FLs	2281.257	395.572	.170	5.767	.000
others	1019.097	150.706	.210	6.762	.000
CAh	172.352	60.373	.095	2.855	.004
NYh	159.757	68.760	.066	2.323	.020
NVh	−1905.282	500.791	−.108	−3.805	.000
JPNh	5105.316	1661.869	.101	3.072	.002
AUSh	−742.305	312.893	−.086	−2.372	.018

a. Dependent variable: media volume

Appendix D: Geographical Information Systems Spatial Statistic Results

Los Angeles Cluster Statistics

	Global Moran's I		Z Score	
	Major Locations	**Minor Locations**	**Major Locations**	**Minor Locations**
Art	0.07	0.08	11.42	13.29
Music	0.19	0.21	30.25	33.30
Fashion[a]	0.18	0.18	28.93	28.93
Television	0.15	0.14	25.11	21.61
Film[a]	0.20	0.22	32.70	34.20
Theater	0.02	0.07	5.19	11.12
Magnet	0.12	0.17	18.83	27.37

New York Cluster Statistics

	Global Moran's I		Z Score	
	Major Locations	**Minor Locations**	**Major Locations**	**Minor Locations**
Art	0.07	0.09	10.09	12.42
Music	0.17	0.25	22.13	32.37
Fashion[a]	0.25	0.25	31.75	32.29
Television	0.17	0.17	24.72	21.80
Film[a]	0.17	0.26	22.58	32.84
Theater	0.22	0.27	37.07	36.78
Magnet	0.14	0.23	18.68	29.58

a. Fashion Week and festivals removed.

The above tables contain the spatial statistics output of our analysis of the Getty photographic database. The Moran's I value demonstrates whether or not there is a clustering pattern of the celebrity-driven industries' social scene. The Z score demonstrates the degree to which the output is statistically significant above the mean. In order to control for outlying events, Fashion Week was removed. Moran's I scores show the social scene clusters and the Z-scores show that this clustering is statistically significant. A Moran's I above 0 demonstrates clustering, and the higher the Z-score, the more significant the clustering.

Data was collected from Getty Images photographs documenting arts and entertainment events in New York and Los Angeles from March 2006 to February 2007. We acquired information about 6,004 events with a total of 309,414 images. Each logged event specified detailed information on date, location, and people in the photographs. After the data was collected, we cleaned and categorized each event record according to established criteria. First, we identified whether a photo was related to an event or to a "celebrity sighting" unrelated to an event. We removed these latter images from the database. The remaining events were coded into several categories: fashion, film, television, theater, art, music, magnet, and hybrid. An event was included in one of these categories if the host or organizer of the event was affiliated with a particular industry. There were, however, many events in which a particular industry could not be identified. For these events, we created two categories: *hybrid*, those events that crossed two cultural industry sectors (e.g., fashion and film), and *magnet* or *celebrity events*, social events that attract media attention and include appearances by multiple celebrities but are not affiliated with a particular industry (e.g., charity event, gala). Next, the physical location off each event was identified and mapped. We used the Global Moran's I statistic. This test enabled us to observe whether spatial autocorrelations occur based on feature locations and attributes, and produces a result that details the level of clustering, dispersion, or random nature of the data. The calculation produces a Moran's I value, where a value near +1.0 indicates clustering and a value near −1.0 indicates dispersion. The results of our analysis showed that events covered by Getty Images had a tendency to spatially cluster. In order to better understand the localities where this spatial clustering occurred, we employed the Getis-Ord or G^*i statistic, also known as the "hot spots stat," because it identifies areas that have higher values than expected in a random observation. Areas identified as hot spots using the G^*i statistic explain why values in a specific location are high, and also show that the results found in the "hot spot" are significant relative to the values found in the surrounding area. These results are visually represented in the maps on pages 125 and 126. For a complete analysis and report on the findings of this research, see Currid and Williams, "The Geography of Buzz."

Notes

1. Celebrity Today

1. David Marshall makes a similar point in *Celebrity and Power*. He looks beyond Hollywood and shows that celebrity emerges in other social and cultural contexts.
2. For discussions of multipolarity in foreign affairs and international politics, see Mansfield, "Concentration, Polarity and the Distribution of Power," and Haass, "The Age of Nonpolarity."
3. Frith, *Celeb Diaries*.
4. See Veblen, *Theory of the Leisure Class*, and Robinson, "Economics of Fashion Demand," for detailed discussion on elites and the masses.
5. Berridge, *Madame Tussaud*. Much of the discussion on Tussaud is informed by Berridge's work.
6. I interviewed Mark Richards, former sculptor for Madame Tussaud's, who was of great help in explaining the evolution of the wax museum from a small London shop to a worldwide franchise. When Richards worked at Tussaud's in the late 1980s, there were seven sculptors who worked right above the shop. In the time he was working there, the wax museum became a massive brand, and as a result the wax studio moved out of the center of London to a huge complex. As Richards put it, "It wasn't a shop anymore. It became a factory."
7. David Marshall makes the point that celebrity journalists were writing about celebrities in such a way that they were becoming as known for "their ordinariness along with their extraordinariness" ("Intimately Intertwined," p. 318).
8. In *Frenzy of Renown*, Leo Braudy argues that fame is essentially being talked about.
9. Gamson's *Claim to Fame* is an excellent account of the old Hollywood studio system and how stars were controlled by studios rather than as independent agents of their own accord.

10. The writer Susan Sontag's death prompted a similar documentation, though Sontag's death was mourned in part because of her great intellectual contributions to the public dialogue and her extraordinary writing and creativity—a much different sentiment from that felt toward Goody.

11. John Reynolds, "*OK!* Achieves Bumper Sales with Jade's Wedding Issues," *Media Week*, March 17, 2009, www.mediaweek.co.uk/news/891089/OK-achieves-bumper-sales-Jades-wedding-issues/.

12. Magazine Publishers of America, an industry association for consumer magazines.

13. See, for example, Florida, *Rise of the Creative Class*, for a detailed account of the changing socioeconomic demographics of the workforce.

14. Data taken from U.S. Census Bureau. See Casper and Bianchi, *Continuity and Change in the American Family*; Amato et al., *Alone Together*.

15. Florida, *Rise of the Creative Class*.

16. As the sociologist Robert Putnam noted in his famous book *Bowling Alone* (New York: Simon & Schuster, 2001), Americans no longer engage in civic and community associations that allow for social interaction and a sharing of collective experiences. David Marshall also discusses the way celebrity journalism acted as a means to fill the void, providing a "constellation of recognition" and "points of commonality" in an otherwise increasingly anonymous society (*Celebrity and Power*, p. 317).

17. To start with the first trend: In a day and age of globalization and placeless technology, we have evolved from small communities to large anonymous cities and suburbs. Of course this is nothing new. In the wake of the Industrial Revolution, urban sociologists decried the rise of the city as a social organization that makes people alienated, lonely, and without any close social ties. On gemeinschaft and gesellschaft and their implications, see Tonnies, *Community and Society*, and Weber, *Economy and Society*.

18. McPherson, Smith-Lovin, and Brashears, "Social Isolation in America." The General Social Survey is an in-person survey conducted by the National Opinion Research Center at the University of Chicago. From 1972 to 1994, the survey was conducted annually; since then it has been conducted biennially. Each year of the survey, approximately two thousand people are interviewed in forty states.

19. The changing social and economic landscape is marked by three

definitive trends: the rise of a globalized, community-less society; the abundance of technology and media outlets to transmit rapid information; and the monetization of practically every element of society. For an extraordinarily detailed look at the changing social landscape, see Florida, *Rise of the Creative Class*, and Conley, *Elsewhere U.S.A.*

20. Jenkins, *Convergence Culture.*
21. Fox, "Evolution, Alienation and Gossip."
22. Brown et al., "Social Closeness Increases Salivary Progesterone in Humans."
23. This topic is discussed more explicitly in Steven Lukes's *Power*. In his discussion of the "third dimension of power," he argues that both overt and covert methods can be used to control the political and issue agendas. In this case, the dominance of celebrity news avoids a public dialogue over "real issues" such as health care, the Iraq War, Afghanistan, and so forth. Also see Bachrach and Baratz, "Two Faces of Power." For a current angle on the use of celebrity to distract from political upheaval, see Jim Windolf, "The Obama-Salahi-Tiger-G.E.-Afghan Axis," *Vanity Fair*, December 7, 2009.
24. Turner, *Understanding Celebrity.*

2. The Celebrity Residual: The Inexplicable Brew of Talent, Fame, and Celebrity

1. Celebritynetworth,   www.celebritynetworth.com/richest-celebrities/paris-hilton-net-worth/.
2. Lynn Hirschberg, "The Self-Manufacture of Megan Fox," *New York Times Magazine*, November 15, 2009.
3. From media reports, it seems that Paris is no longer represented by Mintz but instead Michael Sitrick. Many media mentions of Hilton refer to "her spokesperson" or "her publicist" without elaborating on who this individual is. From the enormous number of articles written about Paris, it appears she has many publicists/spokespeople working for her including Mintz, Sitrick, Lori Zelenko, and manager Jamie Freed. See Laura Barton, "The Message Behind Paris's 'Demure' New Look," *Guardian*, June 28, 2007; Mike Sitrick and Doree Shafrir, "Paris Hilton's New Best Friend," Gawker.com, 2007; "What It Iz: Chris Brown Hires Paris Hilton's Publicist," Power953.com, February 18, 2009; "Paris Hilton Fiddles with Fairy Dust," Just-Jared.com, November 30, 2008; IANS, "Paris Hilton to Sue New

Zealand Company for Billboard Ad," *Entertainment Daily*, November 9, 2009.

4. Page Six is considered the ultimate gossip column. It has been widely known to make or break careers and is followed relentlessly by the New York City, Los Angeles, and London media, tycoons, and celebrity set.

5. Irony of ironies is that Kathy had her own reality TV show that capitalized on Paris's celebrity. The show tanked.

6. The residual is more traditionally used in statistics to explain the difference between the observed value of the dependent variable and the predicted value of the dependent variable based on the regression model. Quite simply, the residual is the difference between what we expect to observe and what we actually do observe. In the 1950s, the Nobel Prize–winning economist Robert M. Solow put forth the theory of the residual as being meaningful in his study of economic growth, where he suggested that it was not capital accumulation or increases in labor that explained growth but instead technological innovation, an almost impossible variable to measure ("Technical Change and the Aggregate Production Function," *Review of Economics and Statistics* 39, no. 3 [1957]: 312–20). This finding became known as the Solow Residual. In my example here, stardom is the dependent variable. One might think talent or even "being known" are the obvious variables that predict star status, but many noncelebrities have both of these variables—some in even greater quantity than celebrities. Thus there are inexplicable variables other than those we think ought to predict celebrity status; these make up the celebrity residual.

7. For an empirical study of the difference between talent and talentless success, see Gergaud and Verardi, "Untalented but Successful." Gergaud and Verardi looked at a Pokémon card game and studied the differences in outcome between those identified as talented and untalented. They found that these distinctions are not mutually exclusive, as we witness in real life where truly talented and merely celebrated stars cohabitate.

8. Gladwell, *Outliers*, discusses the interplay of multiple variables that have helped shape the success of Gates, among others.

9. Marian Burros, "Mrs. Obama Speaks Out About Her Household," *New York Times*, March 20, 2009.

10. See Schweinberger et al., "Event-Related Brain Potential Evidence";

David, "News Concreteness and Visual-Verbal Association"; Hagtvedt and Patrick, "Art Infusion."

11. See Cowen, *What Price Fame?* for a look at the same phenomenon with regard to brands and products. Cowen argues that celebrity endorsements are most effective when the product's quality is hard to measure, which is why you get endorsements for hair spray but not hardware nails.

12. See Lewis, *Moneyball*, for an extraordinarily detailed and riveting account of how scouts and coaches misuse statistics.

13. Ibid., p. 34.

14. David Carr, "How Palin Became a Brand," *New York Times*, April 5, 2010.

15. Ted Johnson, "Where Reality and DC Collide," Politico, November 30, 2009, www.politico.com/news/stories/1109/29974.html.

16. Caves, in *Creative Industries*, does an excellent job outlining the unique properties of the "creative industries"—fashion, art, music, design, film, and so forth. He argues that these industries operate in "uncertain markets" with a "nobody knows" property. In other words, the ability to gauge how good something is in these industries is impossible until the product hits the market. Even then, with the various ways a cultural good is evaluated, the critique is subjective. Similarly, see Faulkner and Anderson, "Short-Term Projects and Emergent Careers," for an extensive study of Hollywood films and the directors and producers associated with them. They discovered that despite awards, there was no correlation between previous success (e.g., winning Oscars) and future success in producing films.

17. Joe Lewis, the British billionaire owner of ENIC International Ltd. and main investor in Tavistock Group, is a perfect example of this model. He is a generally reclusive man who now lives in the Bahamas, and the public's knowledge of his personal life is just a brief sketch.

18. There are always exceptions, Nicola Horlick and Donald Trump, for example. Both, however, are more "celebrated" for their personal lives. In general, in finance, people are considered worth talking to in direct proportion to their number of successful deals. Successful asset managers are those who have an impressive performance track record. These observations have been deduced from my conversations with people who work in the industry.

19. Media hits were calculated through Google News.

20. See Forbes Celebrity 100 (2009) and Absolute Return + Alpha, "Top 25 Highest-Earning Hedge Fund Managers." Earnings were calculated by "the managers' shares of their firm's performance and management fees, as well as gains on their own capital invested in their funds."

21. Perhaps one of the clearest ways to measure celebrity is by looking at biographies. Biographies of course are not a laundry list of job titles and awards. A biography, by its very etymology, is the story of a person's life. Of course, there wouldn't be a market for them if we were not interested in others' lives. Biographies wouldn't make it to the top of the bestseller list if particular individuals weren't celebrated more than others. So a very interesting way to capture where celebrity emerges is to look at who gets written about. Sure enough, merit-driven industries are less likely on the whole to have a preponderance of biographies. Barring the truly exceptional, most biographies are written about individuals in ambiguously measured industries. As the economist Tyler Cowen has pointed out in *What Price Fame?* there has been a massive transformation of biographies from being serious treatises on the life and times of people of obvious merit, such as philosophers or political leaders, to books on entertainment figures and those with spectacular personal lives. Cowen notes that in the early 1900s, 46 percent of all biographies published in the United States were of political leaders. By 1940, political biographies had declined to represent a quarter of all published. During this same time period, entertainment biographies increased from a 26 percent share to 55 percent in 1940. However, in this time period, more than three-quarters of these biographies were of serious, "high-art" entertainers. By 1940, only 9 percent of the entertainment biographies were of "serious people" making obviously merit-worthy contributions to society.

22. It should be noted that Buffett also owns a $4 million property in Laguna Beach, California, and a private jet he named *The Indefensible*. These are Buffett's only extravagances and run against his public castigation of wild CEO expenditures. *Forbes* argues that the Laguna Beach house is worth less than a hundredth percentage point of his net worth. See "Homes of the Billionaires," Forbes.com, March 28, 2009.

23. See Trump's *Never Give Up*, *The Art of the Deal*, and *How to Get Rich*; Jeffery Slonim, "Donald Trump Shelters Jennifer Hudson," *People*, November 11, 2008; Caris Davis, "Trump Wins at Wrestle-

mania, Keeps His Hair," *People*, April 2, 2007; Todd Peterson, "Melania Trump: Giving Birth Was 'Easy,'" *People*, April 6, 2006; K. C. Baker et al., "Donald Trump's Wife Pregnant," *People*, September 27, 2005; Stephen Silverman, "Trump's Bride to Wear $100,000 Dior Gown," *People*, January 18, 2005.

24. Google, "Year-End Zeitgeist: Top Searches in 2006." Google Zeitgeist has aggregate data on search for 2004 onward. Complete methodology of the Zeitgeist data set is also available.

25. Based on an interview with a former *OK!* editor.

3. The Relative Celebrity (or, The Biggest Star You Never Heard Of)

1. Before getting into Games Workshop, the average reader is likely wondering what exactly are war gaming and role playing. The latter is somewhat self-explanatory (you take on a role of someone other than yourself in some fantasy scenario like Dungeons and Dragons), but war gaming is a craze worth further description. War games are essentially simulated military exercises set in particular eras, historical contexts, or environments both real and made up. While the U.S. Department of Defense actually enacts war games with great gravity in order to protect the country, there is an entire subculture of hobbyists who play war games purely for entertainment. The board game Risk is considered the first of such games. Not surprisingly, war games are a part of a larger role-playing genre that includes science fiction and fantasy subculture. But in the last several decades, war gaming has become a particularly unusual and all-encompassing hobby that has transcended its original categorization, becoming its own genre. Within this curious world of war gaming, the Games Workshop has become a pivotal player and in itself its own subculture.

2. Games Workshop offers a variety of fantasy battle situations from futuristic space wars to *Lord of the Rings* (which the company acquired rights to). The games involve collecting a large number of miniatures, each of which is endowed with specific skills, rights, and movements on the battlefield. The miniatures are unpainted pieces of steel and ceramic, and part of the game involves painting one's own actors. In order to participate, one needs to have the rule book, special paint sets with correct colors, and the key models to begin playing. Of course, each game has its own particular models, paint, and rules. An enormous spray paint gun is also on offer for ease and effi-

ciency in miniature preparation. In order to play Warhammer, one of
the Workshop's key games, a hobbyist must have Citadel miniatures,
Dwarfs, Dwarf Thunderers, Dwarf Miners, Goblins of a great variety (Night Goblin Spearmen and Night Goblin Archers, among others), the rule book, and the requisite plastic scenery and paint. There
are various military operations, goals, and situations that are game
specific. While obviously these games can be played in the privacy of
one's home, due to the need for infrastructure and scenery, and the
desire to find other people to play with, many of the games are
played at Games Workshop events, including the world-famous
Games Day held in Birmingham, a few hours north of London.

2. Sure, some relative celebrities end up becoming mainstream, but
   that's rarely the point. Just ask Tron Guy. Jay Maynard, a computer
   programmer, went from geek to Internet celebrity when pictures of
   him in his luminescent costume inspired by the Disney science-fiction
   movie *Tron* showed up all over the Internet. Soon, Maynard ended
   up on *Jimmy Kimmel Live* and an episode of *South Park*, and was a
   headliner for the Internet celebrity conference ROFLCon. But all
   Tron Guy really wanted to do was saunter about Fairmont, Minnesota, in his special white one-piece suit.

3. There's been a lot of talk about "microfame" in the media. But the
   assumption is always that "microfame" (particularly Internet stardom) is a stop on the road to becoming a mainstream "macro"
   celebrity. This argument misses the real point of these micro versions
   of stardom, which is that they exist in their own social and economic
   stratospheres.

4. Relative celebrity emerges through similar channels as other forms of
   clustering. Within the economic geography literature, scholars have
   noted that particular social and economic phenomena occur when a
   concentration of like-minded labor pools, industries, and resources
   locate, whether Detroit's auto industry or Silicon Valley's technology
   sector. For an analysis of this phenomenon in industrial clustering,
   see the original treatise, Marshall's *Principles of Economics*. For a
   more contemporary analysis of clusters, see Porter, "Clusters and the
   Economics of Competition." The small-world network phenomenon
   in the fields of mathematics, physics, and sociology demonstrates
   similar patterns to those found in relative- celebrity social groups. In
   small worlds, people within a network are not necessarily physically
   proximate but most can be reached by every other person within the
   network through a few small steps. While this phenomenon has been

observed in wide sections of the population, it is particularly applicable to groups with common causes, or what the journalist William Finnegan has called affinity groups. See Watts and Strogatz, "Collective Dynamics of 'Small-World' Networks"; Watts, *Small Worlds*; and Finnegan, "Affinity Groups and the Movement Against Corporate Globalization."

5. David Marshall makes the point that celebrities are "elevated individuals" who are revered by a particular audience. See *Celebrity and Power*.

6. Both Jeffrey Williams and David Marshall have noted the existence of celebrity outside the conventional Hollywood and political star systems. Both make the point that celebrities exist in autonomous and self-contained systems. See Marshall, *Celebrity and Power*, and Williams, "Academostars."

7. Economists call this "barriers to entry." When they look at markets, the ability to enter them is a function of "high" or "low" barriers. See Demsetz, "Barriers to Entry."

8. Facebook researchers, for example, have pointed toward the ability of the social-networking site to allow people to "passively" be fed news about their friends. By simply trolling their news feed, members are able to collectively be updated on the extraneous aspects of their various five hundred–plus friends. Social media sites function less as networking conduits than as a means to cultivate public personae. As Lee Rainie, the director of the Pew Internet & American Life Project, put it, Facebook is "broadcasting their lives to an outer tier of acquaintances." Sounds like what the *New York Post* does for Paris. See "Primates on Facebook," *Economist*, February 26, 2009, and the Facebook researchers' further explanation of member social behavior on the site, "Maintained Relationships on Facebook," March 9, 2009, www.facebook.com/note.php?note_id= 55257228858. Other fascinating papers on user behavior are Burke, Marlow, and Lento, "Feed Me," and Sun et al., "Gesundheit!"

9. Lorenzen and Täube, "Breakout from Bollywood?"

10. Box Office 2007, Box Office India.

11. In August 2009, Khan was detained and questioned in Newark Airport immigration. Immigration officials said it was a routine examination. See Harris, "Bollywood Star Detained at Newark Airport."

12. *Morning Edition*, "His Name Is Khan (And It's One You Might Know)," National Public Radio, February 11, 2010. www.npr.org/ templates/story/story.php?storyId=123589668.

13. Taken from Mark Lorenzen, "How the West Was Won." Lorenzen's work is some of the most in-depth and thoughtful analysis on Bollywood and provides fascinating facts and a very interesting assessment of Bollywood vis-à-vis the larger global cultural market.
14. Joe Leahy, "Ambani's Indian Tiger Eyes Wounded MGM," *Financial Times*, January 16, 2010.
15. Lorenzen, "How the West Was Won."
16. "I Don't Regret Turning Down Slumdog: SRK," *Times of India*, January 20, 2009.
17. Joanna Walters, "Why Brits with Brains Are the Big Apple's New Blonde," *Observer*, July 6, 2003, www.guardian.co.uk/world/2003/jul/06/usa.joannawalters.
18. David Kirp, "How Much for That Professor?" *New York Times*, October 27, 2003, www.nytimes.com/2003/10/27/opinion/27KIRP.html.
19. In "Academostars," Jeremy Williams explains that the period after World War II brought intense government and foundation support to public and private universities. This funding enabled professors to generate individually run research projects. In turn, the standards and criteria set by the university changed from teaching to being primarily research driven. By the mid-1970s, the "academic star system" was in place, and professors began creating what Williams terms "individual professional reputations," and this recognition was driven initially by their research. By the mid-1980s, academics were attaining mainstream profiles in the *New York Times*, which had begun to devote coverage to public intellectuals in profiles and news stories. In one such story, "The Tyranny of the Yale Critics" by Colin Campbell, the newspaper profiled the Yale literary stars with full-page photographs of Harold Bloom, Geoffrey Hartman, and Jacques Derrida, the latter captured "in a glam pose," as Williams wrote. Today, some academic stars write features for the newspaper's Sunday magazine (Spurgin, "The *Times Magazine* and Academic Megastars"). See also Shumway, "The Star System in Literary Studies." For additional reading on the transformation of American universities, see Jencks and Riesman, *The Academic Revolution*, and David Kirp's excellent book on "star wars" in academia, *Shakespeare, Einstein, and the Bottom Line*.
20. See Kirp, *Shakespeare, Einstein, and the Bottom Line*.
21. As Jeffrey Williams quotes cultural scholar and New York University professor Andrew Ross, "The phenomenon of academic celebrity in some respects is an extension of the genre of academic gossip, which

has a culture unto itself—this extraordinary phenomenon whereby high-powered intellectuals spend a lot of their downtime trading scurrilous and detailed rumors about far-away colleagues" ("Academostars," p. 372).

22. Katie Nicholl, Miles Goslett, and Caroline Graham, "The History Man and the Fatwa Girl: How Will David Cameron Take News That Think-Tank Guru Niall Ferguson Has Deserted Wife Sue Douglas for Somali Feminist?" *Daily Mail*, August 1, 2010, www.dailymail.co .uk/news/article-1249095/The-history-man-fatwa-girl-How-David-Cameron-news-think-tank-guru-Niall-Ferguson-deserted-wife-Sue-Douglas-Somali-feminist.html#ixzz0etDi4TFQ.

23. Maureen O'Conner, "Fabulously Snobby Divorce Scandal of the Week: Niall Ferguson's Fatwa Mistress Two-Step," Gawker.com, February 8, 2010, gawker.com/5466433/fabulously-snobby-divorce-scandal-of-the-week-niall-fergusons-fatwa-mistress-two+step?skyline =true&s=i. The British high society magazine *Tatler* ran a feature profile on Ferguson and Ali entitled "The Ascent of Love," a clear reference to Ferguson's bestselling book *The Ascent of Money*. The article was accompanied by a photo spread of the two looking glamorous and every bit the star couple.

24. Roubini, "Why Central Banks Should Burst Bubbles."

25. Stephen Mihm, "Dr. Doom," *New York Times*, August 15, 2008, www.nytimes.com/2008/08/17/magazine/17pessimist-t.html.

26. Brian Moylan, "Please Help Give Armageddon-Loving Economist Dr. Doom a New Nickname," Gawker.com, February 3, 2010, http:// gawker.com/5463522/please-help-give-armageddon+loving-economist -dr-doom-a-new-nickname.

27. Richard Lawson, "A Russian Oligarch's New Year's Megaparty Starring Dr. Doom," Gawker.com, January 6, 2010, http://gawker.com/ 5441734/a-russian-oligarchs-new-years-eve-megaparty-photo-album-starring-dr-doom/.

28. Gillian Tett, "Breakfast with the FT: Nouriel Roubini," *Financial Times*, May 7, 2010.

29. Artists still have a media following in England and are mentioned regularly in the gossip blogs and splashed across the tabloid press.

30. For a fascinating account of the rise of Abstract Expressionist artists into mainstream culture (and a great history of the movement), see Perl, *New Art City*.

31. For an in-depth account of the New York pop and graffiti art scene, see Taylor, *The Downtown Book*.

32. See Smart, *The Sport Star*, for an in-depth discussion of the media's increasing interest in major athletes' personal lives. Smart argues that the media has created personal narratives around sports stars, thus generating a fan base not focused solely on sports statistics.

4. Inside the Star Machine: Celebrity as Industry

1. Matthew Garrahan, "Hollywood's Golden Talent Agents," *Financial Times*, February 19, 2010.
2. These numbers are taken from U.S. Bureau of Labor Statistics County Business Patterns (2008). These are number of establishments as reported to the BLS. Establishment numbers are useful for measuring sheer number of firms and businesses in the industry.
3. In order to isolate those occupations directly related to the celebrity industry, I looked at the BLS Occupational Employment Statistics (2008), which is a tabulation of employees by occupation (rather than just industry). I studied the data for the Los Angeles and New York metropolitan statistical areas (MSAs). An MSA is defined as an urban area of at least fifty thousand people, a geographical area of a number of towns and counties and a larger central city. The counties and towns included in a particular MSA are determined by the census. Looking at the occupational data allows us to see the people engaging in work directly relating to the celebrity industry, not just the firms. For example, looking at occupations associated with the publishing industry will allow us to measure the number of publicists, agents, and other individual positions that deal directly with celebrities. Additionally, because so many entertainers are "freelance" and essentially work on contract rather than on retainer, their employment numbers are not often picked up in firm employee numbers.
4. As not all workers within the broadly defined support and prepping industries (e.g., fitness trainers, nutritionists, hairstylists, and so-forth) are working strictly for celebrities, I took a percentage of the overall prep and support industries. I computed this number by incorporating Richard Florida's methodology for approximating the "creative class," or those members of the workforce who "generate meaningful new forms." Florida makes the point that members of the creative class depend on multiple service workers to support them. I extend this argument to include the identified "support" industries and occupations more generally that work within the

celebrity economy. I computed the percentage of the creative class comprised of celebrity-driven occupations. In Los Angeles the figure is 1.9 percent (34,800 workers) and in New York 0.04 percent (12,020 workers) of all "creative" workers (1,878,400 and 2,923,280, respectively). I then multiplied these percents by the total number of support and prep workers in each city to attain an approximation of the number of workers in these broader industrial categories devoted to the celebrity industry. It is impossible to get an exact figure, but this methodology provides a proxy to measure the impact of the celebrity industry on these cities' economies. My result is a very conservative estimate. I suspect many more work with celebrities and aspiring stars. See Florida, *Rise of the Creative Class*, pp. 72–77, for an explanation of this methodological approach.

5. Duff McDonald, "The Britney Economy," *Portfolio*, January 14, 2008.

6. Nicole LaPorte, "Crash of the Stalker Press," *Daily Beast*, November 16, 2009.

7. While celebrities seem like an isolated and limited number of individuals, an analysis of the industrial and occupational structure of the industry demonstrates that it is an important economic cluster to those metros in which it is located. Despite cities and policy makers who dismiss celebrities (and the arts more generally) as inconsequential to the economy, it's clear they're a formidable force in workforce and establishment numbers and payroll. See Alliance for the Arts, "Cultural Capital," 2002; Ann Markusen and Greg Schrock's "The Artistic Dividend"; and Currid, *The Warhol Economy*, for a more detailed discussion as it relates to the artistic and cultural industries more generally.

8. There has been a similar discussion of the importance of clustering in regard to Silicon Valley's technology industry. See Saxenian, *Regional Advantage*, and Freiberger and Swaine, *Fire in the Valley*.

9. See Rein et al., *High Visibility*, for similar celebrity industry classifications. In what the authors call the "structure of the celebrity industry," this book outlines very similar industrial categories: the entertainment industry, communications industry, publicity industry, representation industry, appearance industry, and coaching industry. Turner's *Understanding Celebrity* also details industries that comprise "the economy of celebrity," paying particular attention to agents, publicists, and public relations more generally. Josh Gamson's *Claims to Fame* examines the importance of those individuals

who commercialize celebrities. As you can see, there are nuances in how to construct the celebrity industries, but generally speaking, scholars who have studied this topic are by and large in agreement on the basic components.

10. Occupational Employment Statistics, Bureau of Labor 2007. See Appendix A for a complete list of occupational codes used for this analysis.

11. A location quotient (LQ) is the measure of the concentration of a particular industry or occupation in a designated area compared to a larger geography. In this case, Los Angeles and New York, respectively, are measured compared to the average concentration of these occupations in other metro areas. The equation used to compute these figures is: $LQ = (O_R/TE_R)/(O_N/TE_N)$, where O_R is regional occupational employment, TE_R is total regional employment, O_N is national occupational employment, and TE_N is total national employment.

12. McLuhan, *Understanding Media* and *The Medium Is the Massage*; Boorstin, *The Image*.

13. Gamson, *Claims to Fame*; Turner, "The Mass Production of Celebrity."

14. Gamson, *Claims to Fame*.

15. See Seipp, "The Puppet Masters," for a detailed and illuminating account of the control of the Hollywood publicity machine.

16. Ibid.

17. Ibid.

18. The write-around enables reporters to profile someone by talking to everyone around him or her, even if the writer never gets the interview with the star. The famous example of the write-around is "Frank Sinatra Has a Cold." Gay Talese was assigned to write an article on Frank Sinatra for *Esquire*, but he could not get access to the singer and thus had to observe from a close distance Sinatra's comings and goings and general disposition. Through observation and talking to people in Sinatra's cohort, Talese was able to write the story, which has been hailed as one of the finest pieces of journalism ever written. *Esquire* has said it's the best story ever published in the magazine.

19. David Marshall remarks that journalism has created a new type of celebrity reportage, through which the celebrities' personalities (whether athletes or Hollywood starlets) are key elements to the story lin (Marshall, "Intimately Intertwined in the Most Public Way").

20. Maureen Callahan, "Hot Shots," *New York Post*, February 7, 2010.

21. David Samuels's fascinating article, "Shooting Britney," *Atlantic*, April 2008, provides in-depth figures and details on X17's revenue and staff, along with some very insightful analysis of the paparazzi business in Los Angeles. See also David Carr, "101 Secrets (and 9 Lives) of a Magazine Star," *New York Times*, June 29, 2008.

22. Samuels, "Shooting Britney."

23. Callahan, "Hot Shots."

24. Brandon Gray, " 'New Moon' Shatters Opening Day Record," *Box Office Mojo*, November 21, 2009.

25. These numbers were computed using the location quotient method, as discussed above.

26. Richard Simpson, "The Hairstyle That Cost Jennifer Aniston £40,000," *Daily Mail*, March 4, 2009.

27. Jonathan Morgan, "Jennifer Aniston Spends $20,000 a Month on Her Beauty Routine," *Stylelist*, www.stylelist.com/2008/07/17/jennifer-aniston-spends-20-000-a-month-on-her-beauty-routine/.

28. "Jennifer Aniston Buys Two Tanning Beds," *Star*, September 30, 2008, www.starmagazine.com/jennifer_aniston_tanning_beds/news/14669.

29. Robin Pogrebin, "Workout Trainer of Madonna Will Open New York Studio," *New York Times*, February 6, 2009.

30. Susan Yara, "Personalizing Your Workout," *Forbes*, March 21, 2006, www.forbes.com/2006/03/20/workout-fitness-gyms-cx_sy_0321htow_ls.html.

31. I called both Equinox West Hollywood and Yogaworks in Los Angeles.

32. Howard Breuer, "Britney's Lawyers Question K-Fed's Spending," *People*, March 10, 2008.

33. Liz Jones, "Why Has Victoria Beckham Blown Over £2 million on 100 Virtually Identical Birkin Bags?" *Daily Mail*, May 22, 2009.

34. Average income is based on 2007 U.S. Census estimates: $50,223.

35. Ken Tucker, "Minority Report: In Defense of Tom Cruise," *New York*, June 5, 2005.

36. Garrahan, "Hollywood's Golden Talent Agents."

37. Lorenzen and Täube, "Breakout from Bollywood?"

38. Neil Midgley, "Simon Cowell: A Conqueror, but for How Long?" *Daily Telegraph*, December 12, 2009.

39. Ludovic Hunter-Tilney, "Rage Against the Wrong Machine," *Financial Times*, December 20, 2009, p. 11.

5. How to Become a Star: The Celebrity Network

1. In social network analysis, "clique" describes a group of closely net-worked individuals (e.g., "strong ties") who express very similar opinions, behaviors, etc., exhibiting what social network analysts call "homophily." See Kossinets and Watts, "Origins of Homophily."
2. For a terrific overview of the social network analysis literature, see Marin and Wellman, "Social Network Analysis."
3. My book *The Warhol Economy* discusses how social networks facil-itate important economic outcomes in the creative industries: getting a job, meeting top art dealers, etc. Saxenian's *Regional Advantage* discusses very similar mechanisms within the social networks of Sili-con Valley's technology industry.
4. Obviously, to study celebrity social networks with any rigor, Gilad and I had to figure out a systematic way of collecting and cataloging all the people and events associated with celebrity, and there are thousands and thousands of each. As it turns out, some photo-graphic agencies had already done this and we just picked the best. Getty Images not only has millions of photographs but also catalogs them by topic, event, date, people in photos, and so forth. Gilad and I conducted an experiment to see if we could make sense of celebrity through studying the photographs of the events celebrities go to and the people they hang out with. We collected the caption information on all the photos taken by Getty photographers of arts and enter-tainment events and people for one year. We studied approximately 600,000 photos of almost 12,000 events with 66,100 people in these photos at 128 places around the world. Of course not all 66,100 people in the photographs are celebrities, and sometimes noncelebri-ties end up at celebrity events. In order to account for these cases, we isolated those individuals photographed at least four times. By doing this, we captured 6.5 percent of all individuals in the Getty Images database, the celebrity core. We then studied all the events they attended, people they spent time with, and cities around the world they traveled to in attending those events.
5. Our method was multistep. Step one collected meta-information from the pictures in the Getty database. We then stored the meta-information in a MS-SQL relational database. In step two we identi-fied the individuals in each photo. Instead of studying the photos themselves, we studied the caption information associated with the photos and cataloged an aggregate collection of this data. In order to

identify the photographed objects, we used natural language process-
ing (NLP). SQL-implemented association rules enabled us to clean
the data. Our cataloging process collected the following information:
names and occupations of individuals in each picture, the event and
date when the photo was taken (e.g., Actress Angelina Jolie at the
Oscars, February 22, 2007). In step three we used the database information to build a list of events and the celebrities photographed at
them. From this list we built a two-mode network that connects people to events. The nodes are people and events they connect to
through an undirected edge. A person is connected to an event if he
or she is photographed at the event. In step four we converted the
two-modes network to a one-mode network of co-attendance. In this
new network, the nodes are people, and two nodes are connected by
an undirected edge if they are photographed at the same event. The
edge value equals the number of events they are both photographed
at. We isolated those individuals who were photographed at four or
more events. We also built a one-mode network of events where the
nodes are events and two events are connected with an undirected
edge if at least one individual attends both events. The edge value
equals the number of people who attended both events. Several programs and tools were used to conduct this research, including the
data-mining tool SPPS Clementine (to identify groups in the network). Social network analysis tools Pajek and Netminer were used
for the SNA analysis.

6. In studies done in the 1960s, the sociologist Stanley Milgram found
that most people around the world are connected by 6 degrees, in
itself a fascinating study of how linked human society is despite
seeming chaotic. Since then, scholars have found the same median
connections looking at different populations (the result ranges from
5 to 7, so although 6 is an average result, it is a fairly accurate quantitative representation of the phenomenon). By this theory, I could
connect to a fisherman in Japan through six people: This finding has
become known as the "small-world phenomenon," or "six degrees of
separation" in common parlance. Another study looking at linkages
between film stars found that actors tend to be separated by only
4 degrees. See Stanley Milgram, "The Small-World Problem," *Psy-
chology Today* 1, no. 1 (May 1967): 61–67; Watts, *Small Worlds*;
Watts and Strogatz, "Collective Dynamics of 'Small-World' Networks; Goel, Muhamad, and Watts, "Social Search in 'Small-World'
Experiments." Since the late 1990s, social scientists have been study-

ing the average connectedness of people around the world. There have been multiple experiments and studies undertaken using e-mail, letters, and social media sites. While some results point toward a median of 5.5 and others may report 7 connections, on the whole the average is about 6.

7. Overall, the Getty Images photographic network exhibits the characteristics of a small-world network and properties of a scale-free network (see Appendix B). Scale-free networks possess power law distribution connections between actors as compared to random-network connections. Most people photographed in the Getty database (95 percent) are connected to fewer than five other people, but our "celebrity core" (the 6.5 percent of individuals photographed four or more times) tend to be very connected (possessing greater than 5 degrees). Average distance, or characteristic path length (CPL), of the entire network is 3.26, while the average diameter in other observed social small worlds is 6. While Getty Images does document many culture industry events, individuals' connections are not necessarily industry linked. General results do not produce linkages between nodes by industry (as defined by an individual's industry affiliation and events attended).

8. Rytina and Morgan, "The Arithmetic of Social Relations."

9. Social network analysts use the term "clustering coefficient" to measure the degree to which people are closely connected.

10. See Barabási, *Linked*.

11. Weinberg, "In Health-Care Reform, the 20–80 Solution."

12. Gladwell, *The Tipping Point*; Pareto, "Manual of Political Economy"; Reed, "The Pareto, Zipf and Other Power Laws."

13. Barabási and Albert, "Emergence of Scaling in Random Networks." For a more reader-friendly version of the phenomenon, see Barabási, *Linked*. In social network analysis, this network structure is called a "scale free network." Such a network is present if the nodes' degree frequency distributes according to the power distribution.

14. Metcalfe's law is a way to observe the increased benefits obtained as more people engage in the network. See Gilder, *Telecosm*. Reed's law also looks at the exponential benefits to social networks. David Reed argues that Robert Metcalfe does not fully capture the extent to which additional members of a social network produce exponential connections to members (Reed, "The Law of the Pack").

15. Social network analysts more formally call this the difference

between an individual's positions in a network and cause for his or her participation in some network and position in that network.

16. In pure numbers, A-listers have an average of 3 connections to each other (remember we're just looking at connections among the top twenty, not the entire Getty network), while B-listers have 0.65 and the bottom rung have just 0.5 connections—that's less than 1 full connection to at least one other person for the middle and bottom twenty actors.

17. Currid, *The Warhol Economy*, p. 79.

18. See Oppenheimer, *Front Row: Anna Wintour*.

19. Ibid.

20. Social network analysts call the study of a particular individual's network structure and the connections within his or her network an egocentric analysis. See, for example, Marsden, "Core Discussions Networks of Americans."

21. See Fortini, "Twisted Sisters," Larocca, "Two Stylish," and *The September Issue*.

22. Boundary spanners can also exhibit the network property of "betweenness centrality" when they are an important point of connection along the shortest path between two groups of people or two nodes (people). When a node exhibits betweenness centrality he or she is very powerful within the network because he or she controls information and communication between two groups or people. Not all boundary spanners exhibit betweenness centrality and vice versa.

6. Whatever You Do, Don't Go to Vegas: The Geography of Stardom

1. Hubler, "The Secret Life of Cory Kennedy."

2. The "thirty-mile zone" (TMZ) refers to the "studio zone" for the film industry and includes the area in a thirty-mile radius expanding outward from the intersection of North La Cienega and West Beverly Boulevard in Los Angeles. This zone includes all the major studios (except MGM, which is out of the zone). The zone is also used to determine wages for entertainment workers who are union members. The popular celebrity website TMZ.com derived its name from the industry's geographical initials.

3. GIS is a breakthrough for social science research. It is a technological system of associating statistical data (census, real estate values, etc.) with spatial locations (city, census tract, zip code area). GIS produces

maps that show concentrations of statistical data in particular places and allows researchers to perform statistical analysis on the correlations between place and social and economic data. GIS analyzes how statistical variables increase and decrease across zip code, county, city, and so forth.

4. For the complete study, with a more technical analysis and more statistical results, see Currid and Williams, "The Geography of Buzz."

5. Lynne Zucker and Michael Darby found the same thing in their study "Star Scientists": "Where and when star scientists were actively producing publications is a key predictor of where and when commercial firms began to use biotechnology." Their point, which can also be applied here, is that concentration of the stars within an industry produces real implications for economic growth when innovation occurs. In the case of London, New York, and Los Angeles, these cities economically and socially benefit from concentrations of stars through the revenue generated from their productivity and products.

6. For a discussion of endogeneity (and its associated problems) in statistical analysis, see Bound, Jaeger, and Baker, "Problems with Instrumental Variables Estimation." For an interesting discussion of the role of endogeneity in economic growth and the positive impacts of generating human capital and knowledge, see Romer, "Endogenous Technical Change."

7. It's worth noting that Bollywood shows up with very little frequency in the database. Just 12 events and 197 people are recorded at events in India. In fact, the industry's most celebrated star, Shahrukh Khan, appears in none of Getty's photos. One explanation is that Getty generally documents more Western (primarily European and U.S.) events. Another explanation is that Bollywood is a very insular geography of stardom. As discussed in chapter 3, Bollywood is not interested in being a part of Hollywood and has no need for a Western audience (besides the Indian diasporas) and thus may not court Western media. Similarly, there may be less of a demand for images of Bollywood due to the fact that it remains introverted vis-à-vis other global celebrities and celebrity hubs. The rise of Nollywood (Nigeria's film industry) has prompted another examination of the global filmmaking business. Nollywood does not generate the revenue that Hollywood does, but in sheer numbers it is making more films per year than both Bollywood and Hollywood. See Arsenault

and Castells, "The Structure and Dynamics of Global Multi-Media Business Networks."

8. We studied the relationship between a celebrity's ranking and his or her geographical traveling patterns, or where he or she spent time. We wanted to see if there were patterns between level of celebrity success (media mentions or perceived talent by Hollywood) and geographical movements or attendance at particular events. Our analysis is based on data from the Getty Images photographic database. The collection methods are similar to those discussed in chapter 4 with regard to the social network analysis. We collected photograph caption data for an entire year and cataloged this caption information from all photos in Getty's arts and entertainment category. From this data we identified the top ten photographed locations: New York (NY), Nevada (NV), Australia (AUS), Great Britain (GBR), France (FRA), Florida (FL), Germany (DEU), California (CA), Japan (JPN), and "Other." We calculated the number of events photographed in each location and the number of times people were photographed in any other place before they attended an event in one of the aforementioned places of interest. We can interpret the movement from one place to another as a theoretical "flight" one needed to take to go from place A to place B. These variables were designated the following codes, which can be seen in the regression model outputs in Appendix C: Suffix *s* indicates that a star had to travel to make an appearance in one location (e.g., NYs), a variable with suffix *h* indicates total number of events one attended in one place during our studied period (e.g., NYh). For key locations NY, CA, NV, and GBR, almost all events studied were in New York City, Los Angeles, Las Vegas, and London. Thus our discussion is about these cities rather than the states or countries as a whole. In order to build a celebrity success model, we used two criteria of success: talent and media profile. For the talent proxy, we used *Forbes*'s Star Currency. Media mentions in that period were measured through Google news and blog search results. These results were obtained by carefully searching for the particular person in returned results. This automatic task was done by a specially designed Perl web bot. After collecting our data and creating our variables, we undertook statistical analysis. We used a linear multivariate regression model with the various identified places as independent variables and Star Currency and Google media volume as dependent variables. We chose the

backward selection method of regression analysis in order to minimize the model such that it reported on only the most influential places impacting Star Currency and media volume. We used the SPSS statistical package for this analysis.

9. Preston, "A Dozen Reasons to Be Cheerful About the State of the British Media."

10. There is a wide literature in economics and geography studying the ways places attain competitive advantage in particular industries. Initially most geographical advantages could be explained by natural resources, whether timber or iron ore, and being near a transportation hub. Postindustrial advantages are widely explained as possessing an educated labor force and company headquarters, particularly where innovative activity occurs. Many scholars have pointed to the importance of initial events and historical accidents that set competitive advantage in motion (what Arthur has called the "founder effect"). These initial events generate increasing returns that enable one place, one technology, or one individual to dominate the market and capture most of its benefits. See Arthur, Ermoliev, and Kaniovski, "Path-Dependent Processes"; Arthur, *Increasing Returns and Path Dependence*; Arthur, "Competing Technologies, Increasing Returns"; Arthur, "'Silicon Valley' Locational Clusters"; Bell, *The Coming of Post-Industrial Society*; David, "Clio and the Economics of QWERTY"; Glaeser, "Urban Colossus"; Glaeser and Saiz, "The Rise of the Skilled City"; Lucas, "On the Mechanics of Economic Development."

11. Concentration of human capital is a central explanation for productivity and regional and urban development. Although I am discussing a particular form of human capital, the wider point is that industrial success is predicated on having a critical concentration of the necessary labor force within that industry. See Lucas, "On the Mechanics of Economic Development"; and Florida, *Rise of the Creative Class*.

12. See Graeme Turner's excellent discussion of the role of the media in the production of celebrity in *Understanding Celebrity*. Also see Turner, "Celebrity, the Tabloid and the Democratic Public Sphere." David Marshall has also written extensively about the relationship between celebrity and the media in "New Media—New Self" and "Intimately Intertwined in the Most Public Way."

13. History indicates that art markets tend to flourish in financial capitals because surplus disposable income and patronage are necessary. From Holland's golden age of painting in the seventeenth century to

New York's and London's current overinflated art markets, abundant disposable income has been necessary to keep a robust art market booming. See, for example, Schama, *The Embarrassment of Riches*; Ferguson, *The Ascent of Money*, p. 3; and Goetzmann, "Accounting for Taste: Art and the Financial Markets Over Three Centuries."

14. Economists and economic geographers call this process "path dependency": The future is always limited by the previous set of actions and events, even if what happened before seems irrelevant to the current context. In some cases, path dependency leads to cumulative advantage whereby one place attains advantage over others in producing a particular product or becomes the world headquarters for an industry. This phenomenon is clear in London's and New York's dominance in finance, Pittsburgh's historical advantage in steel manufacturing, and so forth. Thus the series of events and decisions made by policy makers, planners, or business developers caused these cities to become the central node of industrial activity. A similar process occurs with products. Microsoft is not seen as the "best" operating system (Linux is widely viewed as superior by computer scientists), but enough people use it that using any other operating system would be less efficient. At some point, it becomes irrelevant whether the location (or innovation) is in fact the superior version if it has locked in its dominant position by virtue of network externalities and critical mass of resources. For more on this process, see Arthur, *Increasing Returns and Path Dependence in the Economy*; and David, "Clio and the Economics of QWERTY." For an example of this process in popular culture, see Watts, "Is Justin Timberlake the Product of Cumulative Advantage?"

15. Boorstin, *The Image*. Also see the following cultural critics' dissections of how popular culture is created and the way the media constructs events and people to be interested in: Adorno, *The Culture Industry*; Debord, *Society of the Spectacle*; Baudrillard, *Simulacra and Simulation*.

16. Hollywood's construction in popular culture is essentially a simulacrum, or a referenced place, more symbolic than real. Hollywood is constructed for the public in a way that does not exist as such in real life. Both Sorkin, *Variations on a Theme Park*, and Baudrillard, *Simulacra and Simulation*, consider the role of the simulacra and simulacrum in constructions of places and events and the relationship between symbols and reality.

7. The Economics of the Celebrity Residual

1. MonkDogz Art blog, "Where's Bubbles? Jeff Koons May Know," June 29, 2009, http://artblahblah.com/?tag=jeff-koons.

2. Sarah Thorton, "The Recipe for a Record Price: Auction House Price, Media Frenzy and Billionaire Buyers," *Art Newspaper*, May 2008, www.theartnewspaper.com/article.asp?id=8471.

3. Mark Stevens, "Adventures in the Skin Trade," *New Republic*, January 20, 1992. Michael Kimmelman, "Jeff Koons," *New York Times*, November 29, 1991, www.nytimes.com/1991/11/29/arts/art-in-review-233491.html?scp=3&sq=jeff%20koons%20kimmelman%201991&st=cse.

4. Jeff Koons, *The Jeff Koons Handbook* (New York: Rizzoli, 1993).

5. Arifa Akbar, "Koons Is Most Expensive Living Artist at Auction," *Independent*, November 16, 2007, www.independent.co.uk/news/world/americas/koons-is-most-expensive-living-artist-at-auction-400580.html.

6. For a review of the literature on the changing function of the media on celebrity culture, see Barry, "Celebrity, Culture Production and Public Life."

7. Akbar, "Koons Is Most Expensive Living Artist."

8. For an in-depth account of how art markets revolve around reputation, connections, and the media, see Anthony Haden-Guest, *True Colors*, and Thompson, *The $12 Million Stuffed Shark*.

9. Galenson, "Who Are the Greatest Living Artists?" and Galenson, *Conceptual Revolutions in Twentieth-Century Art*.

10. Carol Vogel, "Swimming with Famous Dead Sharks," *New York Times*, October 1, 2006.

11. Richard Brooks, "Hirst's Shark Is Sold to America," *Sunday Times*, January 16, 2005; Serena Davies, "Why Painting Is Back in the Frame," *Daily Telegraph*, January 8, 2005.

12. Landon Thomas Jr. and Carol Vogel, "A New Prince of Wall Street Uses His Riches to Buy Art," *New York Times*, March 3, 2005.

13. Ciar Byrne, "Hirst's Glittering Price Tag Loses None of Its Shine," *Independent*, August 31, 2007, www.independent.co.uk/news/uk/this-britain/hirsts-glittering-price-tag-loses-none-of-its-shine-463675.html.

14. Richard Dorment, "For the Love of Art and Money," *Daily Telegraph*, June 1, 2007.

15. Stallabrass, *High Art Lite*.

16. See Galenson, "You Cannot Be Serious," a very interesting paper on the relationship between the artist's persona and his or her work. Galenson argues that creating ambiguity around why artists create particular works catalyzes debates about their work that enables them both to advance their careers and be viewed as innovators in the art world.
17. DiMaggio, "Classification in Art."
18. Haden-Guest, *True Colors*, p. 151.
19. Galenson's research shows that Richter is the number one artist whose artwork consistently sells for over $1 million. He does not, however, reach the auction price heights of Hirst or Koons. So while Richter will certainly be considered one of the greatest artists of his time, he is not a celebrity who reaps the rewards of the winner-takes-all market. Richter's work is revered by those who know art, the way a Booker Prize winner is lauded by book readers while the masses read Katie Price's latest biography. As Galenson remarks, "Richter has a massive influence on young artists, even if not a household name."
20. "Postwar & Contemporary Art at Christie's Totals $430.8 Million," editorial, *Antiques and the Arts*, May 20, 2008, antiquesandthe arts.com/Antiques/AuctionWatch/2008-05-20__13-38-28.html.
21. Rosen, "The Economics of Superstars."
22. Frank and Cook, *Winner-Take-All Society*. Krueger, "The Economics of Real Superstars." The effects have also been found in empirical studies of sports. See Lucifora and Simmons, "Superstar Effects in Sports," and Nüesch, "The Economics of Superstars and Celebrities," chapter 2.
23. DiMaggio, "Classification in Art."
24. Elberse, "Should You Invest in the Long Tail?"
25. See Adler, "Stardom and Talent." Adler argues that increasing numbers of people consuming the same product generates greater consumption capital, which makes the product more valuable. A rock concert, after all, is more powerful when the stadium is full and people are engaging in a shared experience.
26. Leibenstein, "Bandwagon, Snob, and Veblen Effects in the Theory of Consumers' Demand."
27. For an empirical study of how people make cultural consumer choices, see Salganik, Dodds, and Watts, "Experimental Study of Inequality and Unpredictability in an Artificial Cultural Market"; and Watts, "Is Justin Timberlake a Product of Cumulative Advantage?"

28. Peter Aspden, "Past Masters Beckon for the Followers of Modernity,"*Financial Times*, October 17, 2009. See Thompson, *The $12 Million Stuffed Shark*, for a very thoughtful and exciting look into art economics.

29. Aspden, "Hirst Provides Study in Art of Business," *Financial Times*, October 31, 2009; letters in response to article, "Damien Hirst Belongs in Art Market History," November 7, 2009.

30. See Charles Kurzman et al., "Celebrity Status," *Sociological Theory* 25 (2007): 4, for discussion of celebrity status and the social and economic privilege associated with it.

31. The program can be seen on YouTube, "Tracey Emin on the Loose," www.youtube.com/watch?v=HKNr2LOkXYE.

32. "Saatchi and Emin Make Up as He Buys Her Unmade Bed for £150K," *Independent*, July 16, 2000, www.independent.co.uk/news/media/saatchi-and-emin-make-up-as-he-buys-her-unmade-bed-for-pound150k-707429.html.

33. Nigel Reynolds, "Charles Saatchi Could Have Bought Four Davids for the Price of Tracey Emin's Bed," *Telegraph*, January 7, 2006.

34. This observation comes out of a very helpful conversation with the University of Chicago economist David Galenson. Also see Stallabrass, *High Art Lite*.

35. Forbes.com, "The World's Best-Paid Athletes," June 24, 2004, www.forbes.com/2004/06/23/04athletesland.html.

36. CNN.com, "Beckham Signs '$250 Million' Deal with LA Galaxy," January 11, 2007, http://edition.cnn.com/2007/SPORT/football/01/11/beckham/index.html.

37. Grant Wahl, "David Beckham Could Walk Away from Galaxy After 2009 Season," *Sports Illustrated*/CNN, November 3, 2008, http://sportsillustrated.cnn.com/2008/writers/grant_wahl/11/03/wahl.beckham/index.html; Adam Scime, "David Beckham's $46 Million Deal Makes Him World's Highest-Paid Soccer Player," *Sports Illustrated*, March 30, 2009, http://sportsillustrated.cnn.com/2009/soccer/03/30/beckham.salary/index.html.

38. Scime, "David Beckham's $46 Million Deal."

39. Lawson et al., "Vend It Like Beckham."

40. See Smart, *The Sport Star*.

41. I benefited greatly from talking to *FT* sports columnist Simon Kuper about the Beckham phenomenon.

42. His real bump in salary was when he signed a ten-year contract in

2000 with the Texas Rangers for $252 million, which at the time was the greatest paying contract in baseball's history by $63 million.

43. John Schlegel and Rhett Bollinger, "Jeter's Feat Recognized Around MLB: Players, Coaches Respect What Shortstop Has Done for Game," MLB.com, September 12, 2009, http://mlb.mlb.com/news/article.jsp?ymd=20090909&content_id=6882850&vkey=news_nyy&fext=.jsp&c_id=nyy.

44. It will be very interesting to see what happens when Jeter becomes a free agent. He is signed through 2010. If he is playing spectacularly then, he may sign an astronomical deal, comparable to A-Rod's.

45. There is a literature of "sports economics" that argues that the marginally more talented ballplayer is worthy of a disproportionately higher salary than everyone else he is just a little bit better than. Not coincidentally, the term used by economists to describe this is "the superstar effect." See Claudio Lucifora and Rob Simmons, "Superstar Effects in Sport," *Journal of Sports Economics* 4, no. 1 (2003): 35. For more on the link between spectator draw, media attention, and athlete's reward, see Egon Franck and Stephan Nüesch, "Talent, Past Consumption and/or Popularity—Are German Soccer Celebrities Rosen or Adler Stars?" Institute for Strategy and Business Economics, University of Zürich (working paper), 2006.

46. In 2004, the Yankees lost to the Boston Red Sox in the ALCS. They became the first team in MLB's history, and only the third team in North American professional sports history, to lose a best-of-seven series after taking a 3–0 series lead.

47. Tyler Kepner, "Rodriguez Is at Ease with Himself and October," *New York Times*, October 18, 2009.

48. Lena Williams and Richard Sandomir, "Baseball; Rodriguez T-Shirts a Hot Item," *New York Times*, February 18, 2004.

49. Vince Gennaro, "A-Rod's Dollars Make Sense for Yankees," *Yahoo! Sports*, November 27, 2007.

50. I used Google Insights, an innovative program in Google Labs, to conduct a time series analysis of search interest in various athletes vis-à-vis news mentions and topics associated with news items. Methodology on their datasets can be found at Insights. Numbers given are not absolute but normalized and scaled. The data is scaled from 0 to 100 with each point on the scale being divided by the highest point (100). The data is normalized, which means that the Google researchers divide the data sets by a common variable to

cancel out any effect each individual variable might have on the data. By normalizing the data, the underlying features of the datasets become comparable. As they put it, "If we didn't normalize the results and displayed the absolute rankings instead, data from regions generating the most search volume would always be ranked high."

51. Some argue that sports stars get paid what they're worth. See Simon Kuper, "Sport Can Teach Bankers Fair Play on Pay," *Financial Times*, February 27, 2009.

52. See Smart, *The Sport Star*, for a discussion of Michael Jordan's impact on the various entities that have benefited from his celebrity, from Nike to Jordan the brand.

53. It is remarkably difficult to obtain accurate salary and endorsement figures. I have benefited from very in-depth conversations with *Forbes* researchers and looking at archives in *Hollywood Reporter*, *Variety*, and *Forbes*. That said, many of the numbers used are approximations, as this information is rarely given out.

54. *US Weekly* and *People* archive search results.

55. One film executive explained that 2010 could potentially determine Aniston's star power at the box office, as she is in two major films: *The Bounty Hunter* (with Gerard Butler) and *The Baster* (with Jason Bateman). As he put it, "If both of those movies exceed $100 million, she's a star. If they make less than $40 million, she'll likely be con-signed to playing second fiddle to male movie stars. Certainly there are worse positions to be in careerwise, but I'm sure Aniston wants to get into that Jolie, Bullock, Streep (and to a lesser extent Wither-spoon) zone where people build movies around her and expect to make bank."

56. Recently *Forbes* studied the most "overpaid" actors and found that Will Ferrell makes his studio just $3.29 per dollar he is paid. Consider Ferrell versus Shia LaBeouf, who brings in $160 per dollar he makes. As you can see, the residual is a fairly hard quality to put a concrete value on (http://movies.yahoo.com/feature/forbes-most -overpaid-stars.html).

57. Elberse, "The Power of Stars."

58. De Vany and Walls, "Motion Picture Profit, the Stable Paretian Hypothesis, and the Curse of the Superstar." See also Khurana, "The Curse of the Superstar CEO."

59. See Howard Becker's extraordinary book *Art Worlds*, which details the "conventions" of establishing good art. Bourdieu's *The Field of*

Cultural Production and *Distinction* and Richard Caves's *Creative Industries* are also very useful texts in understanding how to create value and merit in a seemingly subjective world.

60. Endogenous and exogenous models first emerged in macroeconomic theory to explain economic growth as a function of human capital and technology (Paul Romer's endogenous or "new growth theory"). In other words, growth exhibiting increasing returns emerges when variables can continue to create new forms of growth and development. Human beings share ideas, which promotes new inventions; new technology tends to build upon itself. But the establishment of such growth emerges from within a confined area (defined by industry or geography, for example). Prior to such a model, economic growth was explained by savings or technological progress à la the Solow model. Exogenous change is that which changes a variable from the outside. For example, supply and demand of a particular genre of music can be explained by the changes (or consistency) of consumer taste. Mainstream celebrity fits this criterion quite well in that those individuals who transcend their relative celebrity (explained endogenously by those within the system) are a product of exogenous influences, particularly consumer tastes for certain types of celebrity, a topic I address in the next section of the book.

61. Matthew Mosk, "Sarah Palin Has Earned an Estimated $12 Million Since July," ABC News, April 13, 2010, http://abcnews.go.com/Blotter/sarah-palin-earned-estimated-12-million-july/story?id=1035 2437.

62. I benefited tremendously from the fascinating and detailed article by Dan Wetzel, "For Nike, Jordan Delivered the Goods and More," *Yahoo! Sports*, September 8, 2009. This article gives a great account of Nike's gamble on Jordan and how, in turn, he transformed the sports company. http://sports.yahoo.com/nba/news?slug=dw-jordan nike090709&prov=yhoo&type=lgns.

63. Ibid.

64. "Michael Jordan Becomes Highest Paid NBA Player, with One-Year Bulls Contract Worth $25–30 million," *Jet*, July 29, 1996.

65. Darren Rovell, "Swoosh! Inside Nike: Michael Jordan Continues to Score Points for Football Giant," MSNBC: Business, February 12, 2008.

66. Roy S. Johnson, "The Jordan Effect: The World's Greatest Basketball Player Is Also One of Its Great Brands. What Is His Impact on the Economy?" CNN Money, June 22, 1998.

67. Dan Wetzel, "For Nike, Jordan Delivered the Goods and More," *Yahoo! Sports*, September 8, 2009.

68. For research on celebrity endorsers, see Erdogan, Baker, and Tagg, "Selecting Celebrity Endorsers."

69. Mathur, Mathur, and Rangan, "The Wealth Effects Associated with a Celebrity Endorser: The Michael Jordan Phenomenon."

70. Ibid.

71. Johnson, "The Jordan Effect." For an updated account, see Roy Johnson, "Jordan (Still) Rules," *Sports Illustrated*, April 10, 2003.

72. Money, Shimp, and Sakano, "Celebrity Endorsements in Japan and the United States."

73. Advertising Age International, 1997.

74. I learned a great deal from an interview with the director of foreign rights at a major Hollywood studio. He explained to me that romances and humor don't sell abroad, but action films do. Most countries can do their own comedy and romance, but action requires a large start-up cost to film. By extension, those stars who are in the films that have foreign market appeal are more likely to appeal personally to these audiences as well.

75. David Blecken, "Live Issue . . . Can Overseas Celebrities Sell Brands in China?" *Media*, September 10, 2009.

76. One study found that celebrities appeared in 48 percent of Japanese commercials and about half of Korean ads. Lee, Choi, and Tsai, "Celebrity Advertising in Japan and Korea."

77. B. Moore, "Following the Stars," *Los Angeles Times*, September 13, 2009.

78. Miller et al., "The Celebrity 100," Forbes.com.

79. To be clear, although sometimes the public becomes aware of the actual numbers behind a deal, this is not inherently public knowledge. One of the celebrity journalists I interviewed said that it is very difficult to get precise numbers. The price tag of the deal is purposely not always disclosed. As the journalist explained to me, the numbers are hard to get because if we articulate how much a star is worth, then that number can be used for future deals. Jennifer Aniston, or any other star, wants her price tag undisclosed so that she has a bargaining chip for future deals. She can then argue how important celebrity is to that particular brand. Once a star has an established price, it is much harder to argue a greater value of one's celebrity residual, thus she has every reason to keep the numbers to herself.

80. Mail Online, "Kate Moss Signs £3 Million Design Deal with Top-shop," *Daily Mail*, September 2006.

81. See Kahle and Homer, "Physical Attractiveness of the Celebrity Endorser," for research on "source credibility model," "source attractiveness," "expertness," and "trustworthiness" to examine the reasons we do or don't identify with the endorser.

82. Eric Wilson, "Fashion Week: A Controversial Debut for Lohan in Paris," *New York Times*, October 4, 2009.

83. McCracken, "Who Is the Celebrity Endorser?"

84. J. G. Kaikati, "Celebrity Advertising: A Review and Synthesis," *International Journal of Advertising* 6, no. 2 (1987): 93–105.

85. Tripp, Jensen, and Carlson, "The Effects of Multiple Product Endorsements by Celebrities."

86. John Cassidy, "Rational Irrationality: Tiger's Mental Error," *New Yorker*, December 17, 2009.

87. Darren Rovell, "Tiger's Lost Endorsements Cost IMG $4.6 Million Last Year," CNBC.com, June 18, 2010.

88. James Surowiecki, "Branded a Cheat," *New Yorker*, December 29, 2009.

8. The Democratic Celebrity

1. Darnton, "London Journal: For 20%, He Sells Scandal, Keeping Britain Agog."

2. Lyall, "Sex! Sleaze! Filth!"

3. Darnton, "London Journal."

4. Ibid.

5. Frith, *The Celeb Diaries*.

6. Lyall, "British Reality TV Star Ready to Die for the Cameras."

7. Sinclair, "'Jade Goody Effect' Boosts Cervical Cancer Screening Rates."

8. David Marshall discusses this new form of celebrity as challenging "the rigidity of class-based societies by presenting the potential to transcend these categories" ("Intimately Intertwined in the Most Public Way," p. 317).

9. Turner, *Understanding Celebrity*. Turner calls this new form of stardom the "demotic turn" of celebrity production.

10. In *Claims to Fame*, Joshua Gamson uses the term "democratic celebrity" to look at the pull between deserved and undeserved fame.

His definition of democratic celebrity focuses more on the role of the consumer than the star.

11. Gill, "Decade in Review: Age of the Amateur with 15 Minutes of Fame."
12. The *American Idol* format is not unique to this era. The mid-eighties to mid-nineties *Star Search* was another televised talent show. However, *Idol* is unique in its ubiquity and influence and consistent ability to transform unknowns into megastars.
13. Edward Wyatt, " 'Idol' Winners: Not Just Fame but Big Bucks," *New York Times*, February 24, 2010.
14. Gabler, "Reality TV."
15. For a very interesting account of celebrity obsession and the desire to be a celebrity, see Brim, *Look at Me!*
16. Jenkins, *Convergence Culture*, p. 71.
17. Theodor Adorno's work on the culture industries argues that popular culture is shoved at mass audiences without any choice of their own. See Adorno, *The Culture Industry*; and Horkheimer and Adorno, *Dialectic of Enlightenment*.
18. Several scholars have studied reality TV in great detail. See Hartley, *Popular Reality* and *Uses of Television*. Also see Jenkins and Thorburn, *Democracy and New Media*.
19. Carter, "A Reality TV Head Count." Another point to be made here is that reality TV is so much cheaper to produce than sitcoms and dramas. The stars don't get paid as much (if at all), and the pool of people who want to be contestants is endless.
20. Andrejevic, *Reality TV*, p. 111.
21. Davis, "The Secret World of Lonelygirl."
22. Sternberg, "Hey There, Lonelygirl."
23. I benefited tremendously from a conversation with Tyler Cowen, who explained democratic star power in an economic framework.
24. For a hilarious and candid account of this process, see Rebecca Mead, "The Almost It Girl," *New Yorker*, October 20, 2003, p. 96.
25. Graeme Turner calls these methods "DIY production technologies." See Turner, *Understanding Celebrity*, and Couldry, *Media Rituals*.
26. In *Frenzy of Renown*, Leo Braudy notes that fame is social mobility that is not inherited by class or position (p. 595). Democratic celebrity embodies this particular aspect of Braudy's understanding of fame.
27. Wyatt, " 'Idol' Winners: Not Just Fame but Big Bucks."
28. Wyatt, "No Slowing in Cash Flow for 'Idol.' "

29. Gill, "Decade in Review."
30. Beard, "Welcome to the Human Zoo, Susan."
31. Wilson, "The Pressure of Sudden TV Stardom."
32. Cowell, "After the Britain's Got Talent Backlash, Simon Cowell Finally Admits: 'Sorry, I Did Make Mistakes.' "
33. Sales, "The Unreal Rise of Jon and Kate Gosselin."
34. Rice, "TLC Halts Production on 'Jon and Kate Plus 8,' " and "TLC Responds to Jon Gosselin"; Rubinkam, " 'Jon & Kate' Stars Being Investigated Over Child Labor Complaint."
35. There are countless examples of democratic stars who are completely unfit for stardom. Tila Tequila, a MySpace personality, ended up on the cover of men's magazines and with her own reality TV show. More recently she was tweeting about killing herself. She claims she is receiving help. Another U.K. reality TV star, Lizzy Bardsley, was found guilty of child cruelty and benefit fraud.
36. Gill, "Decade in Review."
37. Turner, *Understanding Celebrity*, p. 84.

9. The Future of Celebrity

1. See Marshall, "Intimately Intertwined in the Most Public Way," p. 322.
2. See classic sociological studies on status, hierarchy, and group formations: Blau, "A Theory of Social Integration" and "A Macrosociological Theory of Social Structure"; Bottomore, *Elites and Society*; Breiger, "The Duality of Persons and Groups"; Mills, *The Power Elite*.
3. Turner, "The Mass Production of Celebrity" and *Understanding Celebrity*.
4. For a larger discussion of the underestimated yet significant role of fans, see Jenkins, *Fans, Bloggers, and Gamers*.
5. See Weber, "The Nature of Charismatic Authority and Its Routinization."
6. Uzzi, Amaral, and Reed-Tsochas, "Small-World Networks and Management Science Research."
7. Zucker and Darby, "Star Scientists and Institutional Transformation."
8. This story has been changed somewhat to protect the identity of the person described.
9. See Friedman, *The World Is Flat*; Jacques, *When China Rules the World*.

10. Geddes, "An Interview with Leo Braudy."

11. Pinksy and Young, *The Mirror Effect*; Young and Pinksy, "Narcissism and Celebrity."

12. Brim, *Look at Me!*

13. DiSalvo, "Are Social Networks Messing with Your Head?" See also Twenge and Campbell, *The Narcissism Epidemic*.

14. DiSalvo, "Are Social Networks Messing with Your Head?"

15. Ibid.; comScore, "More Americans Reading Entertainment News Online."

16. comScore, "More Americans Reading Entertainment News Online."

17. Hameed, "Facebook's U.S. Traffic Reaches 132 Million Visitors."

18. Facebook.com, "Press Room: Statistics."

19. Hansell, "Zuckerberg's Law of Information Sharing."

Select Bibliography

Adler, Moshe. "Stardom and Talent." *American Economic Review* 75, no. 1 (1985): 208–12.

Adorno, Theodor. *The Culture Industry: Selected Essays on Mass Culture*. London: Routledge, 1991.

Amato, Paul R., et al. *Alone Together: How Marriage in America Is Changing*. Cambridge, MA: Harvard University Press, 2009.

Anderson, Chris. *Free: The Future of a Radical Price*. New York: Hyperion Books, 2009.

Andrejevic, Mark. *Reality TV: The Work of Being Watched*. Lanham, MD: Rowman and Littlefield, 2004.

AR: Absolute Return + Alpha. "Top 25 Highest-Earning Hedge Fund Managers," March 23, 2009. www.absolutereturn-alpha.com/Article/2165638/Top-25-Highest-Earning-Hedge-Fund-Managers.html.

Arsenault, Amelia H., and Manuel Castells. "The Structure and Dynamics of Global Multi-Media Business Networks." *International Journal of Communication* 2 (2008): 707.

Arthur, W. Brian. "Competing Technologies, Increasing Returns, and Lock-In by Historical Events." *Economic Journal* 99, no. 394 (1989): 116–31.

———. " 'Silicon Valley' Locational Clusters: When Do Increasing Returns Imply Monopoly?" *Mathematical Social Sciences* 19, no. 3 (1990): 235–51.

———. *Increasing Returns and Path Dependence in the Economy*. Ann Arbor: University of Michigan Press, 1994. ·

Arthur, W. Brian, Y. M. Ermoliev, and Y. M. Kaniovski. "Path-Dependent Processes and the Emergence of Macro-Structure." *European Journal of Operational Research* 30, no. 3 (1987): 294–303.

Bachrach, Peter, and Morton Baratz. "Two Faces of Power." *American Political Science Review* 56, no. 4 (1962): 947–52.

Barabási, Albert-László. *Linked: How Everything Is Connected to Everything Else.* New York: Plume, 2003.

Barabási, Albert-László, and Réka Albert. "Emergence of Scaling in Random Networks." *Science* 286 (1999): 509–12.

Barry, Elizabeth. "Celebrity, Culture Production and Public Life." *International Journal of Cultural Studies* 11, no. 3 (2008): 251–58.

Baudrillard, Jean. *Simulacra and Simulation.* Trans. Sheila Faria Glaser. Ann Arbor: University of Michigan Press, 1994.

Beard, Mary. "Welcome to the Human Zoo, Susan." *Times* (London), June 2, 2009.

Becker, Howard S. *Art Worlds.* Berkeley: University of California Press, 1982.

Bell, Daniel. *The Coming of Post-Industrial Society: A Venture in Social Forecasting.* New York: Basic Books, 1973.

Berridge, Kate. *Madame Tussaud: A Life in Wax.* New York: William Morrow, 2006.

Blau, Peter M. "A Theory of Social Integration." *American Journal of Sociology* 65, no. 6 (1960): 545–56.

———. "A Macrosociological Theory of Social Structure." *American Journal of Sociology* 83 (1977): 26–54.

Boorstin, Daniel J. *The Image: A Guide to Pseudo-Events in America.* New York: Vintage Books, 1992 [1961].

Bottomore, Tom. *Elites and Society.* New York: Routledge, 1993.

Bound, John, David A. Jaeger, and Regina M. Baker. "Problems with Instrumental Variables Estimation When the Correlation Between the Instruments and the Endogenous Explanatory Variable Is Weak." *Journal of the American Statistical Association* 90 (1995): 443.

Bourdieu, Pierre. *Distinction: A Social Critique of the Judgement of Taste.* Trans. Richard Nice. Cambridge, MA: Harvard University Press, 1984.

———. *The Field of Cultural Production: Essays on Art and Literature.* New York: Columbia University Press, 1993.

BoxOfficeIndia. "Box Office 2007." www.boxofficeindia.com/showProd .php?itemCat=217&catName=MjAwNw==.

Braudy, Leo. *Frenzy of Renown.* New York: Oxford University Press, 1986.

Breiger, Ronald L. "The Duality of Persons and Groups." *Social Forces* 53, no. 2 (1974): 181–90.

Brim, Orville G. *Look at Me! The Fame Motive from Childhood to Death.* Ann Arbor: University of Michigan Press, 2009.

Brown, Stephanie L., et al. "Social Closeness Increases Salivary Proges-terone in Humans." *Hormones and Behavior* 56 (2009): 108–11.

Burke, Moira, Cameron Marlow, and Thomas Lento. "Feed Me: Motivating Newcomer Contribution in Social Network Sites." SIGHI Conference on Human Factors in Computing Systems (CHI 2009): 945–54.

Campbell, Colin. "The Tyranny of the Yale Critics." *New York Times Magazine*, February 9, 1986.

Carter, Bill. "A Reality TV Head Count." *New York Times*, November 29, 2009.

Casper, Lynne M., and Suzanne M. Bianchi. *Continuity and Change in the American Family*. Thousand Oaks, CA: Sage Publications, 2002.

Caves, Richard E. *Creative Industries: Contracts Between Art and Com-merce*. Cambridge, MA: Harvard University Press, 2000.

comScore. "More Americans Reading Entertainment News Online, with Much of It Occurring During Work Hours." www.comscore.com/Press_Events/Press_Releases/2009/7/More_Americans_Reading_Entertainment _News_Online_With_Much_of_it_Occurring_during_Work_Hours.

Conley, Dalton. *Elsewhere U.S.A.* New York: Pantheon, 2009.

Couldry, Nick. *Media Rituals: A Critical Approach*. New York: Rout-ledge, 2003.

Cowell, Simon. "After the Britain's Got Talent Backlash, Simon Cowell Finally Admits: 'Sorry, I Did Make Mistakes.'" *Daily Mail*, June 20, 2009. www.dailymail.co.uk/tvshowbiz/article-1194302/After-Britains-Got-Talent-backlash-Simon-Cowell-finally-admits-Sorry-I-did-make -mistakes.html.

Cowen, Tyler. *What Price Fame?* Cambridge, MA: Harvard University Press, 2000.

Currid, Elizabeth. *The Warhol Economy: How Fashion, Art, and Music Drive New York City*. Princeton, NJ: Princeton University Press, 2007.

Currid, Elizabeth, and Sarah Williams. "The Geography of Buzz: Art, Culture and the Social Milieu in Los Angeles and New York." *Journal of Economic Geography* 10, no. 3 (2010): 423–51.

Darnton, John. "London Journal; For 20%, He Sells Scandal, Keeping Britain Agog." *New York Times*, March 21, 1994.

David, Paul A. "Clio and the Economics of QWERTY." *American Eco-nomic Review* 75, no. 2 (1985): 332–37.

David, Prabu. "News Concreteness and Visual-Verbal Association: Do News Pictures Narrow the Recall Gap Between Concrete and Abstract News?" *Human Communication Research* 25, no. 2 (2008): 180–201.

Davis, Joshua. "The Secret World of Lonelygirl." *Wired,* December 2006.

Debord, Guy. *The Society of the Spectacle.* London: Zone Books, 1994.

Demsetz, Harold. "Barriers to Entry." *American Economic Review* 72, no. 1 (1982): 47–57.

De Vany, Arthur S., and W. David Walls. "Motion Picture Profit, the Stable Paretian Hypothesis, and the Curse of the Superstar." *Journal of Economic Dynamics and Control* 28, no. 6 (2004): 1035–57.

DiMaggio, Paul. "Classification in Art." *American Sociological Review* 52 (1987): 440–55.

DiSalvo, David. "Are Social Networks Messing with Your Head?" *Scientific American Mind,* January 2010, p. 48.

Elberse, Anita. "The Power of Stars: Do Star Actors Drive the Success of Movies?" *Journal of Marketing* 71, no. 4 (2007).

———. "Should You Invest in the Long Tail?" *Harvard Business Review* (2008).

Erdogan, Zafer B., Michael Baker, and Stephen Tagg. "Selecting Celebrity Endorsers: The Practitioner's Perspective." *Journal of Advertising Research* 41, no. 3 (2001): 39–48.

Facebook.com. "Press Room: Statistics." www.facebook.com/facebook?ref=pf#!/press/info.php?statistics.

Faulkner, Robert R., and Andy B. Anderson. "Short-Term Projects and Emergent Careers: Evidence from Hollywood." *American Journal of Sociology* 92, no. 4 (1987): 879–909.

Ferguson, Niall. *The Ascent of Money: A Financial History of the World.* New York: Penguin, 2008.

Finnegan, William. "Affinity Groups and the Movement Against Corporate Globalization." In *The Social Movements Reader,* ed. Jeff Goodwin and James M. Jasper. Malden, MA: Wiley-Blackwell, 2003.

Florida, Richard. *The Rise of the Creative Class.* New York: Basic Books, 2004.

Forbes. "The Celebrity 100." www.forbes.com/lists/2009/53/celebrity-09_The-Celebrity-100_Rank.html.

Fortini, Amanda. "Twisted Sisters." *New Yorker,* January 18, 2010, p. 32.

Fox, Kate. "Evolution, Alienation and Gossip: The Role of Mobile Telecommunications in the Twenty-First Century." Social Issues Research Centre, 2001.

Frank, Robert H., and Philip J. Cook. *The Winner-Take-All Society.* New York: Free Press, 1995.

Freiberger, Paul, and Michael Swaine. *Fire in the Valley: The Making of the Personal Computer.* New York: McGraw-Hill, 2000.

Friedman, Thomas L. *The World Is Flat: A Brief History of the Twenty-first Century*. New York: Farrar, Straus and Giroux, 2007.

Frith, Mark. *The Celeb Diaries*. London: Ebury Press, 2008.

Gabler, Neal. "Reality TV: Truth Behind the Lens?" Spectrum Lecture, University of Southern California, January 27/28, 2004, www.lear center.org.html/publications/?c=online+publications.

Galenson, David W. "Who Are the Greatest Living Artists? The View from the Auction Market." National Bureau of Economic Research, Working Paper 11644, September 2005.

———. "You Cannot Be Serious: The Conceptual Innovator as Trickster." National Bureau of Economic Research Working Paper 12599, October 2006.

———. *Conceptual Revolutions in Twentieth-Century Art*. New York: Cambridge University Press, 2009.

Gamson, Joshua. *Claims to Fame: Celebrity in Contemporary America*. Berkeley: University of California Press, 1994.

Geddes, Jennifer L. "An Interview with Leo Braudy." *Hedgehog Review* 7, no. 1 (2005): 78–81.

Gergaud, Olivier, and Vincenzo Verardi. "Untalented but Successful." *Cahiers de Maison des Sciences Économiques* bla 06017(2006).

Gilder, George. *Telecosm: How Infinite Bandwith Will Revolutionize Our World*. New York: Free Press, 2000.

Gill, A. A. "Decade in Review: Age of the Amateur with 15 Minutes of Fame." *Sunday Times* (London), December 20, 2009.

Gladwell, Malcolm. *The Tipping Point: How Little Things Can Make a Big Difference*. New York, Little, Brown, 2000.

———. *Outliers: The Story of Success*. New York: Little, Brown, 2008.

Glaeser, Edward L. "Urban Colossus: Why Is New York America's Largest City?" HIER Discussion Paper 2073 (June 2005).

Glaeser, Edward, and Albert Saiz. "The Rise of the Skilled City." *Brookings-Wharton Papers on Urban Affairs 2004*. Washington, D.C.: Brookings Institution Press, 2004.

Goel, Sharad, Roby Muhamad, and Duncan Watts. "Social Search in 'Small-World' Experiments." *Yahoo! Research*, Working Paper, 2009. http://research.yahoo.com/sharad_Goel.

Goetzmann, William N. "Accounting for Taste: Art and the Financial Markets over Three Centuries." *American Economic Review* 83, no. 5 (1993): 1370–76.

Google. "2006 Year-End Zeitgeist: Top Searches in 2006." www.google .com/intl/en/press/zeitgeist2006.html.

Haass, Richard N. "The Age of Nonpolarity: What Will Follow U.S. Dominance." *Foreign Affairs* 87 (2008): 44.

Haden-Guest, Anthony. *True Colors: The Real Life of the Art World.* New York: Atlantic Monthly Press, 1996.

Hagtvedt, Henrik, and Vanessa M. Patrick. "Art Infusion: The Influence of Visual Art on the Perception and Evaluation of Consumer Products." *Journal of Marketing Research* 45, no. 3 (2008): 379–89.

Hameed, Bilal. "Facebook's U.S. Traffic Reaches 132 Million Visitors." January 12, 2010. www.allfacebook.com/2010/01/facebooks-us-traffic-reaches-132-million-visitors/.

Hansell, Saul. "Zuckerberg's Law of Information Sharing." *New York Times*, November 6, 2008. http://bits.blogs.nytimes.com/2008/11/06/zuckerbergs-law-of-information-sharing/.

Harris, Rachael Lee. "Bollywood Star Detained at Newark Airport." *New York Times*, August 16, 2009, p. C2.

Hartley, John. *Popular Reality: Journalism, Modernity, Popular Culture.* London: Edward Arnold, 1996.

———. *Uses of Television.* New York: Routledge, 1999.

Horkheimer, Max, and Theodor W. Adorno. *Dialectic of Enlightenment.* Stanford, CA: Stanford University Press, 2002.

Hubler, Shawn. "The Secret Life of Cory Kennedy." *Los Angeles Times: West*, February 25, 2007.

Jacques, Martin. *When China Rules the World: The End of the Western World and the Birth of a New Global Order.* New York: Penguin Press, 2009.

Jencks, Christopher, and David Riesman. *The Academic Revolution.* New Brunswick, NJ: Transaction, 2002.

Jenkins, Henry. *Convergence Culture: Where Old and New Media Collide.* New York: New York University Press, 2006.

———. *Fans, Bloggers, and Gamers: Exploring Participatory Culture.* New York: New York University Press, 2006.

Jenkins, Henry, and David Thorburn, eds. *Democracy and New Media.* Cambridge, MA: MIT Press, 2003.

Kahle, Lynn R., and Pamela M. Homer. "Physical Attractiveness of the Celebrity Endorser: A Social Adaptation Perspective." *Journal of Consumer Research* 11, no. 1 (1985): 954–61.

Khurana, Rakesh. "The Curse of the Superstar CEO." *Harvard Business Review* (September 2002).

Kirp, David. *Shakespeare, Einstein, and the Bottom Line.* Cambridge, MA: Harvard University Press, 2003.

Kossinets, Gueorgi, and Duncan J. Watts. "Origins of Homophily in an Evolving Social Network." *American Journal of Sociology* 115 (2009): 405–50.

Krueger, Alan B. "The Economics of Real Superstars: The Market for Rock Concerts in the Material World." *Journal of Labor Economics* 23, no. 1 (2005).

Kuper, Simon. "Sport Can Teach Bankers Fair Play on Pay." *Financial Times*, February 27, 2009.

Kuper, Simon, and Stefan Szymanski. *Soccernomics: Why England Loses, Why Germany and Brazil Win, and Why the U.S., Japan, Australia, Turkey—and Even Iraq—Are Destined to Become the Kings of the World's Most Popular Sport.* New York: Nation Books, 2009.

Lawson, Robert A., et al. "Vend It Like Beckham: David Beckham's Effect on MLS Ticket Sales." *International Journal of Sport Finance* 3, no. 4 (2008): 189–95.

Lee, Wei-Na, Sejung Marina Choi, and Wanhsiu Sunny Tsai. "Celebrity Advertising in Japan and Korea: Doing It the Asian Way?" Proceedings of the 2007 Asia-Pacific Conference of the American Academy of Advertising.

Leibenstein, H. "Bandwagon, Snob, and Veblen Effects in the Theory of Consumers' Demand." *Quarterly Journal of Economics* 64 (1950): 183–207.

Lewis, Michael. *Moneyball: The Art of Winning an Unfair Game.* New York: Norton, 2003.

Lorenzen, Mark. "How the West Was Won." Working Paper, Department of Innovation and Organizational Economics, Copenhagen Business School, 2008.

Lorenzen, Mark, and Florian Arun Täube. "Breakout from Bollywood? The Roles of Social Networks and Regulation in the Evolution of Indian Film Industry." *Journal of International Management* 14, no. 3 (2008): 286–99.

Lucas, Robert E. Jr. "On the Mechanics of Economic Development." *Journal of Monetary Economics* 22 (1988): 3–42.

Lucifora, Claudio, and Rob Simmons. "Superstar Effects in Sports: Evidence from Italian Soccer." *Journal of Sports Economics* 4 (2003): 35–55.

Lukes, Steven. *Power: A Radical View.* New York: Macmillan, 1974.

Lyall, Sarah. "Sex! Sleaze! Filth! Britain's Scandal King Sells All!" *New York Times*, January 28, 2006.

————. "British Reality TV Star Ready to Die for the Cameras." *New York Times*, February 19, 2009.

Mansfield, Edward D. "Concentration, Polarity and the Distribution of Power." *International Studies Quarterly* 37 (1993): 105–28.

Marin, Alexandra, and Barry Wellman. "Social Network Analysis: An Introduction." In *Handbook of Social Network Analysis*, ed. Peter Carrington and John Scott. London: Sage Publications, 2010.

Marsden, Peter. "Core Discussions Networks of Americans." *American Sociological Review* 52, no. 1 (1987): 122–31.

Marshall, Alfred. *Principles of Economics*. Amherst, NY: Prometheus, 1997 [1891].

Marshall, P. David. *Celebrity and Power: Fame in Contemporary Culture*. Minneapolis: University of Minnesota Press, 1997.

————. "Intimately Intertwined in the Most Public Way: Celebrity and Journalism." In *The Celebrity Culture Reader*, ed. P. David Marshall. New York: Routledge, 2006.

————. "New Media—New Self: The Changing Power of Celebrity." In *The Celebrity Culture Reader*, ed. P. David Marshall. New York: Routledge, 2006.

Mathur, Lynette Knowles, Ike Mathur, and Nanda Rangan. "The Wealth Effects Associated with a Celebrity Endorser: The Michael Jordan Phenomenon." *Journal of Advertising Research* 37 (1997): 67–73.

McCracken, Grant. "Who Is the Celebrity Endorser? Cultural Foundations of the Endorsement Process." *Journal of Consumer Research* 16, no. 3 (1989): 310-21.

McLuhan, Marshall. *Understanding Media: Extensions of Man*. New York: McGraw-Hill, 1964.

————. *The Medium Is the Massage: An Inventory of Effects*. New York: Random House, 1967.

McPherson, Miller, Lynn Smith-Lovin, and Matthew E. Brashears. "Social Isolation in America: Changes in Core Discussion Networks over Two Decades." *American Sociological Review* 71 (2006): 353–75.

Menand, Louis. "The Iron Law of Stardom." *New Yorker*, March 24, 1997, p. 36.

Mills, C. Wright. *The Power Elite*. New York: Oxford University Press, 1999 [1956].

Money, Bruce R., Terence A. Shimp, and Tomoaki Sakano. "Celebrity Endorsements in Japan and the United States: Is Negative Information All That Harmful?" *Journal of Advertising Research* 46, no. 1 (2006): 113–23.

Nüesch, Stephan. "The Economics of Superstars and Celebrities." PhD diss., University of Zurich, 2007.

Oppenheimer, Jerry. *Front Row: Anna Wintour: The Cool Life and Hot Times of Vogue's Editor-in-Chief.* New York: St. Martin's Press, 2005.

Pareto, Vilfredo. "Manual of Political Economy." *Bulletin of the American Mathematical Society* 18 (1912): 462–74.

Perl, Jed. *New Art City.* New York: Knopf, 2005.

Pinksy, Drew, and S. Mark Young. *The Mirror Effect: How Celebrity Narcissism Is Seducing America.* New York: Harper, 2009.

Porter, Michael E. "Clusters and the Economics of Competition." *Harvard Business Review* (November–December 1998): 77–90.

Preston, Peter. "A Dozen Reasons to Be Cheerful About the State of the British Media." *Observer*, December 27, 2009.

Reed, David. "The Law of the Pack." *Harvard Business Review* (February 2001): 23–24.

Reed, William J. "The Pareto, Zipf and Other Power Laws." *Economics Letters* 74, no. 1 (2001): 15–19.

Rein, Irving, Philip Kotler, Michael Hamlin, and Martin Stoller. *High Visibility: Transforming Your Personal and Professional Brand.* 3rd ed. New York: McGraw-Hill, 2005.

Rice, Lynette. "TLC Halts Production on 'Jon and Kate Plus 8.'" *Entertainment Weekly*, October 1, 2009. http://news-briefs.ew.com/2009/10/01/tlc-halts-production-on-jon-and-kate-plus-8/.

———. "TLC Responds to Jon Gosselin." *TLC Discovery*, October 1, 2009. http://tlc.discovery.com/tv/jon-and-kate/tlc-responds-to-jon-gosselin.html.

Robinson, Dwight E. "Economics of Fashion Demand." *Quarterly Journal of Economics* 75, no. 3 (1961): 376–98.

Romer, Paul M. "Endogenous Technical Change." *Journal of Political Economy* 98, no. 5 (1990): S71–102.

Rosen, Sherwin. "The Economics of Superstars." *American Economic Review* 71, no. 5 (1981): 845–58.

Roubini, Nouriel. "Why Central Banks Should Burst Bubbles." *International Finance* 9 (Spring 2006): 87–107.

Rubinkam, Michael. "'Jon & Kate' Stars Being Investigated over Child Labor Complaint." *Huffington Post*, May 29, 2009. www.huffingtonpost.com/2009/05/29/jon-kate-plus-8-stars-bei_n_209133.html.

Ruscha, Ed. "50 Years of Painting." Exhibition, Hayward Gallery, Southbank Centre, London, October 14, 2009–January 10, 2010.

Rytina, Steve, and David L. Morgan. "The Arithmetic of Social Relations:

The Interplay of Category and Network." *American Journal of Sociology* 88, no. 1 (1982): 88–113.

Sales, Nancy Jo. "The Unreal Rise of Jon and Kate Gosselin." *Vanity Fair*, October 19, 2009.

Salganik, Matthew J., Peter Sheridan Dodds, and Duncan J. Watts. "Experimental Study of Inequality and Unpredictability in an Artificial Cultural Market." *Science* 311 (2006): 854–56.

Saxenian, AnnaLee. *Regional Advantage: Culture and Competition in Silicon Valley and Route 128.* Cambridge, MA: Harvard University Press, 1994.

Schama, Simon. *The Embarrassment of Riches: An Interpretation of Dutch Culture in the Golden Age.* New York: Knopf, 1987.

Schroeder, Alice. *Snowball: Warren Buffett and the Business of Life.* New York: Bantam, 2008.

Schweinberger, Stefan R., et al. "Event-Related Brain Potential Evidence for a Response of Inferior Temporal Cortex to Familiar Face Repetitions." *Cognitive Brain Research* 14, no. 3 (2002): 398–409.

Seipp, Catherine. "The Puppet Masters." *American Journalism Review* 21, no. 8 (1999): 22.

September Issue, The. DVD. Directed by R. J. Cutler. A&E IndieFilms, 2009.

Shumway, David R. "The Star System in Literary Studies." *PMLA* 112 (1997): 85–100.

Sinclair, Joe. "'Jade Goody Effect' Boosts Cervical Cancer Screening Rates." *Guardian*, October 22, 2009.

Smart, Barry. *The Sport Star: Modern Sport and the Cultural Economy of Sporting Celebrity.* Thousand Oaks, CA: Sage Publications, 2005.

Sorkin, Michael, ed. *Variations on a Theme Park: The New American City and the End of Public Space.* New York: Hill and Wang, 1992.

Spurgin, Tim. "The *Times Magazine* and Academic Megastars." *Minnesota Review* n.s. 52–4 (2000): 225–38.

Stallabrass, Julian. *High Art Lite: British Art in the 1990s.* New York: Verso, 1999.

Sternberg, Adam. "Hey There, Lonelygirl." *New York*, August 28, 2006.

Sun, Eric, et al. "Gesundheit! Modeling Contagion Through Facebook News Feed." *Association for the Advancement of Artificial Intelligence* (2009).

Szymanski, Stefan. "Income Inequality, Competitive Balance and the Attractiveness of Team Sports: Some Evidence and a Natural Experiment from English Soccer." *Economic Journal* 111 (2001): F69–F84.

———. "The Economic Design of Sporting Contests." *Journal of Economic Literature* 41 (2003): 1137–87.

Taylor, Marvin J., ed. *The Downtown Book: The New York Art Scene 1974–1984*. Princeton, NJ: Princeton University Press, 2006.

Thompson, Don. *The $12 Million Stuffed Shark: The Curious Economics of Contemporary Art*. New York: Palgrave Macmillan, 2008.

Tönnies, Ferdinand. *Community and Society*. Trans. Charles P. Loomis. East Lansing: Michigan State University Press, 1957 [1887].

Tripp, Carolyn, Thomas D. Jensen, and Les Carlson. "The Effects of Multiple Product Endorsements by Celebrities on Consumers' Attitudes and Intentions." *Journal of Consumer Research* 20, no. 4 (1994): 535–47.

Trump, Donald J., and Meredith McIver. *How to Get Rich*. New York: Random House, 2004.

———. *Never Give Up: How I Turned My Biggest Challenges into Success*. Hoboken, NJ: Wiley, 2008.

Trump, Donald J., and Anthony Schwartz. *The Art of the Deal*. New York: Random House, 1988.

Turner, Graeme. *Understanding Celebrity*. Thousand Oaks, CA: Sage Publications, 2004.

———. "Celebrity, the Tabloid and the Democratic Public Sphere." In *The Celebrity Culture Reader*, ed. P. David Marshall. New York: Routledge, 2006.

———. "The Mass Production of Celebrity: 'Celetoids,' Reality TV and the 'Demotic Turn.'" *International Journal of Cultural Studies* 9, no. 2 (2006): 153–65.

Twenge, Jean M., and W. Keith Campbell. *The Narcissism Epidemic: Living in the Age of Entitlement*. New York: Free Press, 2009.

Uzzi, Brian, Luis Amaral, and Felix Reed-Tsochas. "Small-World Networks and Management Science Research: A Review." *European Management Review* 4 (2007): 77–91.

Veblen, Thorstein. *The Theory of the Leisure Class: An Economic Study of Institutions*. New York: Oxford University Press, 2007 [1899].

Watts, Duncan J. *Small Worlds: The Dynamics of Networks Between Order and Randomness*. Princeton, NJ: Princeton University Press, 1999.

———. "Is Justin Timberlake the Product of Cumulative Advantage?" *New York Times Magazine*, April 15, 2007.

Watts, Duncan J., and Steven H. Strogatz. "Collective Dynamics of 'Small-World' Networks." *Nature* 393 (June 1998): 440–42.

Weber, Max. *Economy and Society*. Ed. Guenther Roth and Claus Wittich, trans. Elphrain Fischoff. New York: Bedminster, 1968 [1914].

———. "The Nature of Charismatic Authority and Its Routinization." In *Theory of Social and Economic Organization*, trans. A. R. Anderson and Talcott Parsons. New York: Oxford University Press, 1947.

Weinberg, Myrl. "In Health Care Reform, the 20–80 Solution." *Providence Journal*, July 27, 2009.

Weisberger, Lauren. *The Devil Wears Prada*. New York: Doubleday, 2003.

Williams, Jeffrey J. "Academostars: Name Recognition." In *The Celebrity Culture Reader*, ed. David Marshall. New York: Routledge, 2006.

Wilson, Glenn. "The Pressure of Sudden TV Stardom." *BBC: Entertainment*, June 1, 2009. http://news.bbc.co.uk/2/hi/entertainment/8077075.stm.

Wyatt, Edward. "No Slowing in Cash Flow for 'Idol.'" *New York Times*, May 11, 2009.

Young, Mark, and Drew Pinsky. "Narcissism and Celebrity." *Journal of Research in Personality* 40, no. 5 (2006): 463–71.

Zucker, Lynne G., and Michael R. Darby. "Star Scientists and Institutional Transformation: Patterns of Invention and Innovation in the Formation of the Biotechnology Industry." *Proceedings of the National Academy of Science* 93 (November 1996): 12709–16.

Acknowledgments

Anyone who is married to, a colleague of, best friends with, a sibling to, or the parent of an author knows that writing a book is not a one-person process. There are many people involved in transforming early sparks of ideas into research and turning those results into sentences that form paragraphs and then pages. Certainly, in my case, I could never have done it alone.

My literary agent, David Halpern of the Robbins Office, has been an extraordinary help navigating the world of publishing and book writing. His invaluable insight helped me find the right publisher and make decisions about various parts of the publishing process. He has also been a great set of eyes, offering thoughtful editorial suggestions that made this book so much better. I couldn't ask for a more brilliant agent and friend.

The same must be said for the Robbins Office in general. Ian King and Rachelle Bergstein offered discerning and intelligent comments, and their devotion to making this book a success is appreciated. Kathy Robbins must be commended for heading such a terrific team and for her own guidance and feedback along the way.

I also thank my editors at Faber, Mitzi Angel and Chantal Clarke, both of whom worked hard to help transform my sometimes rambling sentences and ideas into coherent arguments and a flowing narrative. I am very grateful for their attention to language and beautiful editorial style. FSG's Zachary Brown, Abby Kagan, Jenny Carrow, Alyson Sinclair, and Meredith Kessler continue to impress me with their energy, industriousness, and dedication to my book.

The support and resources of the John Randolph Haynes Foundation and the University of Southern California's Provost's Office enabled me to conduct part of the research in this book, particularly my work mapping the photographs of entertainment events. USC's Lear Center, specifically Marty Kaplan and Johanna Blakely, were advocates of my research from the get-go. Many thanks also to USC's superb media team: Ariel Carpenter, Gary Spiecker, Janis Peterson, and James Grant. USC, and the School of Policy, Planning and Development, where I teach, have been unwavering supporters of my ideas and research. In particular, I thank my dean, Jack Knott, my associate dean, Elizabeth Graddy, and my colleagues Richard Green, Adam Clayton Powell, David Sloane, Dowell Myers, and Lisa Schweitzer, who are tremendously encouraging of my work and express both interest and belief in my research.

The research in this book would not have been possible without my clever collaborators who have worked with me all hours of the day studying data, running analyses, and toiling away writing up results. Gilad Ravid, my colleague at Ben-Gurion University, is my original partner in crime, with whom I initially began my quantitative study of celebrity. Gilad worked tirelessly with me on creating new methods to study the networks of the intricate and complex world of celebrity. Sarah Williams of Columbia University is an extraordinary coauthor on much of the geographical analysis of celebrity. Our partnership resulted in unique methods and data sets to study geography in new and unconventional ways. My colleague Kevin Stolarick was a tremendous help in categorizing the celebrity industry and measuring its workforce data. Kevin has worked with me since my days as a graduate student and continues to be a terrific research partner.

I cannot thank my research assistant, Vivian Ho, enough. Along with her help as a researcher, she toiled away on last-minute work for the book, from reformatting notes (a task I wouldn't give my worst enemy) to looking up references. Vivian is a doctoral student at USC, and her attention to detail, intelligence, and ability to work under pressure are impressive and bode well for her own future career as a scholar.

My scholarly colleagues and mentors Harvey Molotch, Susan Fainstein, Richard Florida, Lance Freeman, David Galenson, Tyler Cowen, Michael Storper, Allen Scott, and Dalton Conley were thoughtful and generous in the time they gave me to talk about my ideas for this book. I am fortunate to have Leo Braudy as my colleague at USC. His *The Frenzy of Renown* is the original treatise on the topic of fame, and his insights into my own work have been essential. Lisa Hacken was a terrific outside reader of my manuscript. Carly DeBeikes was helpful in research assistance. Marissa King, Nicole Esparza, and Duncan Watts took time to study the social network analysis of celebrities that Gilad and I created and offered helpful analytical feedback on some rather complicated results.

My dear friends Elizabeth and Quintin Price, James Brooks, and Dave Auckland, in our late-night dinner conversations and weekend chats at the pub, are such great and intelligent people to bounce ideas off of and debate some of the book's arguments. They put up with my endless dissections of celebrity for far longer than they probably would have liked, and yet every time the topic came up, they discussed it with me as if it were the first time.

Despite the multiple data sets and quantitative analysis that underpin this book, so much of this work also depends on those people who live and breathe the business of celebrity. Without their input, my statistical output would have been numbers without a meaningful social context of the phenomenon of celebrity. Thus I thank the dozens of people who took time out of their schedules to let me interview them about their worlds, in particular, Stan Rosenfield, Richard Johnson, Max Clifford, Franklin Leonard, Simon Kuper, Brandy Navarre, Jeffrey Deitch, and Sandy Nairne. In the face of their terribly busy lives and intense work schedules, these people got on the phone with me multiple times, responded to my many e-mails, or met with me to answer follow-up queries and to explain to me new aspects of the industry and the phenomenon of celebrity. Thank you very much.

My family and friends have always supported every venture I've undertaken, this book being no exception. Thanks to Eric Lovecchio, Tess Mordan, Sloane Crosley, Brooke Cutler, Matt Hayes, Katie Rosinsky, and Marisa and Frederick McSwain. Thanks to my family: Evan, Sarah, Gabriela, Emer Keeling, Argus and Charlie Halkett, and Bill and Joan Halkett. In particular, I'd like to thank my mother: Had I the chance before I was born to create the perfect version of a mother, it would be her exactly. Her relentless belief in me is never taken for granted. Thank you, Choco, for keeping my feet warm as I wrote page after page.

My husband, Richard Halkett, deserves so much credit for his undying support of me and my work. Whether it was weekends taken up by revisions, my high-octane stress level as deadlines approached, or the peculiar two-to-five-a.m. writing slot that I took up for a while, Richard never ceased to be my biggest fan and the most understanding and considerate husband. In addition, his endless fascination with the topic of celebrity and his great patience are more than I could ever ask for in anyone. Walking around New York's Central Park and across the bridges and through the greenery of central London, and driving down Sunset Boulevard in Los Angeles, Richard and I discussed every detail, contradiction, and argument I constructed. Richard has made all matters of my life, intellectual and otherwise, wonderful and, finally, complete. I thank him with all my heart.

Index

Abedin, Huma, 94
Abramovich, Roman, 63
Abstract Expressionists, 64
academic celebrities, 59–64, 193, 252nn19, 21
Academy Awards (Oscars), 10, 12, 28, 52, 109, 116, 128, 131, 213, 259n5; as media event, 124, 142–44; *Vanity Fair* party for, 53–55, 97, 99, 108, 110, 137, 138; winning, 34, 58, 105, 162, 169–71, 196, 214, 247n16
Accenture, 186
Access Hollywood (TV show), 86
AC Milan, 163
Adler, Moshe, 267n25
Adorno, Theodor, 274n17
affinity groups, 251n4
Afghanistan, 245n12
agents, 24, 69–71, 73, 74, 82, 85–87, 127, 172, 254n3, 255n9; for academics, 64; Hollywood, 69, 188, 203, 205–207, 86; lack of, in Bollywood, 89–91; sports, 173; 10 percent cut of, 85
AIDS research, 31
Aiken, Clay, 197
Albert, Réka, 103
Alexander the Great, 10

Ali, Ayaan Hirsi, 62, 253n23
Ali, Muhammad, 177
A-listers, 24, 196, 199, 217, 261n16; Bollywood and, 58; expenditures of, 85; geography of stardom and, 130–37, 145; networks of, 102, 106–10, 112; publicists for, 68, 69, 75, 81–82, 189; relative celebrity and, 54; TV appearances of, 202
Allen, Woody, 181, 218
All-Star teams; baseball, 167; basketball, 177
Amazon, 159, 209
American Broadcasting Company (ABC), 143, 200
American Girl dolls, 48
American Idol (TV show), 91, 194–200, 205–207, 215, 221–23, 274n12
American League, 35
American Pie films, 23
Anderson, Andy B., 247n16
Anderson, Chris, 19, 158–59
Anderson, Tracy, 84
Andrejevic, Mark, 200
Aniston, Jennifer, 43, 51, 55, 56, 76, 140, 199, 203, 225, 272n79; film career of, 34,

Also by Elizabeth Currid-Halkett

*The Warhol Economy: How Fashion, Art, and Music
Drive New York City*

CPSIA information can be obtained
at www.ICGtesting.com
Printed in the USA
LVOW11s1027141216
517222LV00001B/46/P